编委会

主　任：曹顺庆（四川大学）

委　员（音序）：

Paul Cobley，Middlesex University，UK

Lian Duan，Concordia University，Canada

Kalevi Kull，University of Tartu，Estonia

Mabel Lee，University of Sydney，Australia

Massimo Leone，University of Torino，Italy

Susan Petrilli，University of Bari，Italy

Eero Tarasti，University of Helsinki，Finland

Yiyan Wang，Victoria University of Wellington，New Zealand

蔡秀枝（台湾大学）

傅修延（江西师范大学）

蒋述卓（暨南大学）

李凤亮（深圳大学）

乔国强（上海外国语大学）

陶东风（中国人民大学）

王一川（北京师范大学）

杨慧琳（中国人民大学）

乐黛云（北京大学）

张智庭（南开大学）

周　宪（南京大学）

丁尔苏（香港岭南大学）

龚鹏程（台湾佛光大学）

李　彬（清华大学）

李　杰（浙江大学）

申　丹（北京大学）

王　宁（清华大学）

徐　亮（浙江大学）

叶舒宪（中国社会科学院）

张　杰（南京师范大学）

赵宪章（南京大学）

朱国华（华东师范大学）

主　　编：赵毅衡

副 主 编：赵星植　彭佳

编　　务：齐千里　何一杰　陈蓉

网络总监：饶广祥

封面创意：郭人瑞

中国知网(CNKI)来源集刊　中文科技期刊数据库来源集刊
超星数字图书馆来源集刊　万方数据库来源集刊

符号与传媒
Signs & Media

主编　曹顺庆　赵毅衡
四川大学符号学-传媒学研究所　主办

总第8辑

四川大学出版社

责任编辑:陈克坚
责任校对:欧风偃
封面设计:原谋设计工作室
责任印制:王　炜

图书在版编目(CIP)数据

符号与传媒. 第8辑 / 曹顺庆，赵毅衡主编. —成都：四川大学出版社，2014.3
ISBN 978-7-5614-7546-1

Ⅰ.①符…　Ⅱ.①曹…　②赵…　Ⅲ.①符号学-文集
Ⅳ.①H0-53

中国版本图书馆CIP数据核字（2014）第037501号

书名　符号与传媒(第8辑)

主　　编	曹顺庆　赵毅衡
出　　版	四川大学出版社
地　　址	成都市一环路南一段24号(610065)
发　　行	四川大学出版社
书　　号	ISBN 978-7-5614-7546-1
印　　刷	郫县犀浦印刷厂
成品尺寸	170 mm×240 mm
印　　张	15.5
字　　数	285千字
版　　次	2014年3月第1版
印　　次	2014年3月第1次印刷
定　　价	36.00元

版权所有◆侵权必究

◆读者邮购本书,请与本社发行科联系。
电话:(028)85408408/(028)85401670/
(028)85408023　邮政编码:610065
◆本社图书如有印装质量问题,请寄回出版社调换。
◆网址:http://www.scup.cn

编者的话

对话与越界，既是符号过程的鲜明特征，也是符号学这门学科能够发展突进的动力。自本辑开始，《符号与传媒》跨越语言的边界：改成了中英双语版。这种改变不仅是题目与摘要的中英文对照，而是来自世界各地的作者：不管是卓有成就的符号学家，还是像符号学新秀，他们的思想拓宽了研究的版图。

本辑的第一篇文章，埃罗·塔拉斯蒂的《全球符号学中的俄国形式主义：欧洲学派的先声》，即是一次重建世界符号学史的重要尝试。在朱丽娅·庞齐奥、董明来、方芳等人的文章中，也有对经典的重访：重新阅读巴尔特、莫里斯和托多罗夫，让大师们的论述在新的理论视野中再次焕发出光彩。

跨越学科界限也是我们努力的方向。在本辑中，我们可以看到崔斯坦·埃文斯、刘宇、西蒙娜·斯塔诺、李红等人将符号学延伸至艺术、教育学、文化研究和传播学的范畴。胡易容对“像似性”这个最常用概念的反复思辨，推进了我们对符号学基础的理解。

任何学科都需要面对质疑和挑战，符号学也是如此。为此，我们在本辑中特别安排了“西安批判符号学派”专辑。专辑中既有从《周易》和《周礼》的“交道”与“交换”出发对人类现代交往危机进行的反思，亦有对西方身体理论，对鲍德里亚消费社会理论的批判。这种思想的交锋，无疑是学术研究值得鼓励之处。

每年的春季号，我们都提交一份中国符号学年度发展报告，今年的年度报告由刘一鸣、齐千里撰写。我们希望，对每年中国符号学的进步都有所记录，有所讨论。

本辑的另一个改变是改成纸质与网络同时出版，以更好地为各地符号学同仁服务。网络版的链接是 www. semiotics. net. cn/isms，欢迎访问。

Editor's Note

Dialogism and unboundedness, the distinctive characteristics of semiosis, are also the driving force behind the discipline of semiotics. Starting from this issue, *Signs & Media* turns bilingual, publishing papers either in English or in Chinese. The table of contents and the abstracts will be in both languages. Authors are now from around the world. Among our authors are both distinguished semioticians and younger scholars. Their essays have expanded the scope of semiotics.

The first essay of this issue, Eero Tarasti's "Russian Formalism in the Global Semiotic: Precursor of the European Branch" provides us with an excellent example of how to reconstruct the history of semiotics by revisiting its forerunners. This kind of reconstruction could also be found in other essays by Julio Ponzio, Dong Minglai, Fang Fang and others. Their rereadings of Roland Barthes, Charles Morris, and Tzvetan Todoros lead to a revitalization of the masters' contributions from a contemporary theoretical perspective.

Crossing disciplinary boundaries is another important part of our endeavor. In this issue, we can see the efforts of Tristian Evans, Simona Stano, Li Hong and others to extend the applications of semiotics to communication, art studies, education, culture studies, and other fields. Hu Yirong's essay, which carefully ponders the basic concept of "Icon", deepens our understanding of the very foundation of semiotics.

Every discipline has to face questions and challenges; semiotics is no exception. This issue features a special column devoted to the "Xi'an School of Critical Semiotics", which reflects upon the modern crisis in interpersonal communications in the light of two ancient Chinese classics—*Zhou Yi* and *Zhou Li*. The column also offers a critique of Western theories of corporeality as well as Baudrillard's theory of the consumer society. Our journal strongly encourages pointed intellectual exchanges of this nature.

In every year's Spring Issue, we offer an annual report on the development of semiotics in China. The 2013 Report is provided by Liu Yiming and Qi Qianli. It is our hope that major contributions to the evolution of semiotics in China will be carefully recorded and will generate lively discussion.

Beginning with this issue, the journal will be simultaneously published on paper and online, in hopes of improving service for our colleagues and readers everywhere. The link to the online edition is www. semiotics. net. cn/isms; you are welcome to visit.

目　录

理论与运用

西安批判符号学派专辑

书 评

Contents

Theory and Application

Xi'an School of Critical Semiotics

Book Reviews

《符号与传媒》征稿启事

《符号与传媒》，是四川大学符号学-传媒学研究所主办的学术集刊，目前由四川大学文学与新闻学院赵毅衡教授任责任主编，每年分春秋两辑出版。自2008年创办以来，《符号与传媒》已经连续出版5年，刊载符号学-传媒学专业论文150余篇，与国内外符号学团队合作共推出10个颇具影响力的学术研究专题。为适应刊物进一步国际化、专业化的需求，本刊自2014年春季号起将全面改为中英文双语版，并严格执行国际同行评议制度。

本着兼容并包、不拘一格的开放性学术理念，本刊努力将符号学方法与理论系统地扩展至新闻传播学研究、文学文化研究、叙述研究、中国文化典籍研究、艺术研究等众多研究领域，拓宽符号学运动的锋面。本刊所征收的稿件不仅涵盖社会、历史、文化、经济等学科范畴，更着重于将思想的触角延伸至人类科学的各种门类、各种活动。本刊希望通过不同形式的探索，为符号学提供一片广阔的沃土。

思想无疆界。我们相信大作能为符号学与传媒学的理论与应用提出新的想法，我们衷心期待您的文章。

赵毅衡

《符号与传媒》编辑部

投稿邮箱：semiotics _ media@163. com

联系电话：028-85412121

传　　真：028-85412710

官方论坛：www. semiotics. net. cn

官方微博：http://e. weibo. com/semioticsscu

地　　址：四川省成都市武侯区望江路29号

四川大学文学与新闻学院，符号学-传媒学研究所

邮　　编：610064

Signs & Media Call for Papers

Signs & Media is a bilingual (English-Chinese), peer-reviewed academic journal, founded in 2008 by the Institute of Semiotics & Media Studies (ISMS), Sichuan University. *Signs & Media*, dedicating itself to the interdisciplinary research on semiotics and media studies, has since published more than 150 professional papers by scholars from all around the world.

Under the editorship of Professor Henry Yiheng Zhao, *Signs & Media* endeavors to systematically expand semiotics to all fields of human sciences, covering, notably, communication and media studies, cultural studies, art and literature, as well as narratology, stylistics, discourse analysis, cognitive science in the semiotic perspective, and, in particular, reinterpretations of Chinese traditional semiotic heritage.

Signs & Media welcomes contributions on any topics, so long as they, in a way, help illuminate the theoretical foundation and widen the sphere of applicability of semiotics.

Henry Yiheng Zhao

Editor, *Signs and Media*

Email address: semiotics_media@163.com

Phone: +86-28-8541-2121

Fax: +86-28-8541-2710

Website: www.semiotics.net.cn

Official Microblog: http://e.weibo.com/semioticsscu

Postal Address: Institute of Semiotics & Media Studies,

Sichuan University,

No. 29 Wanjiang Road,

Chengdu, 610064

China

理论与应用

Russian Formalism in Global Semiotics: Precursor of the European Branch

Eero Tarasti

Abstract: Russian formalism constitutes one of the essential lines in the history of the European semiotics. As such, this movement is influential both in arts and science. Many of its central notions are in fact musical. As a Finnish musicologist and semiotician, The present paper traces some of Russian formalism's Finnish connection and discuss some of its music-related concepts. In addition, I will focus on the key concepts and influence of three important theorists: Wilhelm Sesemann, Vladimir Propp, and Mikhail Bakhtin.

Key words: polyphonic novel, dialogism, estrangement, symphonic society, narratology

全球符号学中的俄国形式主义：欧洲学派的先声

埃罗·塔拉斯蒂

摘要：俄国形式主义是欧洲符号学历史上的基本方向之一，在艺术与科学中都颇具影响。形式主义的许多核心概念都和音乐相关。作为芬兰的音乐学家和符号学家，作者追溯了俄国形式主义和芬兰的渊源，并讨论了它与音乐相关的一些概念。此外，作者还考察了威廉·泽塞曼、普洛普和巴赫金这三位重要的理论家提出的核心概念及其影响。

关键词：复调小说，对话主义，陌生化，交响型社会，叙述学

There is no doubt that the complex and rich phenomenon of what is called Russian formalism belongs to the very special cultural heritage of the whole international semiotic movement. If we explore more deeply the history of semiotics, we will notice that many of its central notions stem from the period named under Russian formalism. So it is high time to show gratitude to that period, one of the most creative but also controversial of the discipline. My essay here starts therefore with these origins, in spite of possible misunderstandings and misinterpretations.

Now every anthology or encyclopedia of the history of semiotics must contain a chapter on Russian formalism, which started its triumph in the West in the 1970s. However, the first problem we encounter here is how to define the phenomenon and how to distinguish it from other cultural phenomena of the period, i. e. the 1910s and 1920s. Certainly, it is hard to say whether it belongs to science or art, and perhaps this is one of its fascinations. Who was then, after all, a Russian formalist?

Finnish Connections

Russian formalism, which can trace its origin to the year of 1913, when an important essay by Viktor Sklovski appeared, constitutes one of the essential lines in the subsequent history of the European semiotics. The first time we, as young students, read about scholars like Propp, Sklovski, Tynianov, Eichenbaum, Tomaszewski, Jakobson, and Bakhtin, was due to a Swedish anthology *Form och struktur* by Kurt Aspelin and Bengt A. Lundberg, (*Litteraturvetenskapliga texter I urval*, Stockholm: Bokförlaget Pan /Norstedts, 1971). It contained translations of classic essays by Sklovski on artistic devices, by Tynianov on literary evolution, and by Eichenbaum on Gogol's novels. Quite naturally the book then moved from this origin to Mukarovsky, then to French structuralism and ultimately to Yuri Lotman. Semiotics in Finland started with a young student group, which called itself a " structuralist group " and resorted to Umberto Eco and his *La struttura assente*, and to the Swedish translations *Den frånvarande strukturen*.

These classical texts fascinated us. Next time I heard about Russian formalism was in the Introduction to Semiotics, a course offered at the Department of folkloristics at Helsinki University by Professor Vilmos Voigt. This course for the first time introduced the sources in St. Petersburg or Leningrad and Moscow and also revealed the role the Finnish folklore studies played in Propp's theorization. What was involved was the classification method of fairy tales and folk songs by the brothers Krohn and the primary school teacher Antti Aarne. Five years later in Brazil, I found a book entitled *Intelligecia do folklore* by Renato Almeida which had, to my surprise, a whole chapter on *Escola finlandesa*. Prof. Voigt also showed how important a role these Finnish scholars played in Propp when he was writing his *Morfologija skazkii*. Later I used to mention this often until my colleague from Petersburg wrote me that I was wrong and that Propp elaborated his model independently.

Later, it became clear that this was just the origin of a discipline called narratology, a branch of semiotics. In the 1980s, when I visited and lectured at *Musée de l'Homme* in Paris, in the seminar by Prof. Gilbert Rouget, I notice that the only Finnish authors the French anthropologists knew about were Krohn brothers, whose dissertations were published in German. In the rest of this essay, I will continue to trace some of Russian formalism's Finnish connections.

Musical Connections

Another interesting aspect of Russian formalism was its artistic connections. It was obviously also an artistic practice, but an aesthetic standpoint linked to the emergence of modernism. One could link such world class artists like Majakovski, Stravinsky and Eisenstein to it. Kandinsky also has connections to Russian formalism. I could not imagine a more "formalist" book as his *Punkt und Linie zu Fläche*, albeit written later in the 1920s. I found it in Paris as a French translation *Point, ligne et plan*. His effort to create a universal grammar of all the arts, based on correspondences of colours, forms, and sounds sounded truly "structuralist", but resonated also with Scriabinesque symbolism.

Kandinsky was originally a folklorist and ethnologue who travelled among the Zyrians (*syrjäänit*, a Finnougrian tribe), wrote about their archaic life, painted and made drawings on their figures, costumes, houses, artworks, and copied especially their abstract ornamentations. This happened in 1889 at Vologda region habited by the Zyrians. In the Moscow Ethnographic Society in 1888, he had already delivered a lecture on the beliefs of Perms and Zyrians. Kandinsky was also aware of the Finnougric origin of his name stemming from River Konda area and the word *konda*, which meant "honka", a fur tree in Finnish. Several specialists of art history pointed out that the Finnougrian ornamentation was the first impulse to Kandinsky's non-figurative art. His correspondence with A Schoenberg illuminated also his visions on the artistic form. To me all this sounded truly "formalist", but in encyclopedias I tried in vain to find his name in the histories of Russian formalism. Instead, Malevitch and suprematism are often mentioned by the side of Jakobson. Kandinsky's view of the form was dynamic; it was based upon inner tensions of the art work. This view then was shared in musicology by Boris Asafiev in his intonation theory, which was discovered to be a pioneer of musical semiotics in the 1970s.

The new issue in all this, compared to earlier theories, was to see the important points in the text itself, instead of in the mind of a genius creating the art work, or at the receiver's side. So, essentially the whole epistemic movement was anti-psychological by its nature. It tried to base the aesthetic analysis on the object and its structure. It was hostile to any hermeneutic program or poetry linked to arts. It was the new objective scientific spirit of exactness which was underlined. Stravinsky's musical poetics later was characterized by the same spirit of anti-psychological nature: he did not see a reflection of any psychic content in music, as he said in his lectures in Harvard. This was certainly a formalist attitude. When Boris Gasparow visited our structuralist group in Helsinki around 1973, he emphasized however that this asematic or antisemantic approach was in fact only the minor side of the primary semantic nature of music. The same was stated by the French philosopher Vladimir Jankélévitch when speaking of Prokofiev and calling his style "espressivo inexpressif". This meant that the asemanticity was a certain historic phase in style evolution and not a synchronically valid universal truth. However, Stravinsky could then be situated in the tradition of formalist aesthetics stemming in music from Eduard Hanslick in his essay *Vom musikalisch Schönem*, which was published in 1854, and continued even by Lévi-Strauss who claimed that *La musique, c'est le langage moin le sens.* Morpurgo-Tagliabue in his *L'Esthétique contemporaine* spoke about formalism in general as a line of the 20th century aesthetics and then meaning by it a larger phenomenon than just Russian formalism. The roots of Russian formalism, especially the studies in St. Petersburg, lie in Modernism like symbolism and futurism, which were represented by Andrei Belyi with his original theories on symbols and novels, as well as the novel *The Way of Sufferings* by Aleksei Tolstoi portraying a salon in St. Petersburg where Scriabin is played and listeners are surrounded by radically distorted futurist paintings on the walls. This was the *Zeitgeist*.

If I have been dwelling at length on the field of music field here, this can be justified by the theories of the Russian formalists themselves: namely, most of them coined their new concepts as metaphors from musical practices. So far, it seems that this fact has not attracted the attention of scholars.

Sklovski

The concept of estrangement was not just of musical origin, although *Verfremdung* was the central idea of Bertolt Brecht and in the music at his "epic theater". As an artistic device, estrangement was strong in painting, literature, and music. In contemporary art it is not difficult to find other illustrations for estrangements which have a permanent place in avant-garde techniques. If we take a look at opera stagings and videos, one fashionable, almost unavoidable genre mixture of contemporary stagings, one variant of that *Regietheater* in which the stage director builds his own work upon the original, we will find that all works of video and film would have been successfully mixed with the performance of opera. Of these two genres certainly an authentic opera performance is stronger than its filmed version. In a film like *The Umbrellas of Cherburg*, singing serves as a particular estrangement technique. But then the video penetrates inside the opera, as a kind of representation of representation (Theater is of course always that, as Ivo Osolsobe once said!)

Can video then serve as an ostranenie? Yes, to some extent and at the beginning. By its force it definitely wins over the stage performance, singers are put in the background. Let us think of Harry Kupfer's *Parsifal and its Blumenmädchen* scene with slightly pornographic films replacing the real choiron stage. But when it becomes mannerism it fails. Peter Sellars' version of Tristan with continuous video films with other actors than the real singers, completely draws the attention from them and destroys live performance. In Zoldiak's radical version of Jevgeni Onegin (Savonlinna Festival, July 2013), estrangement has reached an extreme point. Yet, video looses its power totally when singers video film each other and see themselves as represented by it. This new mannerism putting singers standing there with a camera or mobile phone, with Facebook at hand all the time, is no longer estrangement but the contrary: if the original idea was to break the automatism of everyday life, now it brings the stage reality back to our daily experiences. The distance between stage and spectators shrinks, at the cost of finer subtleties and real meanings of the composer, music, singers, orchestra and all. The stage has become a narcissist reflection of the modern spectator, the popular commercial mass media culture with all forms of the symbolic violence which has intruded into art. Why should we go to opera only to see the perpetual continuation of the everyday life? Opera is no longer getting us familiar with the knowledge of the Other. All belongs to the Same. This is the end of *ostranenie*.

Tynianov

This term means a poet describing things phonetically, so that innovations on this level may militate against the semantics. If I utter a verse to you in Finnish—*Porkkanan oranssi sokaisi*—you receive it as a kind of phonetic "music" by the mere sounds of the vowels. But its meaning is nonsensical: "The orange of a carrot blinded one."

Tynianov also had reflections on genre which hold true as well for music as for literature. His essential idea is how we recognize a genre, and how we identify it. To which extent is a poem a poem and not any other text? What Tynianov wrote about genre shifts, changes, and dissolutions is close to the tenets of Asafiev, who was even more semiotic, since for him the signified was primary. When the emotional content changed, it needed new musical signifiers, and this caused the so-called "intonation crisis". Meanwhile, later formalists, in Prague circle days, stated that the relationship between changing society and arts was not a causal one but a symbolic, sign relationship, and this was of course against the official *Widerspiegelung* theory.

Zirmunski

My hypothesis is that Igor Stravinsky in his *Oedipus Rex* applied Zirmunskian ideas to the musical versification of the Latin language chosen by the composer, because it could be tested as pure phonetic material devoid of semantic connotations. I thought that this was possible for Stravinsky only after his emigration in his neoclassical period.

Zirmunski also wrote about the limitations of formalism in the 1920s long before it was officially enounced by Zdanov's visit to Leningrad University in 1947. Yet in the Moscow Slavist Congress, the comparative study was rehabilitated. At the end of the 1950s, Zirmunski was against phonology, although he studied it himself; and at the beginning of the 1960s he was against structuralism, even though he used it much himself in his metric interpretations. (For the above I am indebted to Vilmos Voigt.)

Tomasevski

Tomasevski presents a systematic vocabulary to study narratives, launching concepts like theme, fabula, subject, tension, motif, estrangement (*ostranenie*), canonic and free devices, parodies, etc.. All these notions are relevant also to music and, more specifically, to musical narrativity. Yet, when transplanting them back to the musical field, one has to be careful, since many of them are defined and used somehow differently when applied to music. One example is "theme": in a novel the theme is the basic issue, but in music the theme is a particular unit of musical discourse, in tonal music characterized by certain length.

The study of my colleague Erkki Salmenhaara could give us inspirations on how Tomasevski's approach was "musicalized". In Salmenhaara's view, all the Viennese classical symphonic music, i. e. symphonies, sonatas, string quartets, and other chamber music pieces with larger forms, could be classified as to the key architecture with the following diagram. There were only a few basic types which were used by great composers.

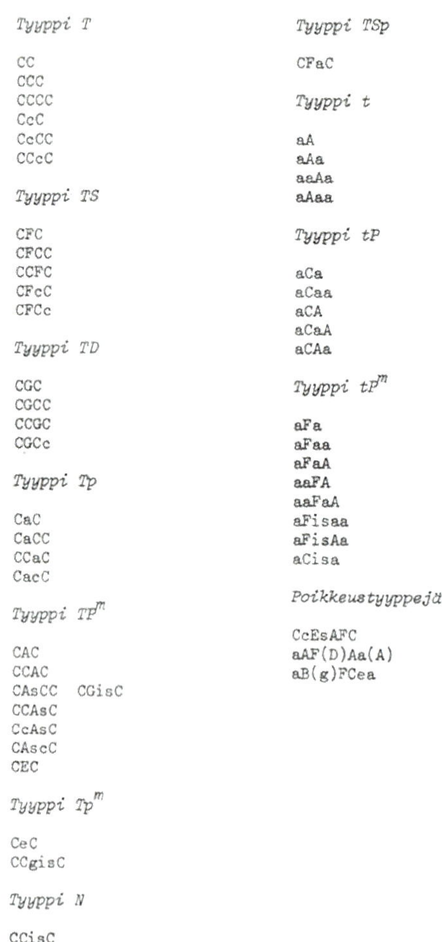

Tyyppi T

CC
CCC
CCCC
CcC
CcCC
CCcC

Tyyppi TS

CFC
CFCC
CCFC
CFcC
CFCc

Tyyppi TD

CGC
CGCC
CCGC
CGCc

Tyyppi Tp

CaC
CaCC
CCaC
CacC

Tyyppi TP^m

CAC
CCAC
CAsCC CGisC
CCAsC
CcAsC
CAscC
CEC

Tyyppi Tp^m

CeC
CCgisC

Tyyppi N

CCisC

Tyyppi TSp

CFaC

Tyyppi t

aA
aAa
aaAa
aAaa

Tyyppi tP

aCa
aCaa
aCA
aCaA
aCAa

Tyyppi tP^m

aFa
aFaa
aFaA
aaFA
aaFaA
aFisaa
aFisAa
aCisa

Poikkeustyyppejä

CcEsAFC
aAF(D)Aa(A)
aB(g)FCea

Diagram of Salmenhaara 26

Boris Tomasevski illustrates several concepts in his essay "the Structure of Plot" (which I have read as Finnish translation in the anthology *Venäläinen formalismi* edited by Pekka Pesonen and Timo Suni); Tomasevski presents a systematic vocabulary to study narratives launching concepts like theme, fabula, subject, tension, motif, exposition, time, space, kinetic space, estrangement (*ostranenie*), canonic and free devices, parodies...; all these notions are relevant also for music and, say, for musical narrativity. Yet, when transplanting them back to musical field, one has to be careful since many of them are defined and used somehow differently in being applied to music, like the first one: "theme". In a novel, theme is the basic issue, what the story is all about, like Last Days of Pompei, love story of Anna and Vronsky, society of learned men in Hesse, development of one young man like in Goethe's *Wilhelm Meister*. However, in music theme is a particular unit of musical discourse, in tonal music characterized by certain length, clear cut harmonic basis, clearly melodic formula, etc..

In fact, I already sketched an essay in which Tomasevski's approach was "musicalized" and another one in which completely traditional music theoretical study of symphony or sonata by such composer like J. Brahms will be semiotized, showing his narrative structure; this will concern perfectly absolute music without any programs. I was inspired by a study on Brahms symphonies by my colleague Erkki Salmenhaara from 1978 which I studied for my speeches for Mariinsky festival by Valeri Gergijev in Finland, having a lot of Brahms symphonies in their program!

In Salmenhaara's view all the Viennese classical symphonic music, i. e. symphonies, sonatas, string quartets and other chamber music pieces with larger forms, could be classified as to the key architecture with the following diagram. There were only a few basic types which were used by great composers. Most common was the tonic type (in major indicated by T and in minor t) and the use of subdominant in the side movement (the type is TS). Also very common is tonic-dominant-tonic. Both these types constitute the major symphony type. In minor they are rare, and as known in the minor as a contrasting tonality serves most often the parallel major type tP; the next big group is formed by key relations which Salmenhaara calls modal parallel, i. e. in major the major side key situated at the distance of major or minor third (both upwards and downwards). Theoretical possibilities are thus if the key is C major in this TPm type as follows: CAC, CasC, CEC, CesC. Also modal minor parallels of type Tpm appear, but more seldom. In minor a modal parallel solution (parallel key being almost always major of type): tPm is as common as parallel major.

I wanted to cite this because in the scheme we have in musical terms something similar to Tomasevski's classification of the narrative techniques, or Vladimir Propp's study on the morphology of folk tale. Here we are talking about symphonies and sonatas instead of novels or fairy tales. The key distinctions lie not only in the abstract spatial relations in the inner tonal space, but also the fact that symphonies and sonatas are already semantically loaded. Even the choice of a key is not at all arbitrary. Let us say: anyone writing in E flat major after Beethoven's *Eroica* must face the heroic character of this key. In the time of Russian formalism, the synaesthesic meanings of keys were also discussed by artists: Kandinsky portrayed different angles with various colors; Rimsky-Korsakov and Scriabin had their diagrams of correspondences of keys and colors. Individual composers thought of keys in terms of colors. For Sibelius, the combination of orange, red and black was D major.

Anyway, the classification evokes the idea of the basic theme of each story, whether it goes from "sad" minor to "victorious" major, whether it starts and ends happily but has excursion (shifting off, debrayages) into darker fields. The global plan of a work is just its symphonic structure strengthened by thematic (actorial) and motivic elements on more superficial levels of the work. However, just as Propp came to 31 basic functions of the Russian fairy tale, here we can see 58 types of symphonic literature. Analogies between story telling in a novel and symphony continue when we study them further and examine more figurative expressions in both fields.

Altogether this might even lead us to think of the birth of Russian formalism *aus dem Geiste der Musik*, as with Nietzsche about tragedy.

Sesemann

One name that seems strange in this collection was Karsavin, who is among those scholars well known in Russia but totally ignored in the West. I heard about him rather recently in connection with the Lithuanian philosopher and aesthetician Wilhelm Sesemann, who had invited this Russian intellectual from Russia to Kaunas University in the 1930s. Unfortunately these two extremely important scholars remained there after the occupation of Lithuania and did not emigrate early enough, so they shared the destiny to be sent to Siberia, where Karsavin died in 1952 and Sesemann survived. Sesemann returned as rehabilitated to Kaunas and lived there until 1962.

The reason I would like to raise these two names in this context of Russian formalism, even though neither of them is directly mentioned in any Western encyclopedia of semiotics as Russian formalists, is that they played an important role mediating formalist ideas to other scholars who became influential in the semiotic field. Sesemann was the logic teacher of A. J. Greimas at Kaunas University, where Greimas attended Seseman's course in 1934, as shown by his study book. Greimas, the founder of the Paris school of semiotics, said later that it was from Karsavin that he realized that the Lithuanian language could be used as a scientific discourse. Certainly even less known is that as the first Finnish semiotician is the nephew of Sesemann, Finnish-Swedish poet Henry Parland, who in the 1920s wrote cultural essays inspired by Russian formalists like Zirmunski, on Russian and American movies, on Kaunas Jewish theater, etc. And Sesemann himself was a half Finn. The honorary member of the Finnish Semiotic Society, psychiatrist Oscarl Parland, has studied the life of his brother and uncle.

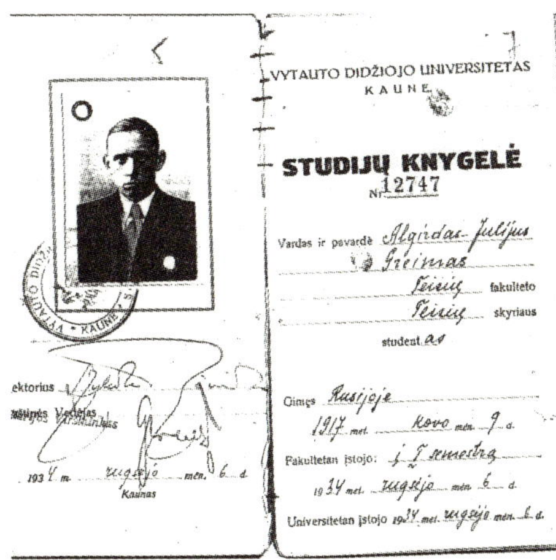

VYTAUTO DIDŽIOJO UNIVERSITETAS
KAUNE

STUDIJŲ KNYGELĖ
Nr. 12747

Vardas ir pavardė Algirdas Julijus Greimas
Teisių fakulteto
Teisių skyriaus
studentas

Gimęs Rusijoje
1917 met. kovo mėn. 9 d.
Fakultetan įstojo: į I semestrą
1934 met. rugsėjo mėn. 6 d.
Universitetan įstojo 1934 met. rugsėjo mėn. 6 d.

ektorius
Vedėjas
1934 m. rugsėjo mėn. 6 d.
Kaunas

Greimas's Student Card in Kaunas University

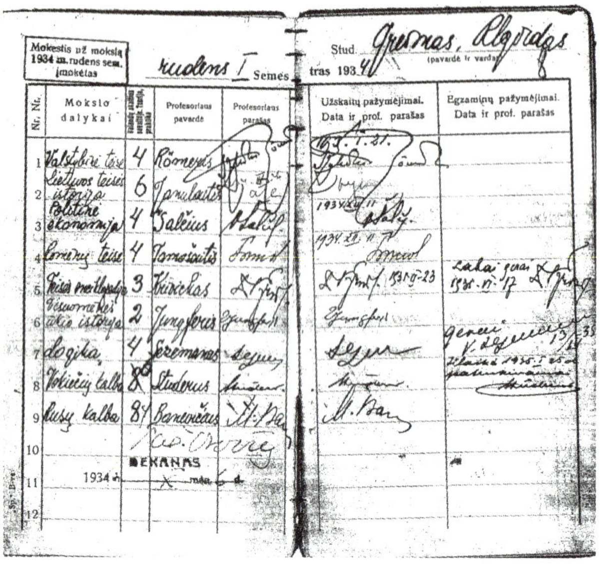
Mokestis už mokslą 1934 m. rudens sem. įmokėtas
rudens I Semestras 1934
Stud. Greimas, Algirdas
(pavardė ir vardas)
Nr. Nr.
Mokslo dalykai
Profesoriaus pavardė
Profesoriaus parašas
Užskaitų pažymėjimai. Data ir prof. parašas
Egzaminų pažymėjimai. Data ir prof. parašas
DEKANAS

Greimas's Study Book

According to Thorsten Botz-Bornstein, for Seseman the meaning was neither totally subjective, to be studied as the state of the human mind, nor completely objective, i. e. existing in a text, but living between them, in a form he saw as possessing a certain rhythm. Sesemann was influenced by Russian formalism, but his view on the form was rather dynamic, almost kinetic. The place where he put it between the subjective and objective comes close to Greimas's concept of *le monde naturel* which was not at all anything natural but already semiotized by the human mind.

Seseman also criticizes Russian formalists. His view of structure was that it was inner rhythm which constituted the true aesthetic moment. It was close to Lossky's notion of organic whole or neo-Kantian efforts to dynamize static logical systems. Sememan emphasized the two forms of knowledge: *kennen* and *wissen*, of which the first one was more important. Not the notion of "device" *priem* from Sklovski was the true essence of an art work. Of it, Sesemann said in his work *Iskusstvo I kul'tura*, which, by the way, appeared in the same year as Heidegger's *Sein und Zeit* in 1927: "the notion of device as used by the school of the Formalists which is for them a substitute for form in spite of all the methodological convenience it offers it cannot be considered sound from a philosophical point of view. Form understood only as a device of artistic expression takes in a subjective-intentional character and seems to exist without any relation to the material itself" (quoted from Botz-Bornstein, p. 41). But Sesemann's "formalism" is an "aesthetic one" (ibid.). It is true that he was a philosopher and aesthetician in the first place and moved onto another level of abstraction than formalist scholars, whose thinking system were more concrete.

Propp

In considering the reception and influence of Russian formalism on subsequent developments in semiotics, the name which surfaces most readily is Vladimir Propp. When Propp's *Morfologija skazki*, was translated into English in 1958 and into French in 1964, it became the "Bible" of structuralists. Its models are further developed by Lévi-Strauss, Greimas, Brémond, Elli-Kaija Köngäs-Maranda, and Pierre Maranda.

The innovation Propp made in *Morfologija skazki* as early as in 1928 is decisive. In order to understand the productivity of the idea, let us ponder from what intellectual context it emerged. Propp's basic discovery in studying Russian fairy tales was that the elements of one tale could be transferred to another tale without any change. The very notion of plot is defined as follows: one chooses at random one part of a tale, and provides it with word "about" and then definition is ready. Propp found all other earlier classifications unsuccessful. For Veselovski, plot consisted of several motifs, and each motif developed into a section. Plot was a theme which consisted of various situations. For him motif is primary; plot is secondary. But Propp thought that we had to first segment a tale; only thereafter could we make comparisons. All questions in the study of tales lead to the unresolved problem of why all fairy tales in the world remind us of each other. How can we explain that a tale about a frog queen is so similar to tales of the same kind in Russia, Germany, France, India, America and New Zealand? For Propp, the basic unit of a tale was "a function". So Propp formulated his hypotheses as follows: (a) Functions are stable units of fairy tales, independent of who fulfills them or how *dramatis personae* realize them; (b) the number of functions is limited; (c) the order or sequence of functions is identical; (d) all fairy tales belong to the same genre. However, functions do not follow each other immediately. When different persons fulfill consecutively functions, the latter person has to know all that has happened before he can enter. (How well this is realized in a Wagnerian mythic opera! Lévi-Strauss considered Wagner the first structural analyst of myth!)

How did Propp use ideas from the Finnish school of folkloristics for his achievement? According to Vilmos Voigt (in a letter to me), Propp was influenced by Aarne-Thompson. After the *skazochnaja* committee, a research committee for folk tales, was founded by *Russkoe geograficheskoe obshchestvo* (whose director was the famous orientalist, Duke S. F. Oldenburg), it invited Propp to make a catalogue of fairy tale types. Propp got a grant but soon thought that Aarne's system was outdated. After he read through Afanasjev's classical fairy tale collection, he realized that many fairy tales followed the same structure. This was the birth of Propp's morphology. He wrote his own book three times. First he wrote it as a narrative story, not morphology, and the committee did not accept it. Then, following V. M, Zirmuski's advice, Propp wrote a short text with only schemes and diagrams. It was almost incomprehensible. Finally emerged the well-known last version, which was published in the book series of Russian literature edited by Zhirmunski.

After the Second World War, Afanasjev's 3-part fairy tale collection was published. At its end, there was a catalogue of about 100 printed pages of fairy tale types, following Aarne-Thompson in 1928, edited by Propp. If we compare Aarne-Thompson type stores and Propp's morphological diagrams, we will learn the division of texts is similar, but the purposes are different. Accordingly, Propp had known since the beginning what the "Finnish" analysis of fairy tale types was like, and he twice wrote such a catalogue—yet his own method of morphology was different. (By the way, this background has been adequately treated in the dictionary of *Enzyklopedie des Märchens*. This Encyclopedia has entries for Propp, Andrejev, Morphologie, etc..)

In the 1960s, the Russian folklorists like K. V. Chistov have underlined that Propp "was a deeply Soviet great scholar", whereas the Western folklorists and Isidor Levin expressed the opinion that the context of Propp's life work was international. The rebirth of Propp's Morpholoqy was the idea of Roman Jakobson, and thanks to Thomas A. Sebeok, the first English version appeared (Email letter from Voigt to Tarasti in July 2013).

Levi-Strauss published his comments on Propp in his essay in *Cahiers de l'Institut de science economique appliqué no* 9, *mars* 1960 entitled "*L'analyse morphologique des contes russes*" and simultaneously in English in the *International Journal of Slavic Linguistics and Poetics* 3, 1960. He began by saying that those exercising structural analysis had been often accused of formalism. This means that form is determined by its opposition to the matter which is alien to it, whereas in truth structure does not have any separate contents: it is the content put in a logical organization, which is conceived as a property of "the real" (Lévi-Strauss 1973, p. 139). Lévi-Strauss praises the translators of Propp's work who have done an immense service to the human sciences by their work. Lévi-Strauss then comments on Propp and admits that his criticism of previous scholars is justified (Miller, Wundt, Aarne, Veselovsky). The problem is that one can always find tales which belong at the same time to several categories because classification is based upon types of tale or themes which they enact. The distinction of theme again is arbitrary. The classification of Aarne provided an inventory of themes which is very useful, but the segmentation is purely empirical, although the belonging of one tale to one caregory is always approximative.

Propp's work was indeed celebrated by the structuralist movement by and large. For Greimas it was one of the starting points for his semiotic school and he launched the discussion in his *Sémantique structural* in 1966. Like Lévi-Strauss, he noticed that Propp's list could be made more economical, and one could distinguish what he called the mythical actants model with six members, that is, subject, object, sender, receiver, helper and opponent. However, the concept of an actant appears in his book much earlier than when he speaks about Propp in the chapter *A la recherché des modeles de transformation*. Also, Greimas tries to reduce the number of functions.

Yet, in the history of structuralism written by Francois Dosse, Russian formalism is mentioned just when he discusses its impact on French structuralism. However, when Propp's book appeared at Seuil in 1965, it became the source of inspiration for the whole structuralist movement. It appeared in English in 1958 thanks to the initiative of Jakobson and effort of Thomas A Sebeok, yet Lévi-Strauss had discovered it as early as in 1960.

But there were also other scholars working further with the Proppian model. If Lévi-Strauss had changed his linear model into an achronic matrix, this was elaborated further by Elli-Kaija Köngäs-Maranda and Pierre Maranda in their article "Structural Models in Folklore", which appeared in *Midwest Folklore*, in the Fall of 1962. They list earlier studies on structure in folklore such as Propp's Morphology and Lévi-Strauss, Sebeok and Alan Dundes' theories. The primary goal of all of them was to find out the smallest operational units of structure. Aarne proposed it as "type" in 1910, Propp as "function" in 1928; they were both content units without operational value. Then Thompson proposed "motif" in 1932, and Lévi-Strauss "mytheme" in 1955 in a study on the Oedipus myth. The latter was a contentual-structural unit consisting of a relation between subject and predicate. Dundes proposed in 1962 a "motifeme", which was an act of a protagonist, taking into account its meaning in the whole fairy tale.

When the structuralist fashion lost its attractiveness, what remained was narratology, which could still consider Propp as its pioneer, especially since almost all canonical analyses of stories started with segmentation. For instance, even in musical narratology, as I have tried to show in my study of the G minor Ballade of Chopin with its modal grammar. But, as Ugo Volli said, after Propp, various authors have tried to extend the morphology to other narrative genres, like myth, legend, popular literature, and modern novel. But in order to do, analysis is to be brought up to a higher level of abstraction (*Manuale di semiotica*, p. 111). It is hard to imagine any other type of systematic narrative study than what stems from Proppian "functions".

Bakhtin

Yet, there is another Russian classic formalist who became very influential in the West in the 1980s. This was Mikhail Bakhtin. His profound ideas on own/alien speech, the dialogical imagination, polyphonic discourse in literature, ideologemes, and carnivalesque culture, had a major impact on Western intelligentsia.

In his semiophilosophy and semioethics, Augusto Ponzio, together with Susan Petrilli, has taken Bakhtin as one of his precursors. Ponzio tries to analyze the present globalized reality and also life in the European Union in Bakhtinian terms. He sees Bakhtin more a philosopher than a literary theoretician (for instance: Ponzio, *Signs, Dialogue and Ideology*, p. 107—138, 1993; *Fuori Campo, I segni del corpo tra rappresentazione ed eccedenza*, p. 305—320, 1999). In fact, Ponzio writes, "We take 'our' words, says Bakhtin, from the mouth of others. 'Our' words are always semi-other. They are pregnant with the intentions of others before we use them ourselves as the materials and instruments of our own intentions. Consequently [...]. our discourses and thoughts are inevitably dialogic."

Yet, in the West, it was perhaps Julia Kristeva who first introduced the ideas of Bakhtin. She noted as early as in 1966 in her essay "Le Mot, le dialogue et le roman", that what is involved is a "cosmogony" in which "*on ne connait pas la substance, la cause, l'identité en dehors du rapport avec le tout qui n' existe que dans et par la relation*" (op cit. p. 160). She speaks of Bakthin's intertextuality in "two texts which join", they contradict and relativize. The one who attends carnaval is at the same time actor and spectator. She distinguishes epic literature which is monologistic from a dialogical one. In fact, we can notice like Kristeva the following cases: (a) subject of utterance, enunciate coincides with the zero value of subject of enunciation: "he" or proper name; the most simple narrative technique which gives birth to a story; (b) coincidence of the subject of enunciate with subject of enunciation: "me" "I"; (c) coincidence of subject of enunciate with the destinator "you"; (d) coincidence of subject of enunciation at the same time with subject of enunciation and destinator. Novel becomes a play with writing and tagging the dialogical nature of the book. Kristeva ends up with a scheme portraying these case:

Practice	God
"Discourse"	"History"
Dialogis	Monologism

Correlational logics	Aristotelian logics
Syntagma	System
Carnaval	Narrative
Ambivalence; Menippea;	polyphonic novel

If the word is the minimal unit in Bakhtin's theory, there can be found two types: one's own word and alien word. Authoritarian word comes from the exterior and demands to be accepted; it penetratesus independently whether we find it convincing or not. The distinction between own and alien is very important in Bakhtin. We may think this coincides with existential semiotics and its categories of Moi/Soi. According to Bakhtin the resistance to alien, external world is of the highest importance to the development of individual ideology and identity. The whole process of learning and education is after all about how the alien becomes one's own.

Surprisingly, in quite recent years, a special cultural psychological theory emerged from Bahktin's ideas, along with its application to psychotherapy, as well as cognitive and neurological brain studies. Hubert Hermans has created a theory of dialogical self entirely on a Bakhtinian basis. Hermans observes two kinds of positions: intersubjective interchange and dominance or social power. One may ask how dialogical the brain is and scrutinize dysfunctions like schizophrenia as a "collapse of the dialogical self". Theorists across disciplines have described the dynamic and multifaceted nature of self-experience, stressing that the self is "inherently 'dialogical' or the product of ongoing conversations both within the individual and between the individual and others". (p. 209). Moreover, Mikael Leiman from Joensuu University confirms: "Semiotic position and Bakhtinian notions of the signs suggest modification of the concept of I-position. Person's position reveals his or her subjective stance with regard to the addressee. The addressee is an invisible third, always seen to adopt a reciprocal stance, a counter-position. Thus instead of a dialogue between an I-position (a voice) and another, each I-position has dialogical relationship to its addressee. I-positions are embodied in signs, and sign mediate changes between the positions. Also Heikki Majava a Finnish psychiatrist has developed a model of transference based upon two I-positions, in the Bakhtinian sense."

There, if one says in existential semiotics that dialogue can be a disturbance in communication in which the I tries to communicate his/her ideas, this disturbance is welcome and beneficial; it must be there as a particular "noise" of the communication channel, albeit it were true that the other addressee remains an alien-psychic entity of which we can only hypothesize that he/she is something similar as the speaking subject. Thus almost imperceptibly we glide with Bakhtin into most vital debate of the nature of the self and cultural communication.

Altogether we see that the heritage of Russian formalism is not only shared by the Tartu-Moscow school of cultural semiotics (although it is in a privileged position), but Bakhtinian reception also takes place all over the world. Many applying his concepts hardly even know his background in the formalist movement; some specialists even deny that he belonged to that school at all. There he is, however, right in the encyclopedias of semiotics. Yet it is typical of contemporary schools of cultural theory and others to utilize these great figures as innovators, but detach them from their ideational context. Of course, we are interested in the works of Propp or Bakhtin just as historic documents of the early 20th century thought, but primarily for the weightiness of their ideas. We read them as classics, which will never be exhausted.

References:

Almeida, Renato, (1974). *Intelligência do folklore*, 2a edicão, Rio de Janeiro: Campanhia Editora Americanna.

Apo, Satu, (1986). *Ihmesadun rakenne* (*The Structure and Message of Magic Tales*). Proceedings from Finnish literary society 446. Helsinki: Suomalaisen kirjallisuuden seura.

Aspelin, Kurt, Lundberg, Bengt A., (1971). *Form och struktur. Litteraturvetenskapliga texter i urval*. Stockholm: Bokförlaget Pan/Norstedts.

Bahtin, Mihail M., (1979). *Kirjallisuuden ja estetiikan ongelmia* (*Problems of Literature and Aesthetics*). Trans. from Russian to Finnish by Kerttu Kyhälä-Juntunen and Veikko Airola. Moskova: Kustannusliike Progress

——, (1996). *The Dialogic Imagination: Four Essays*. Ed., Michael Holquist, trans, Caryl Emerson and Michael Holquist. Austin: University of Texas Press.

Botz-Bornstein, Thorsten, (2006). *Vasily Sesemann, Experience, Formalism and the*

Question of Being. Amsterdam, New York: Radopi.

Brémond, Claude, (1973). *Logique du récit*. Paris: Seuil.

Dosse, Francois, (1991). *Histoire du structuralisme. I. Le champ du signe*, 1945 — 1966. Paris: Editions La Découverte.

Greimas, Algirdas Julien, (1966). *Sémantique structural*. Paris: Larousse.

Hermans, Hubert, ed., (2002). *Theory & Psychology*, Vol 12, number 2, April. Special issue: The Dialogical Self. Alberta: Sage Publications.

Karsavin, Lev, (2003). *Le poème de la mort. Traduction postface et apercu biographique par Francois Lesourd*. Lausanne: Editions l'Age d' Homme.

Kristeva, Julia, (1969). *Zeemeiotikee. Recherches pour une sémanalyse*. Paris: Seuil.

Köngäs-Maranda, Elli-Kaija, Maranda, Pierre, (1962). "Structural Models in Folklore", (*Midwest Folklore*), Fall 1962. Bloomington, Indiana: Indiana University.

Lévi-Strauss, Claude, (1973). *Anthropologie structurale deux*. Paris: Plon.

Marc-Lipiansky, Mireille, (1973). *Le structuralisme de Lévi-Strauss*. Paris: Payot.

Nöth, Winfried, (2000). *Handbuch der Semiotik. 2. vollstndig neu bearbeitete und erweiterte Auflage*. Stuttgart, Weimar: Verlag J. B. Metzler.

Parland, Oscar, (1991). *Tieto ja eläytyminen: Esseitä ja muistelmia* (*Knowledge and Empathy: Essays and Memories*). Porvoo, Helsinki, Juva: WSOY.

Pesonen, Pekka, (1987). *Vallankumouksen henki hengen vallankumouksessa: Tutkielma Andei Belyin romaanista "Peterburg" ja sen aatetaustasta.* (*The Spirit of Revolution in the Revolution of the Spirit: A Study of Alndrei Bely's Novel "Peterburg" and its Ideological Background*). Slavica helsingiensia. supplementum II. Helsinki: Universityo of Helsinki.

Pesonen, Pekka, Suni, Timo, eds. (2001). *Venäläinen formalismi*. Tietolipas 172. Helsinki: Finnish Literary Society.

Ponzio, Augusto, (1993). *Signs, Dilogue and Ideology*. Ed., trans., from Italian by Susann Petrilli. Amsterdam: John Benjamins Publishing Company.

Propp, Vladimir, (1970). *Morphologie du conte*. Points. Paris: Seuil.

Salmenhaara, Erkki, (1979). *Tutkielmia Brahmsun sinfonioista*. (*Studies in Brahms Symphonies*), Acta Musicologica Fennica 12. Helsinki: Suomen Musiikkitieteellinen Seura.

Tarasti, Eero. (1979). *Myth and Music*. Berlin: Mouton de Gruyter.

——, (1994). *A Theory of Musical Semiotics*. Bloomington, Indianapolis: Indiana University Press.

——, (2000). *Existential Semiotics*. Bloomington, Indianapolis: Indiana University Press.

——, (2009). *Fondements de la sémiotique existentielle*. Trans. from English by Jean-Laurent Csinidis. Paris: L'Harmattan.

——, (2010). *Fondamenti di semiotica esistenziale*. Trans. from English by Massimo Berruti. Bari: Giuseppe Laterza Editore.

Taruskin, Richard, (1997). *Defining Russia Musically*. Princeton, New Jersey: Princeton University Press.

Valkonen, Markku, (1998). "Kandinsky, Kalevala and the Shamans", exhibition catalogue, The Retretti Art Center, Punkaharju, Finland.

Valkonen, Olli, (1998). "Wassily Kandinsky's Early Contacts with Finland", exhibition catalogue, The Retretti Art Center, Punkaharju, Finland.

Voigt, Vilmos, (1973). Lectures on Semiotics at the Folklore Dep. in the University of Helsinki.

——, (2013). Letter to Eero Tarasti by email, July 24, 2013.

Volli, Ugo, (2000). *Manuale di semiotica*. Roma-Bari: Editore Laterza.

Author:

Eero Tarasti, professor of musicology at the University of Helsinki, President of the International Association for Semiotic Studies (2004 — current). His research fields are semiotics and musicolgy.

作者简介:

埃罗·塔拉斯蒂,赫尔辛基大学音乐学教授,国际符号学协会主席(2004 至今)。主要研究方向为符号学、音乐学。

E-mail: eero. tarasti@helsinki. fi

The Temporality of Text: Starting from Roland Barthes' *La préparation du roman*

Julia Ponzio

Abstract: This paper is focused on the last two courses given by Roland Barthes at the Collège de France between 1978 and 1980 on "The Preparation of Novel". In these courses he outlines a new perspective on the novel as elaborated during the last years of his work. To look at the novel from the viewpoint of its preparation means to consider it from a perspective that is totally different from that of the literary critic and of traditional analyses of the literary text in general. Traditional text analyses a novel as an already written text in which everything has already happened: from this point of view, the novel is a "fact", a "matter of fact". As such it is analysed and classified in terms of a historical or structural schema and interpreted in response to the question: "what does the author mean?" That is, "which is the true signified of these signifiers which compose the text?" Barthes' perspective is completely different and opens to the possibility of a new relation to the text, where the core of the problem of the novel is no longer the "author", but the subject of writing desire.

Key words: desire, event, finitude, novel, subject

论文本的时间性：从罗兰·巴尔特《小说的准备》谈起

朱丽娅·庞齐奥

摘要：本文对罗兰·巴尔特的著作《小说的准备》进行了讨论，该书是他 1978—1980 年间任教于法兰西学院时两门课程的讲义集。这两门课程为作者在这部最后的文集中提出的小说的新视角勾勒出了大致的轮廓，这种视角和以往的文学批评，以及传统文本分析的视角都不同。传统的文本分析将小说视为既定的、已经写成的文本：从这一视角而言，小说是已成的“事实”；它也由此被置放在历史或结构的框架下加以检视和分类，并且被认为是旨在回答这样的问题：“作者的意图是什么？”也就是“什么是构成文本的能指的真正所指”？与此不同的是，巴尔特的看法为文本的新关系打开了可能：文本的核心问题不再是“作者”，而是书写欲望的主体。

关键词：欲望，事件，界限，小说，主体

Ⅰ. A New Perspective on the Novel

The last two courses Roland Barthes gave at the Collège de France between 1978 and 1980 were focused on the theme of the "Preparation of Novel". To look at the novel from the viewpoint of its preparation means to consider it from the perspective—which is totally different from that of the literary critic—of the traditional analysis of the literary text in general. Traditional text analyses a novel as an already written text, as a text in which everything has already happened: for this reason, from the viewpoint of traditional text analysis the novel is a "fact", a "matter of fact", which has to be analysed: such analysis of a literary text as an accomplished fact is an "autopsy". This approach consists in classifying the text in terms of a historical or structural schema and interpreting it through the construction of a comment that answers the question: "what does the author mean?" That is to say, "which is the true signified of these signifiers which compose the text?" The perspective on the literary text invented by Barthes in the two years of his 1978 – 1980 courses on "The Preparation of the Novel" is completely different and opens to the possibility of a new relation to text.

The novel Barthes discussed in his two courses is not an already written novel, but rather a projected novel, a desired one. Barthes entitled this novel *Vita Nova* and only wrote some preparatory outlines. We don't really know whether Barthes did not write it because of his unexpected death, in 1980, just a few days after the conclusion of the courses, or because to write this novel as Barthes desired was structurally impossible.

Ⅱ. Phantasm of Writing and Subject as Singularity

At the beginning of the course, Barthes said that this novel, the novel he wanted to write, titled *Vita Nova*, is the "Phantasm" (*Fantasme*) from which the course originated (Barthes, 2003, Eng. trans., 2010, p.3). In the English translations of the course the French word *Fantasme* is translated as "Phantasy". In the present text, we have chosen to use the term Phantasm because what Barthes called a *Fantasme* is an imaginary object instead of simply a phantasy.

Phantasm is a desired object which is not already present, but nevertheless has a strongly concrete repercussion on my present life, because I desire it so strongly that all I do is oriented to its realization. In this Phantasm I imagine a situation which I want to realize; I imagine how everything will be once the desired object is realized; I imagine myself walking towards this realization; how I will become after this realization; how other people will consider me after this realization, etc.. In this sense, the phantasm is an object which does not still exist, but acts on my present, and which changes my days, and my relation with the world, with others and even with myself. In this sense "*vita nova*", the desired novel, the novel which has not yet be written, the novel at the level of its preparation, that is to say, of its planning and of its patient elaboration, represents, in the last years of Barthes' life, his Phantasm.

This analysis of the novel in its preparatory phase, starting from someone's writing desire, radically changes the questions posed to the text. Looking at the text from the viewpoint of its preparation, the main question is no longer that of classical text analysis— "What does the author mean?" "What is the meaning of this text?" —as if the text were a game which consists in the deciphering and decryption of a code hidden by the author. Looking at the text from the viewpoint of its preparation, the main question becomes: "who is the subject which is about to write?" That is to say, "who is the subject of what Barthes calls the 'to-want-to write'" (Barthes, 2003, Eng. trans., 2010, p.8), and "why does this subject desire to write", and "what need does this desire of writing respond to". For these reasons, the course of 1979 began with what Barthes called "a declaration of the subject". "Subject" is a word full of history and which, therefore, can have very different meanings. The subject that makes its declaration in the opening pages of *Preparation of the Novel* is a very different one—it is not a transcendental subject; it is not an abstract subject, a subject without a body. The first thing this "subject" declares in *The Preparation of Novel* does is its age, and this declaration is not only the definition of a personal datum but the description of a mood.

Let's read the beginning of the declaration made by this subject:

> Dante: "Nel mezzo del cammin di nostra vita." Dante was thirty-five. I'm much older and have gone far beyond the mathematical "middle" of my life's journey [...]. Now, for my part, although I've gone far beyond the arithmetical middle of my life, it's today that I'm experiencing the sensation—certainty of living out the middle—of the journey, of finding myself at that kind of juncture [...] beyond which the waters divide, taking two divergent ways. (Barthes, 2003, Eng. trans., 2010, p. 3)

This declaration is more than a definition of self, the "confession" of a mood. After the confession of a mood this subject tries to explain it. This sensation is due, he says, to two states of "consciousness" and to one "event".

The first evidence is that of irreversibility and finitude of life's time. This irreversibility, this sense of finitude, as Barthes says, is not "natural" but becomes stronger with age: "having reached a certain age our days are numbered." (Barthes, 2003, Eng. trans., 2010, p. 4) The feeling is that there is no more time to live all the desired lives, and that for this reason it is necessary to realize the last desire, to choose the last life. This is precisely what Barthes calls the *vita nova*, the new life. This necessity to choose a last time is opposed to the repetitiveness of life that represents the second consciousness. Speaking of this second consciousness, Barthes says:

> [...] there comes a time when what you've done, written (past works and practices) looks like repeated material, doomed to repetition, to the lassitude of repetition. (Barthes, 2003, Eng. trans. 2010, p. 4)

It is the sensation of the "forclosure of anything new", the "forclosure of adventure", of sensation to be sentenced to repetition. Barthes establishes, therefore, in these initial pages of the course on *The Repetition of Novel*, an apparently simple opposition between a desire of a *vita nova*, due to consciousness that the time at one's disposal has become very short, and the sensation of being sentenced to what is already done, to what is already said, and to what is already written.

Ⅲ. The Event as What Breaks the Time of the Subject

This apparently simple opposition is soon complicated, in Barthes' discourse, by a third element which is no longer a consciousness, an evidence, or a fact, but rather an "event". An event is something that happens when life seems to be a familiar scene, closed to any possibility of renewal, when life only seems to be a repetition of identity, when all possibility of a *vita nova* seems to be impossible: the event is something unexpected, an incident, as Barthes call it, a short circuit which changes everything.

Barthes writes:

> Last, an event sent by Destiny, can occur to painfully or dramatically mark, cut into, incise, break up that slow running aground, triggering the transformation of that all-too-familiar landscape—what I called the "middle of the journey of life"; it is, alas, pain's *asset* (*l'actif du doleur*). (Barthes, 2003, Eng. trans., 2010, p. 4)

The event Barthes is speaking about is that of mourning: he is not speaking about mourning in general, but about a particular mourning, his own mourning, mourning lived in the first person by the subject who is saying I: he is referring to the event of his mother's death, which also constitutes one of the focal points in *La chambre Claire*, which Barthes writes at the same time of his two courses. Mourning is an event which divides life in two parts, which articulates life in a "before" and "after". in such a way that from that moment on, nothing is the same, nothing is as before it was. In this sense an event is, according to Barthes, what articulates, carves, and breaks the time of life. Discontinuity as provoked by the event is unsolvable, definitive. The wound mourning opened in the continuity of the subject's life will not close; there is no possibility of recovery. As Barthes writes:

> [...] on the one hand, I have no time left to try out several different lifes: I have to choose my last life, my new life, *vita nova*. And on the other, I have to get out of this gloomy state of mind that the wearing effects of repetitive work and mourning have disposed to me. (Barthes, 2003, Eng. trans., 2010, p. 5).

Therefore, the subject that declares itself in these opening pages of Barthes' course of 1979 is not an omnipotent subject, a strong subject, a subject ruler of its own time. On the contrary, this subject is a subject installed in its own finitude, installed in its own mood, at the mercy of the events, a subject in difficulty, in checkmate, a subject that has reached an *impasse*. The experience of *impasse* is the experience of a sense of finitude which is totally different from the ordinary sense of finitude. The ordinary idea of finitude is linked to the economy of time, of counted time, in days and hours, and to saving time. This is the idea of finitude described by Barthes in the first of the two states of consciousness. On the contrary, finitude, as described by the subject in the first pages of *The Preparation of Novel*, is linked to the sense of the loss of what is impossible to retrieve, to the nostalgia of what is already past. The time of this finitude is not the linear time in which I count the days, but a broken time: in this time all calculation of time looses its sense. This is no longer the finitude of the isolated subject, which counts its time: finitude in this new sense is the question of the relation with what is irreplaceable, a loss impossible to compensate. In this finitude time is not stretched out like a line, but, on the contrary, is contracted in a strange presence. That is the presence of the unreplaceable; that is past, but that at once occupies my present, filled with nostalgia for it: this contraction of time is mourning which cannot be elaborated; all is blocked in what Barthes call the feeling of affliction. This time contracted in the instant is the very short time of an instant in which everything suddenly changes.

Ⅳ. The "Desire of Writing" as Event

In *The Preparation of Novel*, this situation of impasse changes when a second event occurs. The second event Barthes describes is the desire of *vita nova*, the desire to write a novel. In the fist of the two courses, Barthes describes the apparition of his desire of writing, the instant starting from which all will be oriented to the project of writing a novel.

> April 15, 1978. Casablanca. The sluggishness of the afternoon. The sky clouds over, a slight chill in the air. A group of us go in two cars to the Waterfall. *The same, uninterrupted sadness*, a kind of listlessness that bears upon everything I do, everything I think. Return, an empty apartment; a difficult time: the afternoon. Alone, sad. I reflect with enough intensity. The beginnings of an idea: something like a "literary conversion—it's those two very old words that occur to me: to enter into literature, into writing; to write, as if I'd never written before. (Barthes, 2003, Eng. trans., 2010, p. 7).

This time contracted in an instant. This instant in which everything suddenly changes, is what Barthes calls "the time of individuation". The two courses on preparation of the novel are a reflection about this strange presence in which time is not a line, in which there is no possibility of a development, in which all time is suspended in a point, which cannot be explained by the past. In Barthes's tale, as we have just read it, there is no logical connection between the trip of few hours before and the desire to write the novel. These two elements are composed together and together they reveal a scene, a moment, which has no explanations. As described, the trip, the past just passed, does not have the function of explaining the present. In the same way, there is no connection between the sadness of a moment before and the desire to write a novel. Telling this story, this tale, that is, the story of a singularity (Barthes's own tale, the tale of his life, of the moment he is living), Barthes tells the reasons of his desire of writing, which is to say he tells his story to explain why he began desiring to write, why he was in need to write a novel. This means that the subject which declares himself, in the first pages of this course, the subject which is about to write, the subject of the desire of writing is not a subject in general, but a subject with a proper name. This declaration by a subject, therefore, according to Barthes, is the declaration of a singularity. For this reason, the novel about which Barthes speaks is not "the novel" in general, nor the definition of a literary genre: this desired novel is the Phantasm of a unprecedented novelty, of a radical change of life which produces a totally new *œuvre*, an absolute event, a cut in time and in history from which all can begin again.

Ⅴ. The Desire of a New Practice of Writing

This novel requires a new practice of writing capable of describing the temporality of the subject of the desire of writing, which is not a continuous temporality, but temporality broken by the event. As Barthes says:

> For someone who writes, who has chosen to write, that is to say, for someone who has *experienced the jouissance*, *the joy of writing*, [...] there can be no other *Vita Nova* (or so it seems to me) than the discovery of a new writing practice. (Barthes, 2003, Eng. tran. , 2010. p. 6)

The practice of writing the classic novel is based on the construction of a temporality which is a precise sequence between before and after: if the writer recounts something about the past of a character, often this is because the past explains, justifies something which happens in the present of the narration. In the classic narration, time is linked by a strict logic. The "and then what? [...]" of this time is always translatable with a "and therefore?" The classic structure of narration consists in the construction of a timeline in which the stories of the characters gradually develop: even the plot twists have their explanation, their justification, which the writer must, has the duty, to reveal.

The problem of this classic narrative structure is that it is not able to tell the story of the subject of the desire of writing, as described by Barthes himself. This subject cannot write his story using this classic narrative structure because the time of his life is not a line, but a time which is broken by events, a time all concentrated in a present which no past can justify. What Barthes looks for is a writing without narration, a writing without timelines, a writing without "and then", without "therefore". Barthes' *vita nova*, which is at once a project of life and the title of his projected novel, is the possibility to write the sense of finitude contracted in a single instant, in which everything changes: that's why the new practice of writing Barthes is looking for is a writing of the present. (Barthes, 2003, Eng. trans, 2010, p. 17)

For this reason Barthes, in these years, focuses his studies on two practices of catching the present in a text, which are haiku and photography. Almost all the course of 1979—80 revolved around the analysis of haiku and its relation with the photographic text. Haiku is a short poem, from Japanese literary culture, and is composed by three verses. Haiku, as Barthes says, only presents the scene of an instant by the composition, that is to say, by a syntax between few elements. According to Barthes, it is an exemplary model of annotation of the present (Barthes, 2003, Eng. trans., 2010, p. 29). The annotation, of which haiku is a model, selects and extrapolates from the continuous flux of living experiences, a lived experience that is annotated: to note means here that it becomes notable, that it assumes a given form. The event that haiku extrapolates, that is the referent of haiku, Barthes says, is a circumstance: the referent of this form of annotation is a *circum stans*, that is, what we find around us without looking for it, and without creating it. The referent of haiku is what we meet, what comes towards us in spite of our will, what happens, the autonomous event which happens, like the change of weather or seasons.

Haiku is, therefore, according to Barthes, the result of an encounter, the result of an event that does not happen neither to an abstract, transcendental subject, nor to an individuality, that is to say to an identity individuated by a gender, a role, a nationality etc.: this is an encounter between singularities, an encounter after which all is different, all acquires a *nuance*, which makes the moment of the encounter and the singularities which meet in this encounter unique. The told present assumes a *nuance* in relation to the individuality who tells: *nuance* is a short circuit between two instants, a relation made of two that has no justification and that justifies nothing (Barthes, 2003, Eng. trans., 2010, pp. 46—47). The classical question of the analysis of a text, "what does the author mean", here makes no sense, because haiku does not have any hidden meaning. The relation between the lines which compose haiku is not a logical connection: their link is purely syntactic. It is precisely in this purely syntactic link that Barthes has an interest here, when he works on haiku, that is to say he is interested in this link which is constituted neither by a timeline nor by a logical chain.

Barthes often in the course opposes the syntactic link which characterizes haiku, to Proust's search for the lost time: Proust establishes a link between memory and he who remembers, which is constituted by a hidden sense to dig up a buried past, whose recollection enables the present to find a sense again in a continuous narration. On the contrary, in the structure of haiku there is no semantic link between the singularity that tells and the singularity that is told. This link is exclusively syntactic. This syntax, this encounter between singularities which implies the *nuance*, is what Barthes calls the process of individuation.

Ⅵ. Individuation as Encounter

The reasons of Barthes' interest in the structure of haiku is its capability to write the process on individuation, to write the moment in which this individuation happens. In this process of individuation emerges what Barthes quoting Proust calls "the edge of particular", that is to say what makes someone or something "such" is special, unreplaceable.

Individuation is, as Barthes says, a notion that consists in relating the irreductibility, the founding nuance, the Suchness, the Specialness of the individual (civic and psychological subject) to a given moment of that individual: so the "soul" in that it passes, not to return. (Barthes, 2003, Eng. trans., 2010, p. 43)

Individuation is determined from the event of an unpredictable encounter with something, which from that moment on becomes necessary, which is no longer possible to substitute, which misses even before its absence: in this sense a relation among singularities is always on the brink of mourning. On this brink, finitude is no longer economic finitude which sends away death, relegating it to a future which doesn't exist yet, but is finitude blocked in the loss of the other, the presence of death as death of the other which compresses the time in this missing which doesn't pass, doesn't heal, doesn't flow: in this time in which finitude is linked with the possibility of the loss of the other, time is no longer a line; it becomes short, blocked, stopped and flat, as on the surface of a photograph.

In the same years in which Barthes gave the two courses on the preparation of novel, he wrote *La chambre claire*, in which the question of this unjustified relation, the question of this syntax of the encounter which suspends time, contracting it in a present, emerges in the definition of what Barthes, reflecting on the peculiarities of the photographic text, calls *punctum*. In *La chambre claire*, photography is presented as an extreme condition of the text. This extremity is due to the relation between signifier and signified, which this particular text implies. In the photographic text, the relation between signifier and signified and, even more, the relation between signified and its referent seems absolutely immediate without mediation; it seems a tautology (Barthes, 1981, Eng. trans., 2010, p. 12 ff.). The referent seems to be in the photographic text there, in flesh and bones. Barthes explains in *La chambre claire*, that, however, this relation of adherence between signifier and its referent in the photographical text is only apparent. And it is rather for this reason that the photographical text has a lot of things in common with haiku. This appearance which Barthes is speaking about is the appearance of a semantic link between the photo and what it represents. But in reality, as Barthes says, at the very moment it is indicated by a camera, the referent has already escaped. It is already hidden from what Barthes calls the "pose". To assume a pose, Barthes says, means to become a signifier of ourselves. This means that the direct, immediate, almost tautological relation is not between the photographic image and the referent, but between the photographic image and the pose, that is, a signifier by which the photographed subject interprets itself, recites the part of itself, as an actor. This relation between the pose and the referent, therefore, is a very problematic relation because the subject in the pose doesn't manifest itself, but, on the contrary, it hides itself as in an act of protection. The referent escapes behind the pose. I become an image, through the pose, a moment before the click of the camera: the image I become in the pose is heavy, blocked, without evolution, and this is, as

Barthes says, very different from the subject which is always light, divided, scattered, and incoherent. This image forces itself to have an expression, a fixed expression, to exit from neutrality, to abandon what Barthes calls the degree zero. In the pose, the photographed subject tries therefore, according to Barthes, to signify itself, to become signifier of itself, that is, to establish a semantic link with itself. The photographed image, therefore, signifies the pose, signifies a subject which tries to escape. That's why often, looking at a photo, Barthes says, more than a presence, I perceive that something is missing. I miss a place, for example, a moment, a person, the way in which I or someone else was before. This sense of loss is blocked, with no possible solutions. The time of this loss is not the time in which I look forward to something, in which even if it is very slow, time is flowing.

Ⅶ. A Syntactics of Sense

This sense of loss is linked with the emerging of what Barthes in *La chambre claire* calls *punctum* (Barthes, 1981, Eng. trans., 2010, p. 25 ff.). *Punctum* is what makes some photos notable for someone, what makes a photo more than a signifier which waits for the surfacing of its signified, which makes me fix a photo for a very long time, which makes me keep a photo with me, for example, which makes a photo important to me. *Punctum*, as Barthes says, is what makes a photo happen to me, exist for me. In these photos I find what I miss, they are the image of a loss. In the first part of *Lachambre Claire* the *punctum* is defined as a coexistence in the same space of the photo of two elements without a logical connection, but that, from the moment of the click, have sense only in this relation. In this case, the loss, which is missing, is the missing of a sense, the missing of a semantic relation. A photograph in which *punctum* emerges is the exposition of this *syntactics of sense*. The result of this syntactics of sense both in the haiku and in the photograph, is not a meaning but a *nuance*; is not a signified, but a process of individuation. In this encounter in which nothing is the same, in which nothing is as it was before, the *nuances* emerge as an absolute difference. What Barthes calls *nuance* in *The Preparation of Novel* (Barthes, 2003, Eng. trans., 2010, p. 46 ff.) neither belongs to the subject, nor to the object: it is neither a particular way of the subject to see something, nor a particular moment which the individual finds and describes. *Nuance* belongs to the encounter. *Nuance* is a short circuit between two singularities, which is circumstantial, which is not justifiable by a search for sense, and which doesn't justify anything. It is a present unexplained by the past and unable to explain the future. Haiku and the photograph in which a *punctum* emerges do not establish any semantic link. They are the description of the event. For these reasons, in haiku and in the photographs in which the *punctum* emerges, the question "what did the author want to say?" makes no sense. Neither the photographic text nor the haiku can be developed. In this sense, Barthes says in *La chambre claire*, even if a photo (analogic photo) has to be "developed" by a chemical process to be seen, it allows us to see the undevelopable, the essence of a wound, what cannot be transformed but can only repeat itself in the form of an insistence (Barthes, 1981, Eng. trans., 2010, p. 49). This impossibility of a development which characterizes the photographic text in Barthes' *La Chambre claire* is what, in the course on *Preparation of the Novel*, keeps together the photographic text and the poetic text of haiku.

What photo and haiku have in common is, as Barthes says, their *noeme*, that is what deeply defines them. In fact, both are a presentation of the "already been", the presentation of a past, which is also a presentation of a loss. They both are ways in which I can see what I miss without compensation of the loss. Nevertheless, there is an important difference between photo and haiku, which Barthes clarifies in *The Preparation of the Novel* in his own words:

> The (perhaps noematic) difference between Photography and haiku = a photograph is a bound to say everything. [...] It produces excesses of meaning =/ haiku: abstract and yet lifelike effect (perhaps we are leaving the Noeme of photography and rejoining the Noeme of text). (Barthes, 2003, Eng. trans., 2010, p. 73)

A photo, as Barthes says, is obliged to say all; it is saturated with inevitable details. Details represent, signify, and take the place of facts that the photo certifies, testifies. But one of these details can become *apunctum* for someone, provoking a drift of sense: *punctum* doesn't signify anything, but rather it is exactly what I misses. It is, as Barthes says in *The third meaning* "a signifier without a signified" (Barthes, 1970, Eng. trans., 1970, p. 61), a sign without sense, an association that has nothing to do with a semantic relation. *Punctum* is therefore possible in a photo. On the contrary, haiku, as Barthes says, gives at once the way of the fact and the way of the abolition of the fact (Barthes, 2003, Eng. trans., 2010, p. 78). In a haiku, the fact, the contingence, has already established a relation with the writing individuality, that is to say, it is not a pure fact, independent from he or she who takes note. This means in it, the independence of the fact is abolished, because the fact is taken in a relation that determines the individuation and so the nuance. In a photo the *punctum* is a possibility; in haiku the *punctum* is already cut out from a horizon of sense. The nuance has already been cut out from a generality, from a common discourse, from a relation between signifier and signified based on semantic sense.

Ⅷ. Writing the Intractable

Therefore, haiku is not similar to the photographic text in general, but to those photos in which a *punctum* emerges. This *punctum* which haiku and some photos cut out, is a space empty of sense in which two singularities enter in a relation, becoming unreplaceable for each other: it is the space of what Barthes call the *intractable*, which is, as he says, the moment in which things are filled by the affect, the moment of truth, in which I discovers what counts for me (Barthes, 2003, Eng. trans., 2010, p. 107). In the two courses on the preparation of the novel, Barthes is looking for the possibility of a Novel whose material is this intractable, that is to say, the contracted instant of time in which I feel finitude as loss of what is not possible to substitute.

"The classic novel," says Barthes at the end of the first course, "is a text, a texture in which the moments of truth are rare and mixed with fiction, deception, invention." For this reason, Barthes says that his resistance, his incapability to pass from the desire of writing to the real act of writing is above all a "moral" resistance (Barthes, 2003, Eng. trans., 2010, p. 109).

The deception, the lie which worries Barthes is not at the level of the content of the literary work; it does not belong to literary invention, nor literary fiction: the deception which worries Barthes is at the level of the form of narration. The way in which in a classic novel is built according to the structure of text, is very different from the way in which, as anticipated, haiku links together differences or circumstances. The classic novel, what Barthes calls in the courses "The Book" (with capital letters) is architected, it is constructed: in it the told events are linked together in a timeline which can be inverted, as in the case of Proust's Novel, but which continues to have the form of a continuous line, which flows, and where all is linked, coherent, and in which every transformation is only a development without events—in such a way the past justifies the present and present promises a future. The deception, the lie of the novel, which Barthes is speaking about is the form of this time, its linearity without incidents, without events, without any cut.

What Barthes opposes to "The Book", is what he calls "The Album", in which the structure is missing, as occurs in a book of poems, for example, or is given by the same succession of things, as occurs in a journal. But nor does the album, in Barthes' discourse, seem to have the capability to work with the intractable, with the vertiginous finitude of loss, because the blank which separates the pages of a journal, or a book of poems, does not have the same value as the blank between the lines of an haiku: in a journal or a collection of poems, a ripped page is not missing in the same way in which one of its verses can be missing in an haiku: if I rip the page of an album it remains readable, while if I cancel one of the lines of a haiku it is no longer readable. This means that both "The Book" and "The Album", which are the two main forms of Western literature, are linked to the idea of linear time, of a development, of a flowing; therefore, none of them is able to tell the story of a subject whose line of time has been broken by an event. None of them is able to write the intractable.

For this reasons, probably, Barthes remains blocked, as he says, to the first challenge that whoever wants to write a novel has to handle, that is, of choosing the form of the work. Barthes doesn't succeed in finding the form of the work he wants to write because both "The Book" and "The Album", only permit the horizontal cuts which in *Le plaisir du text* Barthes attributes to the "text of pleasure". The pleasure of text, Barthes says in this paper, is linked to the possibility of cutting the text, of making scratches in it. In the text of pleasure, these scratches are only possible on the horizontal plan of the story told, of the thread. The reader cuts the text simply by jumping, skipping, all of which are not useful to the disclosure of the secret which the text promises. These cuts are linked to an economy of time, to the economic sense of finitude. The new practice of writing which Barthes looks for in the courses on the preparation of the novel, has to be able, on the contrary, to produce a text in which the cuts, the scratches are not at the superficial level of the thread, but are deeper, at the level of the form. In "the Pleasure of the text", Barthes calls such a text the "text of bliss" (*jouissance*). The text of bliss produces the possibility of lacerations, of scratches which are internal to language, internal to writing, and internal to the form of the literary work. In it, the relation between signifier and signified is not only deferred, as in the text of pleasure. There is no secret promised at the end of the tale. In the text of bliss, the space opened between signifier and signified is not a deferall, but a lack of sense. This space emancipates the signifier from its semantic link with the signified, opening the space of what Barthes calls significance, that is, opening the space of the nuance, in which every signified is unreplaceable and untranslatable. In the text of bliss, all semantic relations between the textual signifier, the author and the reader are impossible. Unlike the classical structure of the comment, there is no reader here who must reconstruct the meaning of the discourse of the author. In the text of bliss, author and reader are unanchored; they float off. They lose their fixed place. They no longer hold a pose. We can say that in the text of bliss, the tale is always the same: in it we no longer have a character who tries to reach a goal solving problems and affronting challenges, as in the classic structure of novel. He or she who is in trouble, in the text of bliss, is not a character, but language itself, identity, the relation between the author and what he writes. The trouble has to do the strange situation of signifiers, which begin to construct a structure of sense independently from the relation with their signified. It is the moment when I begin to perceive the bliss of the *form* of writing. I like the style, the way in which someone composed its text: my bliss is determined on the syntactical level of the form, of the style, and not on the semantic level of content. On this level, every signifier becomes unreplaceable and untranslatable, the linearity of narration is transformed in the labyrinth of style, where the signifiers acquire a sense not in relation with their signified, but for their position, that is, for the relation they establish encountering other signifiers. In this sense of writing, which is for Barthes the sense of a *vita nova*, the indifference of the pose which is the individuality of the author, changes into the difference of the encounter which is the individuation of an unreplaceable singularity.

References:

Barthes, Roland, (1970). "Le troisieme sens: Notes de recherche sur quelques photogrammes de S. M. Eisenstein". Cahiers du cinema. English translation by S. Heath, (1970). "The Third Meaning: Research Notes on Several Eisenstein Still", in *The Responsibility of Forms: Critical Essays on Music, Art, and Representation*. Berkeley: University of California Press.

——, (1973). *Le plaisir du texte*, Paris: Seuil. English translation by R. Miller, (1975). *The Pleasure of Text*. New York: Hill and Wang.

——, (1978 – 1979 et 1979 – 1980). *La prèparation du roman I et II. Cours et séminairesau Collège de France*, ed., Nathalie Léger, Paris: Seuil, 2003. English translation by K. Briggs, (2010). *The preparation of the Novel*, New York: Columbia University Press.

—— (1981). *La chambre claire. Note sur la photographie*, Paris: Seuil. English translation by R. Howard, (2010). *Camera Lucida*. New York: Hill & Wang.

Author:

Julia Ponzio, Ph. D. in Modern and Contemporary Philosophy, Researcher in Philosophy and Theory of Languages at the Faculty of Foreign Languages and Literatures, University of Bari Aldo Moro, Her Research mainly focuses on the theories of philosophy and language.

作者简介:

朱丽娅·庞齐奥，现当代哲学博士，意大利巴里大学外国语言与文学系研究员，研究方向为哲学与语言理论。

E-mail:derby2626@gmail.com

"象似"还是"像似"?
一个至关重要的符号学术语的考察与建议*

胡易容

摘　要：从20世纪80年代末开始，我国语言学界开始集中研究语言中的像似问题。当时将iconicity译为"象似性"，至今几乎已成为学界定译。本文通过字源、词源、构词语法和术语生成环境等多方面综合考察后指出，"像"与"象"的使用在符号学领域内需要重新审视；同时，通过一种符号学考察，指出"象"与"像"的发展呈现为一般符号典型类型演进，这种演进也同时印证了"像似"在意涵上的自恰。

关键词：像似性，符号学，图像符号，语言学

A Semiotical Investigation on the Term "Icon" in Chinese

Hu Yirong

Abstract: Since the end of the 1980s, scholars on language have given attention to the problem of iconicity. The Chinese translation of iconicity today is "象似". Through a comprehensive investigation of morphology and the background of the term, this paper will point out that "像" is a more appropriate translation for iconicity. Additionally, this essay will explore the relationship between the Chinese characters "象" and "像" that reflects some rules of signs evolution, showing more consistence in its significance.

Key words: iconicity, semiotics, icon, linguistics

---

* 本文受国家社科基金项目"图像符号学：传媒景观世界的图式把握"（项目编号：13FXW002），2012年度广西高等教育新世纪教学改革工程项目（项目编号：2012JGB142）资助。

一、当前符号学术语规范亟待加强

目前符号学术语的统一尚有许多工作需要展开。我国将符号学这门学科作为舶来品，基础理论大部分来自译作，术语统一情况堪忧，本文所主要探讨的像似性问题也未能幸免。"iconicity"为皮尔斯提出的符号学术语，源于其对符号类型的分类之中的 icon（皮尔斯将依据指向对象的方式将符号分为 icon、index 和 symbol 三类），属皮尔斯符号学的最基础、最关键概念之一。其中 icon 常见的翻译有：象/像似符号[①]、肖似符号[②]、图像符号[③]。"iconicity"相应译为象/像似性、相似性、图象性、形象性[④]。皮尔斯认为，icon 指向对象靠的是"与之相似"。其他几个术语在使用中较易区分，如"相似性"这个词语过于日常化，作为术语有其局限性；而"图象性"显然无法涵盖皮尔斯的本意，因为 iconicity 不仅包括图像符号，还包括语言、声音等非图像的相似关系。因此，最恰当的术语恐怕还是"像似性"或"象似性"。这两个极其接近的术语不仅关乎术语统一与规范，还涉及"象"与"像"这两个汉字的规范使用。语言学界、符号学界有必要身体力行，用规范的现代汉语字、词进行学术研究。

"像似"或"象似"在日常生活中均无使用，为符号学专用术语。可查阅的较早记录是 1988 年许国璋先生将 iconicity 一词翻译成"象似性"[⑤]，并逐渐引起国内语言学界重视。语言学家沈家煊的《句法的象似性问题》一文影响很大，被引多达七百余次。[⑥] 此后，"象似性"就成为语言学中基本的通行术语。迄今为止，中国知网（CNKI）检索篇名中包含"象似"的论文有 684 篇。[⑦] 此外，还有公开出版发行的学术著作提到"象似"，如王寅的《中国语言象似性研究论文精选》（湖南人民出版社，2009 年）。至此，"象似"成为几无异议的定译。

---

① 许国璋：《论语言符号的任意性》，《外语教学与研究》，1988 年第 3 期，第 2 页；沈家煊：《句法的象似性问题》，《外语教学与研究》，1993 年第 1 期；王寅：《iconicity 的译名与定义》，《中国翻译》，1999 年第 2 期，第 48 页。

② 见李幼蒸：《理论符号学导论》，社会科学文献出版社，1999 年。

③ ［意］翁贝托·艾柯：《符号学理论》，卢德平译，中国人民大学出版社，1990 年。

④ ［美］梅萨利：《视觉说服：形象在广告中的作用》，王波译，新华出版社，2004 年，第 3 页。

⑤ 许国璋：《论语言符号的任意性》，《外语教学与研究》，1988 年第 3 期，第 2 页。

⑥ 沈家煊：《句法的象似性问题》，《外语教学与研究》，1993 年第 1 期，后载于李行健编，《中国语言学年鉴》，语文出版社，1994 年。

⑦ 中国知网：<http://epub.cnki.net/>，2012 年 10 月 19 日。

既然如此，那么“像似”是不是误用、错用呢？这个情况需要具体而论。近年“像似”或“像似性”一词作为符号学的专门术语，其使用频率也开始日渐增高，知网论文检索主题中包含“像似”一词的论文有135篇[①]。另外，海曼《自然句法：像似性与磨损》（世界图书出版公司引进剑桥大学出版社版权，2012年）题名就用了“像似性”。

那么，究竟是“像”还是“象”？我们可以从“像”与“象”字源、字义和构词法等多方面来考察。从汉字演化的字源角度来说或是从整个汉语简化字规范用法的全局意义来考虑，学界都有必要对于近20年的一个仅限于学术界的术语作一个重新审视。本文所反映出的符号学译名术语情况仅仅是符号学术语不统一的一个具体案例。以此为契机，本文希望呼吁学界在译名选用上加强沟通、协调，推进术语的规范使用。

二、从字源发生廓清“象”“像”与“相”

实际上，“象”“像”“相”三字，尤其是前两字，几乎已经成为中国汉字的一段无头公案。仅以工具书为凭，几乎无法准确无误地使用三者。例如“头像”为什么是“像”，而“面相”又成了“相”了呢？为什么“假象”是“象”而“真相”又必须是“相”？细加考证，就会发现这几个字的使用与规范实在是乱“象”丛生。一个重要原因是“像”与“象”在古代汉语中可通用。因此，不仅是普通民众的日常使用混乱，连规范制定也迟迟未能统一。我国汉字规范化过程中，“象”与“像”的廓清也一波三折。20世纪五六十年代，汉字简化方案中用“象”取代“像”，而将“像”作为“象”的繁体字。到20世纪80年代，又重新将“像”定为规范汉字。这就导致两者在使用上的混淆惯性。此后两次权威的标准又作出不同规定，给两个字的区分造成更大困难。本研究不是汉字语言专题研究，讨论这一问题的主要目的在于界定本研究的对象及术语。故而重在从这几个字与符号世界的关联去理解它们的区别，以及这种区别对当下使用和理解的影响。本文从符号学角度，对这三个汉字的意涵演化及其含义的基本属性作了一个归纳：

象：主要用于由自然对象延伸而成的万事万物——在皮尔斯符号表意三元素中恰好与对象（object）对应。

像：主要用于由人模拟对象而创生符号世界——属于符号再现体（representum）范畴。

---

① 中国知网：<http：//epub. cnki. net>，2012年10月19日

相：实际上是由人的主观观测而生成的意义范畴——符号解释项（interpretation）。

根据这一符号表意框架，“象”是自然物的符号化，而“像”是符号化的自然物的再度符号化，“相”则是符号化的自然物符号化的文化阐释。从文字符号的发生时间来看，先有“象”，后有“像”与“相”。

（一）“象”源于自然并引申为万事万物的抽象

从字源看，“象”为象形字，原意为“象”这种哺乳动物。首先来看“象”的文字演变。甲骨文中，“象”是一个象形的动物侧面形象。甲骨文（象）、金文（象）均突出其长鼻特征，《说文》曰：“象，南越大兽，长鼻牙，三年一乳。像鼻牙四足尾之形。”《山海经·南山经》记载：“祷过之山多象。”从象形文字的符号化特征来看，均为侧面。这种符号化的方式不是偶然的，而是人们视角的必然结果。四足野生动物与人的照面方式多为侧面，正面对峙的几率极低。从符号的特征来看，四足动物的侧面轮廓也易识别，尤其是利于突出象的长鼻。语言符号的系统化的分节演化力量使得象形文字逐渐抽象化。“象”从专指一种动物抽象为指代具有共同特征的事物。及至金文时，“象”的象形程度已经有所弱化，而汉字系统的秩序雏形开始显现。不过，此时的汉字尚处于一个未系统化的阶段，字的象形化、个性化特征比较鲜明。有学者指出，对小篆以前的部分图形文字的形体研究，不宜采用层层切分的办法，应该采用相对笼统的、以字的整体为单位的方法。[①] 也即此时由于汉字系统尚未建立，字与字的共同规律性关系尚未明确。

秦统一六国，将“象”的象形特征进一步弱化（象），并将下部“豕”作为此类动物的共同组成部分。汉字以像似为主的符号理据性自此失去了其主导地位，而规约性占据了核心位置，这是汉字史的一个重要节点。也即，像似符号理据性在文字符号的使用中逐渐被磨蚀。具体方式就是符号的生成理据性（像似）逐渐让位于使用上的便利，这种使用便利被称为“使用理据”，或“再理据化”[②]，实际上它是相对于生成理据的“非理据”。作为文字符号的“象”至此就成为完全意义上的规约符号。

① 王亚平、孟华：《汉字符号学》，上海古籍出版社，2001年，第31页。

② 再理据化的具体方式是对已经磨蚀理据性的字符，用加入表意符号——部首等方式来重新使字符与其指涉的对象发生意义上的直接联系。如象形字“其”像簸箕之形，假借为代词“其”，去理据化了，便给“其”字加上“竹”的意符构成“箕”，使其“再理据化”。此例子为青岛海洋大学孟华教授所提供。

“象”的意涵发展第二个阶段是作为外延指代对象的扩展和泛化。在此阶段，“象”从特指一种动物转指形象，《辞海》举例道：“孔传：审所梦之人，刻其形象。”其后，“象”的外延自然而迅速地扩展为“万事万物的现象”。《周易·系辞上》曰：“在天成象，在地成形。”至此，“象”实际上已经有抽象的意味，但仍只是外延扩展。严格的抽象是通过隐喻、提喻、象征等，以高度符号化的方式来意指对象。如《汉书·成帝纪四》：“五星聚东井，得天下之象也。”这里的象就成了“征兆”“迹象”。至此，“象”的含义分化为二：其一是在抽象的程度上上升为非官能性对象，《韩非子·解老》：“故诸人之所以意想者，皆谓之象也。”这里的“象”是人自发的“想象”，是可以超越外部客观世界的心理世界——心像。再进一步抽象化，“象”不仅视觉官能无法感知，就连心中所想的对象之“形象性”也被抽去，成为只能凭借“悟”和“智识”偶或窥见的终极智慧——“道”。《老子》：“执大象，天下往。”[①] 这里“象”就是道，道者，无形之象。其二，“象”是对“征兆”“迹象”形成的机制的说明，即通过“像似”的方式对原有对象加以“模拟”。因此，“象”就有了“像”的含义。”如《周易·系辞下》：“是故易者象也，象也者像也。”“象形”“象声”就是用的这个含义。至此，汉字中“象”的含义初步齐备。此后各种用法无非是在这几个层次上的选取或细节变化。

归纳起来，从最初指代一种动物到假借为“形状、样子”，再到“包罗万象”和“大象无形”的抽象事物，“象”作为名词的指称范围逐渐扩大，但其核心意义却依然是某种“对象物”。用作动词表“模拟”含义时，是无法单独使用的，因此，表达这个意义的功能并不完整。这也表明，“象”的核心意义仍具有“对象化”的意义。在符号学中，对象物（object）本身作为一种自在物，并不构成符号，但它是对符号表意不可或缺的要素，是对符号的召唤。在索绪尔的二元符号结构中，它是符号所指出的事物；在皮尔斯的三元结构中，作为名词的“象”在符号表意过程中可以直接理解为“对象”。

（二）“像”是由人依据对象通过模拟生成的仿制符号

再看“像”。“像”属形声字，许慎《说文解字》释曰：“像，象也。从人，从象，象亦声。”可见“像”与“人”的关系更密切，表现出较强的“人为性”，它作为名词通常指比照人制作而成的对象物。如：画像、泥像、塑

① 老子继承并发展了《易经》中“象”思维的传统。“象”不同于“形”，“形”是有形的，看得见摸得着的；“象”是无形的，看不见摸不着的，但可以感受到的。

像、神像、偶像。此后，“像”的词义的指称范围拓展至“所有比照人或物制造的形象物”，因此，摄像、录像应当用“像”。从符号表意过程来看，“像”作为名词，已经不是原初的“自然物”或“对象物”，而是对象的再现。换言之，“像”所指称的事物是通过人工方式仿制、复制、再制、绘制而成，相当于皮尔斯符号三分中的符号再现体（representum）。因此，“像”是“象”的符号化结果，其中加入了“人”这一根本性要素，自在之“象”也就成了符号之“像”。而“像”对“象”的符号化方式就是“像似”，即人工的模拟、仿制、复制等。这就清楚地解释了为何“景象”用“象”而图像用“像”。

掌握了上述原则，即便是对非常难以区分的组词都可以较好地掌握其选用规则。如“幻象”和“幻像”。在实际使用中均有出现，在百度中可以粗略观察到两者的使用频率。输入“幻象”搜索到的结果约有 16,600,000 条，而“幻像”的结果有 3,740,000 条（搜索时间为 2012 年 9 月 29 日 11 时 24 分）。其中，“幻象”一词在《新华字典》和《现代汉语词典》均有收录，解释为：“幻想出来或由幻觉产生的形象。”在哲学术语中，“幻象”亦译“假象”。该词源于拉丁文 illudere，意为欺骗、困惑。印度哲学中的“摩耶”即幻象，认为现实世界由梵变化而出，实为幻象。《现代汉语词典》未收录“幻像”，但该词作为技术术语依然使用频繁。在《简明摄影辞典》中，“幻像”又称幻影，指由摄影镜头内部透镜各表面反射形成的次级影像。此外，《汉英航空发动机工程技术词典》《汉英计算机分类词典》等多部工具书收录了“幻像”。不难理解，“幻像”的“像”是“光学成像”，“幻”是感知结果。在线新华字典对“幻像”的释义为：幻化虚像，并举例名：“探险家被一条西北通道的幻像吸引。”此例中的“幻像”超越“光学成像”，而造成了与“幻象”的混淆。以近年公开出版的图书和音像制品为例，有学术专著《镜头定格的“真实幻像”：跨文化语境下的“中国形象”构造》（李娅菲，人民出版社，2011 年），该书的标题中的“幻像”尚可以解释为镜头造成的技术“幻视”；而另一部著作《幻像与生命：〈庄子〉的变异书写》（夏可君，学林出版社，2007 年）就无疑不是技术层面的问题，此处完全可以置换为“幻象”。

“幻像”与“幻象”两词经实际使用上的范畴扩展后，其间的微妙差异已经难以从词典的规定中直接区分。但若从本文提出“象”与“像”的符号表意的属性差异加以考察，则可以较好地区分。“象”是符号表意的对象，故当我们所说的“幻觉形象”是强调其作为一种“对象物”时，其选字应与“假象”“现象”同用“象”，侧重表达一种客观存在的事物。例如：海市蜃楼是一个幻象。当上下文语境导致含义偏向基于像似关系而生成的符号载体，则与“实”相对，是一种“虚像”，当用“幻像”。这里的“像”与“心像”“仿像”“拟像”相同。这样就能清楚地理解和选用。再如，2012年上映的电影《幻像》，表现了沉迷于网络游戏中的不同人群在游戏和现实中的系列遭遇，其“幻像”主要是影片主要表现的场景——虚拟的网络游戏空间。就这个意义来说，网络游戏生成的虚拟场景是一种相对于人为的现实生活的虚拟“幻像”，而非凭空生出的“幻象”。因此，当属正确使用。

实际上，使用十分混乱的还有中医及堪舆学术语“脉象”。只要以上述符号表意属性的不同为依据就很容易区分。“脉象”在中医药学名词审定委员会审定的《中医药学名词》（科学出版社，2005年）中的释义为“医生手指所感受到的脉搏跳动的形象”，在《汉语同韵大词典》的解释为“中医指脉搏所表现的快慢、强弱、深浅等情况”，而《中国方术大辞典》则将“脉象”解释为堪舆家所称“四象”之一，指穴场中心圆晕微微起脊之象。上述三部工具书都清楚地表明，无论在中医还是堪舆术语中，“脉象”都落脚为一种情况或一个形象，属于事物对象。故可以明确判断，“脉象”是准确的用法，而“脉像”则属误用，因为脉搏和风水自身即是再现对象，而不是一种因与某物像似而生成的符号。

（三）“相”是因他者的审视而生成的解释项

再看“像”“象”与“相”的关系。假象为何是“象”，而真相就成了“相”？头像为何是“像”，而“面相”又是“相”？从造字法来看，“相”为会意字。甲骨文（[illegible]）与金文（[illegible]）写法相似，小篆后，写法基本未有大的改变。对此，可以理解为原初的理据性仍然在汉字中有所保留。东汉许慎《说文解字》释曰：“相，审视也。从目，从木。”这里，引入了他者的“审视”，故又释曰：“按目接物曰相”。这样，问题就不再是符号再现体与对象之间的二元关系，而是以他者的眼光对“样子、外貌”等进行观察。可见，相的名词含义是由动作转化而来。“相”这一动作通常的对象是“人”，故而“相”就有了“容貌”的含义。由于是主观评判，其含义常常带有审美含义。如飞将军李广在不得意时，扪心自问：“岂吾相不当侯邪?”焦仲卿向父母告白：“儿已薄禄相。”这些对容貌的判断均指与某个社会化价值体系的匹配程度。

相对而言，“像”没有这种评价性含义，仅指人们依据对象创制而成的符号物，如：图像、头像、成像、佛像。回到上文有关真假的问题——“假象”不是人们主观希望看到的结果，而是事物自我呈现出的某种具有欺骗作用的表象、现象，是对象的状态，因而是“象”；而“真相”则是观者希望达成的目标，侧重于“释义者”的立场，是第三方动作的发生结果，故而是“相”。同理，“面相”的“相”是“相面”所“相”（审视）的结果，而审视必有解释。因此，在符号意指三分式中，“相”就属于符号解释项。实际上，结合“相”的动词用法来看，这个特征就更加明确。此后，相的含义引申为凡“彼此交接，皆曰相。其交接而扶助者则为相瞽之‘相’”（《说文解字注》）。瞽是瞎子，瞎子看不见东西，需要一个人帮助他看，这个帮助他看的人就叫“相”，“相”就有了辅助、帮助之意。此后一些词，如“丞相”“宰相”“相国”“相公”，都是由此而来。

自此，在符号表意的过程中，“象”“像”“相”各自有了明确的归属，它们之间并无时间先后而只有逻辑的衔接。其衔接方式可以这样表述：自然世界之“象”并非符号，而只有被符号化之后才能为人们表意所用；符号也并非意义本身，它是意义赖以存在的载体。这个过程是在符号化的瞬间同时完成的。一旦符号化，自然世界瞬间转换成可以感知的符号世界，并同时具有了丰富的意义。以上述符号表意过程为依据，我们可以重新梳理作为重要中国文化符号之“象”“像”与“相”：

象——各种基于像似构成的符号对象；

像——基于像似规则生成的符号再现体及其衍生法则；

相——观看和解释的心理及文化机制。

这三者的含义也可以折射本研究的主旨和对象。它指向一个能囊括所有符号在内的“像”的符号学系统，而本文的材料常常是狭义的图像符号，这是由于相对于语言符号，它缺乏被作为符号的深入讨论。同时，为了表明本研究结论并不仅仅适用于视觉图像，作者将不时用非图像的像似符号来作为例证。

三、“象似”与“像似”的术语生成辨析

（一）从构词法比较“像似”与“象似”

“iconicity”意为形象性，用图像表示。其词根是名词 icon（图标；偶像；肖像，画像；圣像）。对此词的翻译，似乎应当体现出“图像”这个词的含义。从这个角度来说，“像似”优于“象似”。根据前面的分析，“像”在表达“相近、类同”的意思时，独立表意能力更强，能更具象地表“图像形”之意，更契合“icon”一词根。

从与“似”的搭配构词来看，“象似”与“像似”构成方式不同。“似”在今天通常用于表示“类同、接近”等含义，可以与“像”互换。“似”做动词，在《现代汉语词典》（第五版）中释义为“像”[①]，如：相似、相像。两者甚至可以互释。[②]“像”与“似”组合，是近义并列联合而成的复合词，两个语素在地位上处于平等地位。且此类合成词有一个特征，即将词的两个语素拆开，仍可独立表达与原词近似的意思。如：道路、头绪、攻击、生产、英明、孤独。[③]

再看“象”与“似”，意义和用法差距明显。尤其在词性方面。“象”虽有“模拟、效仿”的意思，但不能单独成词，只能作为词素，与其他语素构成动宾结构的合成词，如“象形”“象声”“象征”[④]，其意思分别为模拟事物的“形状、声音以及征兆”。问题在于，当“象”与“似”连用时，由于“似”不是名词，无法与“象”构成动宾结构。与“象征”“象形”等词的构词法并不相同，也无其他可参照案例。从严格区分“象”与“像”的用法以来，“象”本身作为动词与其他动词联合构词，只此孤例。以此来看，“象似”恐是80年代“象”“像”不分时期的遗留产物。

（二）从术语的翻译及其使用语境考证“象似”与“像似”

20世纪80年代最初译介“像似”一词的资料，可以证明上述判断。国内语言学界对“象似”问题最早是许国璋先生的翻译，经对全文查证，许国璋先生的文章中，对“象”与“像”的选用遵循较早的标准。其中，文中所使用的“拟象”“中国的语言哲学，正象中国的主流哲学一样……”（第9页第2段）；“图象文字”（第9页第3段）[⑤] 这几处，此后汉字简化字均已经明确规定用“像”。许国璋先生翻译是此文1988年，恰好是在“象”“像”规范重新制定之前。到1990年全国科技名词审定委员会规定了关于科技术语中“象”与“像”用法。其中有一条是：“在作形状，作名词性词素构成的复合

① 中国社会科学院语言研究所词典编辑室：《现代汉语词典》（第五版），商务印书馆，2005年，第1295页。

② 但从字源来看，两者的本源是不同的。“像”是人对对象的模仿，是人与自然的关系；“像”是对内在抽象的模拟和反映，而“似”更具外在一致的客观比较，后文将论及。

③ 北京大学中文系，现代汉语教研室：《现代汉语》，商务印书馆，2004年，第197页。

④ 中国社会科学院语言研究所词典编辑室：《现代汉语词典》（第五版），商务印书馆，2005年，第1491页。

⑤ 许国璋：《论语言符号的任意性》，《外语教学与研究》，1988年第3期，第2~9页。

词时用‘象’，如：图象、录象、摄象等等。”但90年代中后期，几种权威性语文辞书在修订或出版时都处理为：图像、录像、摄像。[①] 此后，有学者对《人民日报》的文章进行了词频统计，所得出的结果支持“像”做名词性词素构成复合词的使用习惯。

此后，学界由于引用与因袭的惯性，并未依据新的汉字规范调整许国璋所用的术语。如沈家煊在颇具影响力的《句法的象似性问题》一文中说明，对“象似”这一术语的使用是从许国璋先生的译法[②]，但他未对该词另加辨析。从沈先生全文对“象”与“像”的使用来看，全文使用“象”字145次；而使用“像”仅2次，分别是“图像”（icon）和“映像”（image）。该文的“图像/象”一词共计出现4次，其中，1次写作“图像”，其他3次为“图象”。我们无法考证这是否是笔误，但可以明确的是，这一时期，“像”与“象”的使用尚处于缺乏规范或可以混用的阶段，这两个字的规范尚未在学界普及。此后，杜文礼先生的《语言的象似性探微》一文情况类似，全文无一“像”字，均用“象”，其中许多用法此后已明确规定为使用“像”，如：“拟象”（第1段倒数第3行等多处）；“图象”（第1段倒数第3、5行）。[③] 此后，对于“象似性”论述及定名最具代表性的应当是王寅教授，其论文《iconicity的译名与定义》[④] 以讨论学科术语定译的方式将这一术语固化。但该文与上述几篇文献一样，全文无一个“像”字。应当说，此时的用法并不算错误。正如该文引1979年版的《现代汉语词典》给“象”的5条义项：（1）形状，样子；（2）仿效，摹拟；（3）在形象上相同或有某些共同点；（4）好象；（5）比如。而2005年《现代汉语词典》中的“象”除指动物“象”外，仅剩下两个义项：（1）形状；样子；（2）仿效，摹拟。1979年版词典中的第3、4、6个义项已明确转归“像”。可见，汉字从规范到学术、日常使用中的定型有一定的时间差，而学术使用的连贯性特别强，这导致了术语的转变较之日常使用更为困难。

---

① 全国科学技术名词审定委员会，国家语言文字工作委员会：《“象”与“像”在名词义上的用法有新界定——关于“象”与“像”用法研讨会会议纪要》，《科技术语研究》，2001年第4期，第13页。

② 沈家煊：《句法的象似性问题》，《外语教学与研究》，1993年第1期，第2页。

③ 杜文礼：《语言的象似性探微》，《四川外语学院学报》1996，第60～65页。

④ 王寅：《iconicity的译名与定义》，《中国翻译》，1999年第2期，第48页。

小结：过渡性策略与建议

可以得出的结论是，我国简化字规范的过程本身导致了“象”“像”不分。在早年的语言环境下，“象似性”并非错误的用法，但随着简化汉字规范的推进，这一情况已经改变，而学术术语的引用、承袭导致了用字规范的相对滞后。

至此，词义虽已辨析清楚，但处理此类情况仍然面临诸多具体的困难。首先是一个学界的规约。几乎整个语言符号学界均已以“象似”为题做大量的论述和研究工作。笔者认为，当前的简化字规范作为全国通行的规范，其意义要比语言学界术语使用特例重大。有时候学术界常常创生出在日常生活中并不使用的新词，但这种创生通常是 日常语言使用规范的基础之上进行的。例如：赵毅衡在翻译及学术构想中创造的“伴随文本”（co-text）、“阐释漩涡”（vortex of interpretations）、“语象”（verb icon）①，并不违背术语中字词在日常使用中的惯有意义。对于“iconicity”的汉语对应词的翻译显然也应当遵循这种一般使用规则，尤其在某的术语通过会议和工具书的形式明确了其使用规范后②。“像”与“象”的义项已经在《现代汉语词典》等权威工具书得到了调整，学界有必要以此为据，调整术语的使用规范。

此外，目前使用“像似”的论文、论著逐渐增多。这也表明，随着汉字简化规范字对“象”与“像”的整理和讨论逐渐开展，对“像”与“象”的确切区分逐渐得到学界更多的认识。我国符号学、语言学界有必要对该术语进行一个与时俱进的调整。不过，由于引用前人著述时通常不宜直接更改原作者的术语使用，笔者建议，当前情形下，应当同时接受“像似”和“象似”两种用法，并应逐渐推广“像似”的规范用法，尤其是对整个学术界具有影响力的专业词典、理论工具书，应当主动在推进术语的规范、统一上起到引导、示范作用。

---

① “语象”一词为较早翻译。见赵毅衡：《新批评：一种更独特的形式主义文论》，中国社会科学出版社，1996 年，第 135 页。若按硬译理解为语言图像，似乎更适用“像”，但实际上它往往超越单纯的“图像”性，它是语言、文字中生成的形象，意象故而则更适合理解为“图式特征的语言单位对象”，则可取“象”。

② 全国科学技术名词审定委员会，国家语言文字工作委员会：《“象”与“像”在名词义上的用法有新界定——关于“象”与“像”用法研讨会会议纪要》，《科技术语研究》，2001 年第 4 期，第 14 页。

作者简介：

胡易容，清华大学新闻与传播学院博士后，桂林电子科技大学数字媒体系主任、副教授。研究方向为符号学视域下的传媒图像文化与品牌形象战略。

Author:

Hu Yirong, Postdoctoral researcher of Journalism and Communication School, Qinghua University; associate professor and the dean of Digital Media Art Department, Guilin University of Electronic Technology. His research interests include semiotics of design and semiotics of branding strategy.

E-mail: hyr@tsinghua. edu. cn

Interpretation as Protention: The Temporal Mechanism of the Process of Interpreting

Dong Minglai

Abstract: This paper attempts to clarify the mode in which a text is given to a consciousness in time. The original given of temporal objects is not some homogeneous and mathematical points juxtaposed in a homogeneous medium but a whole of some heterogeneous qualities, which he calls duration. These appearances of different signs in time consciousness are connected to each other in the mode of time which Husserl describes as retention and protention, especially protention. The second part of this paper is to focus on multiple characteristics involved in this action of interpretation as anticipation, including its relation to a past as its passive guidance, its applications on different levels of texts, and its possibility of being "disappointed".

Key words: phenomenology, time consciousness, interpretation, Husserl, Bergson, semiotics

作为前瞻的解释：论解释过程的时间机制

董明来

摘　要：本文试图澄清文本被给予时间意识的基本方式。在柏格森和胡塞尔时间哲学的基础上，笔者试图描绘时间意识的两个主要特征。首先，根据柏格森的观点，对象在时间中的原初给予并非一些同质的、数学性的“点”在一个同质中介中的单纯并列，而是一些不同质的感知的整体，柏格森将这种整体称为“延续”。进一步讲，根据胡塞尔的观点，不同符号乃是在时间意识中被联结的：他把这种原初的时间意识描绘为一个由前瞻和后顾所组成的场域，而解释行为则主要是一种前瞻。本文的第二部分将着重描述这种作为前瞻的解释行为的诸种特质，包括以一种消极综合的方式作为其引导的过去经验，它在不同文本层面上的具体面貌，以及其“期待”落空的诸种可能。

关键词：现象学，时间意识，解释，胡塞尔，柏格森，符号学

Every interpretation is an action of the consciousness, and every consciousness must manifest its contents in time: this means that every interpretation must be temporal in some senses. The problem is how time really constructs our living experience of reading a text. From a phenomenological point of view, I will be trying to answer this question by arguing that an interpretation is always involved with a special form of anticipation or protention, which is guided by our memory about texts in the past. In order to make my analysis as clear as possible, I will organize my paper in the following way:

I will first argue that in order to be interpreted or understood, a text must be able to be divided into multiple individual signs. This process of division cannot be understood in the same way like that in which we separate a line into different segments, because the latter way is only quantitative, while the living experience of interpreting is always qualitative. According to Bergson, the mode which understands time as a homogeneous medium is only a spatialized image of the original experience of time. From his theory, I will attempt to argue that the grammatical mode that describes a sentence as an "axis" is also just a secondary form understanding the original experience of interpretation.

Further, on the basis of Husserl's phenomenology of inner time consciousness, I will try to describe the mechanism of interpretation as protention: the content in the retention and the primordial present can enable the consciousness to expect content in the protention from the level of words to the level of context, which may or may not be fulfilled by the real content given to the mind.

Ⅰ. Interpretation as Separation and the Qualitative Feature of This Separation

All texts must be divisible: a special combination of sounds in the stream of consciousness can be treated as a sentence only when it is able to be divided into different but connected parts, namely, into words. For those who do not speak English, a sentence of English is nothing but a mere sequence of noise like the noise of an air-conditioner, because for them there is no meaningful word, but merely a dull continuity of sounds. For example, for such a mind, the sentence "Plato is an ancient Greek philosopher" can be just "pla toisan ancie tegreekphi lopher", which just makes no sense at all. Therefore, the capacity of understanding the language of English is firstly an ability to separate an English word from another one.

This process of separation, however, is not like what the grammar describes for us. The aim of every school of linguistics is to offer a framework in which the organization of texts can be described rationally. As Saussure points out in his *Caurse in General Linguistics*, the aim of linguistics is to describe "the faculty of constructing a language, i. e. a system of distinct signs corresponding to distinct ideas" (Saussure, 1959, p. 10). For him, language (langage) is an untemporal rational system, while the individual usage of rules and elements from this system in everyday experience is called the "speech" (langue) (Saussure, 1959, p. 9). However, this aim itself is different from the way in which a text appears as the content of a temporal consciousness. In other words, the separation which the consciousness holds in time is not the object of linguistic surveys. In the second chapter of his *Time and Free Will*, Bergson argues that in order to be grasped as numbers, objects must be abstracted into identical units:

> It is not enough to say that number is a collection of units; we must add that these units are identical with one another, or at least that they are assumed to be identical when they are counted. (Bergson, 1950, p. 76)

According to Bergson, the counted numbers are added together simultaneously but not successively, because as identical units, they will remain one if only successiveness is involved: "if we picture to ourselves each of the sheep in the flock in succession and separately, we shall never have to do with more than a single sheep." (Bergson, 1950, p. 77) Therefore, the only way to differentiate numbers becomes distinguishing their different positions: "we either leave these sensations their specific differences, which amounts to saying that we do not count them; or else we eliminate their differences, and then how are we to distinguish them if not by their positions or that of their symbols?" (Bergson, 1950, p. 76, note) These different positions must presuppose some "empty intervals" among them, so that they can be separated. This will finally lead to the concept as a homogeneous medium which is the ground for all these positions and intervals. This concept of homogeneous medium is, logically, Bergson's preparation for his distinction between two different understandings of time. For him, the way in which we grasp time as a homogeneous medium into which abstracted events are separated and juxtaposed is just a spatialization of the original experience of time, which he calls as duration:

> [...] when we speak of time, we generally think of a homogeneous medium in which our conscious states are ranged alongside one another as in space, so as to form a discrete multiplicity. (Bergson, 1950, p. 90)

Events juxtaposed in such an abstract time are actually identical "points" when being mentioned: for example, if we write down some notes on the calendar, which is an image of time which describes time as an "area" with determined "parts", the fact that these notes appear in different places on the calendar can alone make events represented by these notes something which happened in different dates, even though we do not write down any detail about those events. Multiplicities experienced in duration, on the contrary, are "heterogeneous, that of sensible qualities" (Bergson, 1950, p. 97), which means that we cannot eliminate their individualized characteristics: my "memory" about what happened yesterday and my "expectation" towards what will happen tomorrow are actually given to me with different appearances like their numbers of details in our mind, which are all in "themselves", but not in positions that they hold. Furthermore, these qualitatively heterogeneous contents are always connected with each other in our original experience of the duration, though can be distinguished from each other:

> [...] but states of consciousness, even when successive, permeate one another, and in the simplest of them the whole soul can be reflected. (Bergson, 1950, p. 98)

In the living duration, two impressions are always interpenetrating each other. Or put it more exactly, the original experience of the duration is a stream that "flows" continuously, without "stops" in it like the interval between two spatial points. Of course, this does not imply that all contents in the duration are mixed up, but only means that we should only distinguish them according to their own qualitative features.

Upon Bergson's distinction between the spatialization of time and the original experience of duration, we can clarify the difference between our temporal consciousness of a text and the grammatical description of it. In order to constitute a system of rules, a grammar must describe the structure of a sentence as composed by abstract elements as "subjects" "verbs" and "objects". In a system like this, individual words are eliminated of all their specialties: the only reason why they have different functions is that they hold different positions combined in an "axis". For example, as Saussure says in his *Course in General Linguistics*, "[i]n the syntagm a term acquires its value only because it stands in opposition to everything that precedes or follows it, or to both." (Saussure, 1959, p. 123) Saussure describes the syntagm as a spatial chain with identical but separable parts, and the only reason why they have different values is that they occupy different places in this chain. Especially for languages like Chinese which do not have form changes of words, the grammatical meanings are strictly tied with word orders: in a Chinese sentence, the first word must be the subject and the second one must be the verb. Even in inflecting languages like Latin, form changes are still not special determinations of particular words, but only the "visible mark" for some abstract positions. For example, in German the affix "-e" is not a part of any particular verb, but only a mark which indicates its position as following a first-person noun or pronoun.

It is important to be mentioned that the mode mentioned above is not the one which treats the individual experience of a text, but that deals with the rational structure of all semiotic systems. Saussure emphasizes many times that syntagm is not a structure of the speech, but of the language (Cf. Saussure, 1959, pp. 124 – 125). The speech, on contrary, has a totally different mechanism: when sounds composing a sentence come through our consciousness, words organize this sentence "enter" and "leave" continually, without intervals. Actually, even a "pause" in a sentence is not an empty interval, but must be treated also as a sign, because in everyday communications, pauses and silences also express meanings. The mind interprets a concrete sentence by distinguishing all the concrete words of this sentence qualitatively: the word "Plato" is divided from the word "is" because they sound differently to us. There is not a visible "line" with determined segments, so that we can put the contingent combination of the letters "p—l—a—t—o" into the first part of this line, and "i—s" into the second. Even when "seeing" these words printed on a piece of paper, the "blank" on the paper will not occur in our mind, let alone the fact that in Chinese and Japanese. There are no spaces, no commas and no punctuations according to the traditional way of writing, whereas people can still make sense from them. In fact, the possibility to understand the "right meaning" of a grammatically "wrong" sentence also lies in this mechanism of grasping concrete words in a time consciousness: "Ich hat ein Buch" is totally wrong as regard to German grammar, but one who speaks German can still understand it as saying "I have a book" but not some third-person singular who "has" a book. This is possible only because for a German consciousness, the knowledge of the concrete word "ich" is already enough without the forms of verbs which only indicate the positions on an "axis".

Such qualitative action of dividing, as an action of the mind, is always happening "in time": words distinguished in this way are words in the duration. The problem is, as contents temporally "flowing" away, how can different syllables in this continuous sequence form a word, and how can different words form a sentence to the mind. Or put it another way: how is it possible that the consciousness combines special sequence of sounds into a word according to "this", but not another order? How can it immediately understands "Plato" as a word and "is" as another, but not "Pla" as one and "tois" as another? According to the structure described above, qualities of different roots seem to be given a priori, which means that, it has already been obtained by the consciousness before a particular action of interpretation. This, however, is still possible to be understood in a temporal sense. Namely, the learning of a language or other types of sign system is also a mechanism of time consciousness. To understand this mechanism, we may introduce Edmund Husserl's phenomenology of time, which not only understands time as a continuous stream, but also clarifies the fact that what has passed and what will come are both constitutional parts of a sphere of "now", which is called as the "living present" by Husserl.

Ⅱ. Interpretation as Expectation: the Details of Its Mechanism

According to Husserl, the original "now" of a temporal consciousness is not a point which does not extend itself, but a "sphere" in which the "past" as retention and the "future" as protention are both in some sense present:

> What is already prominently accentuated in it going from one present to the next and is constituted in the train of presents as a lasting unity of identity is linked together temporally; that is to say, temporal relations are from the very beginning and by essential necessity linked together in being constituted. (Husserl, 2001, p. 180)

Husserl emphasizes many times that every retention or living memory is linked to a further memorial content, while it is passing further and further into a completely remote and empty past: "every now of consciousness, everything actually present belonging to consciousness, is subject to the law of modification: it changes into primary 'memory' of 'memory', and does so continuously." (Husserl, 1990, p. 139) These "memories" or retentions are parts of the living present along with the primordial impression, so that the mind can be conscious about a series of impresses in different phases of the continuity as a presented whole. As Husserl writes: "The ordinate taken as a whole is a memorial continuum, and each later ordinate contains in itself the memory of every earlier ordinate. Everything that the ordinate contains in the way of points (in the way of memories) exists 'simultaneously' (as actually present experience) in the time-point of the ordinate". (Husserl, 1990, p. 343) The mind is always combining multiplicities in retention into the present, while at the same time all contents are flowing further away into a situation as "zero". It is important that in the original consciousness of time, the distinction between "near" and "far" is not mentioned in a spatial and quantitative way. On the contrary, in Husserl's theory a "far" retention is "further" than a "near" one only because of the qualitative differences between them:

> The expanse of fresh retention, then, continuously passes over into an expanse of empty retention [...]. What is the same in its very sense is still given to consciousness; this is still given to consciousness in the special sense, namely, as affective. But this affective force goes back inexorably; the objective sense becomes inexorably poorer with respect to internal differentiations, thus emptying itself in a certain way. (Husserl, 2001, p. 218)

The criteria according to which we can distinguish far retentions from near ones is the strength of affective force: a fresh memory, for example, that of my lunch today, is always full of details like its smell and taste, while what happened long ago would be only an abstract event for me now. Therefore, the reason why my retention about what happened ten years ago could be described as far is not that it has a longer distance from "now" on a time line, but that the impression of it in my living present is weaker and paler. Like Bergson, for Husserl, the everyday time consciousness is always qualitative and concrete, but not quantitative and abstract.

This mechanism of retention can be treated as a model for that of protention, which is more important for our study of the living experience of interpretation. Like memories, contents in the future must be in some sense already presented in the sphere of the "now", although these contents are at the same time something "new" to the mind: " [...] proceeding from familiar tones, we would come to tones that we have never heard at all. " (Husserl,

1990, p. 14) The protention is both something which "grows" from the ground of past and something which is an opened possibility.

First, though protention is always towards something new, towards a field with open possibilities, it does not mean that the mind is facing a totally empty and superficial area when expecting. Rather, an expectation is always expecting something familiar to occur, which is determined by the "awakening" of some contents in the past, in the retention:

> The occurrence of something futural is expected through its similarity to what has occurred in the past, like already happens in the most primitive case of a steady protention. (Husserl, 2001, p. 237)

As a special modification of the temporal consciousness, an interpretation is also involved with such protention: even when only the first syllable is given, the mind is already expecting a completed word, with all its syllables presented as protention. The consciousness is always expecting the next few syllables to come, which can belong to the same word with those in the primordial present and even in the near retention. For example, the syllables "sophy" as a part of the word "philosophy" can be expected when "lo" is in the primordial present and the "phi" has already passed into a near retention. This protention on the word level can be easily applied to the sentence level, because the mind must at the same time have the first few syllables of "the next word to come" in order to distinguish those of the word in its primordial now from them. When the first two syllables of "philosophy" have been given, the mind is also expecting a verb or a link verb, and even adjunctions or objects to offer predicates to the "subject". We are able to expect these contents, because we are awakening some familiar sentence structures at the same time. However, such familiar sentence structures are not "recalled" as a geometrical image with such and such an architectural structure. As Husserl puts it, the far retention which can be awakened as an example for a protention is also an impression in a living now, therefore also has, and even still has the same temporal form like the primordial present, which is not quantitative but qualitative. Actually, the way in which we awaken them is not like that in which we recall some knowledge when dealing with a quiz or test: even children who have not learned about any grammatical knowledge will rely on their memory or retention of expressions they have repeatedly heard about.

The expectation on the level of sentence also is a basic structure for understanding non-linguistic texts. Consider the last few seconds of a tied basketball game: confronted with such a circumstance, a basketball fan will definitely look forward to a buzzer beater, which may be the result of a series of movements like screens for the shooter and the shooter's own running. We expect a scene like this because we have seen similar scenes many times before, but those scenes do not need to occur to us actively. Using Husserl's own words, "they are 'familiar' —not individually, but rather according to their type". (Husserl, 2001, p. 241) This means that when expecting a buzzer beater, we are not actually "playing back" any particular one we have watched; rather, for most people all the games that we have watched are actually in an empty retention and have already loses all their differentiations. Games that we watched provide us a type according to which we can expect contents in the game we are watching "right now" only because they have happened repeatedly, which is correctly described by Husserl as an "empirical certainty".

Furthermore, the protention is also constitutional on the level of the whole text, or of the context. The meaning of the first few sentences or even first few words will make us anticipate what the whole text will be talking about: an essay which begins with something about Plato or Kant will stimulate an expectation for contents about philosophy, because the belief that Kant or Plato must be mentioned along with philosophy has an empirical certainty for us.

What is important is, however, an expectation can not to be "satisfied" in every case. As Husserl himself points out, the opportunity of an expectation to be fulfilled already opens its possibility of being disappointed:

> If a has repeatedly emerged under certain circumstances or as a final term in a regular sequence, and if the corresponding expectation is there through associative awakening, then the absence, the non-occurrence becomes salient, the expectation is disappointed; the present temporal field, that is, the sense-

field is filled out, but filled out "otherwise". (Husserl, 2001, p. 239)

A consciousness whose expectation is disappointed is not the one which has no contents entering its living present, but is the one which has contents that it "has never imagined about". Multiplicities given to the mind can have fewer or more parts than the type according to which the mind has been expecting. Regarding the area of interpretation, the interpreter can be failed by the particular text that it is reading in every level of this text. The word may be spelled in a wrong way; the sentence may have a strange order, and the content of the whole text may come from a totally new angle. These forms of failure may, or may not arise from mistakes: an English sentence may disappoint one's expectation because it is grammatically wrong, but can also be a line from a poem, which is "twisted" by the poet deliberately.

What is interesting is that the possibility becomes larger and larger from the level of word to the level of context. The expectation towards the completion of a word is seldom disappointed, because the spelling or the pronunciation of a word is strictly determined, otherwise the combination of letters or sounds will simply lose its wordness, while what can disappoint an interpreter is a word spelled wrongly. On the contrary, a sentence allows more possibilities than a word: a noun can be followed by a verb, a linking verb or a clause, which can all be anticipated by the mind while failed it at the same time. What is important is that such a disappointment does not have to undermine the understandability of the sentence. This phenomenon is explicit in cases of inflecting languages: like in the example which we have used above, the verb "haben" in its special form "hat" is strangely or incorrectly connected with the pronoun "ich", which truly disappoints a consciousness anticipating a correct German sentence, while the sentence itself is still perfectly understandable. Finally, an expectation towards the meaning of the whole text, as what is the vaguest and emptiest modification of protention, is most likely to be disappointed: a text which mentions Plato can be actually about the history of ancient Greece or about the homosexuality issue when being expected to be a philosophical essay. The conclusion might be that the more open a structure is, the more possible it disappoints an expectation, while still making sense to it.

The last point which must be mentioned here is that, the familiarity of similar contents in an interpretation does not function actively, but only passively. With the words "active" and "passive", Husserl distinguishes two modes of givenness: the object of one of them is directly "aimed at" by the consciousness, while that of another one is only "co-given" in the background. It is on the basis of this very distinction that it is possible that the attention of a consciousness can turn from one part of the circumstance to another one, which is actually making what was formally in the background to the foreground, and *vice versa* (Cf. Husserl, 1998, p. 225). The familiar structure which guides our interpretation has already sunken into the indifferent limit of zero, but the way we use it as a meta-language is not to recollect it actively. This far-distant structure actually functions like a near retention, which, according to Husserl's own metaphor, is "belonging to every perception like a comet's tail" (Husserl, 2001, p. 459). The primary attention of the ego is still on the body of the comet, and the tail of it still has some affective force on the ego, though the intensity of that force is weaker when the same content is in the primordial present.

That is to say, our past and repeated experiences of structures (like basketball games which we have watched and ended up with a buzzer beater) is not reproduced, because they are not the object in question, but only the motivation which stimulates the ego towards some similar but new contents. In order to use a language, one does not need to memorize the concrete knowledge that he or she has read from a text book, though structures which are the same or familiar with examples in such a book are always there with a low degree of attentive force. It is still true that in anticipating there is a turning of the attention, but it is not turned to the past structure, but to the content anticipating itself. In hearing the word "Plato", our attention will be led to the following words like "is" or "says" or whatever, which themselves can be treated as passively co-present, but in a different manner with the past guidance (Cf. Husserl, 2001, p. 239).

Conclusion

From the analysis offered above, this paper can briefly portrays some fundamental features of the interpretation as a special form of our temporal consciousness.

A text can be grasped in two ways: either as the object of a grammatical system or as the content manifold in a living temporal consciousness. The latter should be considered as the primary givenness of it, which is mainly organized by the structure of protention, while the grammatical or linguistic approach is based on the spatial representation of the original consciousness of temporal contents. Both Bergson and Husserl realize that in our primordial experience, multiple impressions are treated as "in" different times not because they hold different positions in a homogeneous "chain", but because they have different "degrees" of empirical richness or clearness. Only on this qualitative understanding of time, can we apply Husserl's analysis of retention and protention to the survey of interpretation. An interpretation is a protention in the way according to which contents in the future can be "expected" but not "experienced" because they are vague than those in the primordial present. It means that when interpreting, we are not counting identical units juxtaposed together, but a series of impression which penetrate each other qualitatively. The interpreter can expect the text to be fit to the "type" from texts which the interpreter has met before. Such an expectation, as something coming from the empirical certainty, serves as a basic structure for our living experience of a text from the level of word to the level of context, while all such expectations can be disappointed by the real content given to the primordial living present.

Reference:

Bergson, Henri, (1950). *Time and Free Will*, trans., F. L. Pogson. London: George All & Unwin Ltd.

Husserl, Edmund, (1990). *On the Phenomenology of the Consciousness of Inner Time*, trans., John Barnett Brough. Norwall: Kluwer Academic Publishers.

——, (1998). *Ideas Pertaining to a Pure Phenomenology and to a Phenomenological Philosophy*, *First Book*, trans., F. Kersten. Norwall: Kluwer Academic Publishers.

——, (2001). *Analysis Concerning Passive and Active Synthesis: Lectures on Transcendental Logic*, trans., Anthony J. Steinbock. Norwall: Kluwer Academic Publishers

Saussure, Ferdinand de, (1959). *Course in General Linguistics*, trans., Wade Baskin. New York-London: Philosophical Library.

Author:

Dong Minglai, Ph. D. student in Faculty of Philosophy at Duquesne University.

作者简介：

董明来，迪尤肯大学哲学系在读博士。

E-mail:Dongminglai1987@gmail.com

前进中的后退：莫里斯的行为主义符号观*

金毅强

摘要：莫里斯的符号观的核心，是将符号过程视为介于一个“载体”和两个“它者”间的联系的行为：“符号载体”指涉“意指”；“符号载体”引起“解释项”。这个符号观的两个“它者”范围太小，不能涵括很多符号现象；“符号载体”和“解释项”间其实并不是简单的引起关系；“意指”和“解释项”也不可能同时存在于符号过程中。莫里斯的符号观，受皮尔斯三元关系符号论和行为主义心理学的不足所限，未能达到预期效果。

关键词：莫里斯，行为主义符号论，意指，解释项，符号载体

Regressing in Advancing: Morris' Behaviorist View of Sign

Jin Yiqiang

Abstract: The kernel of Morris'view of sign is to regard semiosis as an action involving relations between one "vehicle" and two "others": "sign vehicle" refers to "designatum"; "sign vehicle" causes "interpretant". The scope of the two "others" are too narrow if sign is to encompass various kinds of signs; the relationship between "sign vehicle" and "interpretant" is not causal by nature; "designatum" and "interpretant" never get both involved in a semiosis. Morris' view of sign, inheriting Peirce's triadic view of sign and behaviorism, fails to meet Morris' expectation.

---

* 本文系2012年浙江省哲学社会科学规划课题“基于符内联系运行机制的符号理论研究”（项目编号：12JCWW18YB）的研究成果。

Key words: Morris, behaviorist view of sign, designatum, interpretant, sign vehicle

一、行为主义符号论

符号学大致上出现了六种关于符号的表述，六种表述的共同之处在于，都认为符号现象至少涉及两个事物（A 与 B），都认为两事物间有联系；不同之处在于，对 A 的内容与性质、B 的内容与性质，以及 A 与 B 间联系的性质的判断不一致。为了避免术语上的混乱，我们可将 A 称为符号的“载体”，B 称为符号的“它者”，A 与 B 间的联系称为“符内联系”。

行为主义符号学的观点可以表述为：符号是 A，A 导致一个涉及 B 的心理过程，在该过程之前，与 A 相关且不在场的 A' 导致与 B 相关的 B'。行为主义符号学的代表学者有两批。一是奥格登（C. K. Ogden）和理查兹（I. A. Richards），他们试图以符号情景理论将符号理解与心理过程统一起来：“符号是这样的一个刺激物，它类似于某个原刺激的一部分，且足以唤起由原刺激所引起的心理印迹。”[①] 二是莫里斯（Charles Morris）。在其三本主要著作中，莫里斯给出了略有差异的定义。第一种说法是：符号过程（semiosis）涉及三个或四个要素，在该过程中充当符号的是符号载体（sign vehicle），符号所指涉的是意指（designatum），某物对某解释者来说是符号所借助的，作用于该解释者的效果是解释项（interpretant），第四个要素是解释者（interpreter）。[②] 第二种说法是：符号是任何满足如下条件的预备刺激（preparatory-stimulus），该预备刺激在引起某行为族（behavior-family）的诸反应序列（response-sequences）的刺激物（stimulus-object）不在场时，在某有机体内引起以该行为族的反应序列方式作出反应的倾向。[③] 第三种说法是：符号过程是五个概念间的联系，即符号（sign）在某种环境（context）下，在解释者（interpreter）中造成以解释项（interpretant）这种方式对符号的意指（signification）——当时该事物并未作为一种刺激进行活动——作出反映的倾向。[④] 三种说法有区别，但是本质上基本相同。抽象地说：如果

---

① C. K. Ogden, I. A. Richards, *The Meaning of Meaning*. New York: Routledge & Kegan Paul, 1923, p. 53.

② Charles Morris, *Foundations of the Theory of Signs*. Chicago: University of Chicago Press, 1938, p. 3.

③ Charles Morris, *Signs, Language and Behavior*. New York: Prentice-Hall, 1946, p. 10.

④ Charles Morris, *Signification and Significance*. Cambridge: M. I. T. Press, 1964, p. 2.

刺激 A' 在人的心中引起 B'，且当 A' 不在场时，与 A' 相关的 A 在人的心中引起等同于或类似于 B' 的 B，那么 A 就是个符号。

用我们的术语来说，在莫里斯的行为主义符号观中，符号过程涉及一个载体，即“符号载体”“预备刺激”或“符号”，和两个它者，即“意指”（designatum 或 signification）或“刺激物”和“解释项”；载体和它者的联系，即“符内联系”，可以概括为：符号载体指涉意指，符号载体引起解释项。

二、莫里斯符内联系观的不足

（一）两个“它者”的描写力

这个符内联系观的第一个问题在于：两个它者的范围太小，不适用于很多符号现象。莫里斯本人显然也知道这点。在后两种定义之后，莫里斯都强调他所提出的符号表述不是作为符号的定义，因为有些符号不一定符合表述中的规定。事实正是如此。首先，很多符号，例如符号史上所谓的“自然符号”、非语言的“惯例符号”，和无指称的语言符号，都不涉及“意指”或“刺激物”。在自然符号中，比如“云”和“雨”这一关系对，用莫里斯的观点来说，只能是：“云”这个符号载体在“某人”心中引起“雨”这个观念。在非语言的“惯例符号”中，比如“鼓声”和“攻击”这一关系对，用莫里斯的观点来说，只能是：“鼓声”这个符号载体在某人心中引起“攻击”这个想法。在无指称的语言符号中，比如“躺下”，用莫里斯的观点来说，只能是：“躺下”这个声音在某人心中引起“躺下”这个想法。在这种情况下，“雨”“攻击”“躺下”都是符号载体对人的心理的影响，更接近于“解释项”；除此以外，三种符号过程中都没有涉及其他心理现象，也就是说，不涉及“意指”。简而言之，“意指”或“刺激物”，对于很多符号过程来说，根本就是不必要的。其次，很多符号并不涉及“反应倾向”。在第一种说法里，莫里斯将“解释项”解释为“效果”；在后来的两种说法里，他却将其改为“反应倾向”。显然，在莫里斯看来，“反应倾向”优于“效果”，然而，实情很可能刚好相反。“反应倾向”虽然比“反应”更有基础性，适用范围更广，但仍不如皮尔斯的“直接解释项”（或称为“感情解释项”）更基础，适用范围更广。后者只谈论符号对解释者的影响，前者却谈论解释者对符号的反应。后者是被动的，因而也是必然的；前者却是主观的，取决于解释者的实际情况或主观意愿。皮尔斯之所以将“感情解释项”重新命名为“直接解释项”，就是因为他意识到："有些情况下，感情解释项是符号产生的唯一的真正意义效果。"[①] 换句话说，有些符号只在解释者心里形成某种感觉，某种印象，而不涉及进一步的影响或反应。此外，对于大部分的自然符号和惯例符号而言，解释者即便有主动的反应，也只是识别、理解等心智上的反应，而不是莫里斯的有关肌肉或腺体的动作反应倾向。皮尔斯之所以将"精力解释项"替换成"动态解释项"（很可能就是因为"精力"二字与肌肉上的努力联系过于紧密），就是要告诉我们：很多符号即便造成心理上的主动反应，或者说"努力"，也只是心智上的反应，而不涉及肌肉上的反应。奥斯古德在修正行为主义符号论时，转而采用神经生理性质上的"表征性的间接的反应"（representational mediational response），显然是因为"反应"一词要求过高了。[②]

（二）引起关系论

莫里斯的符内联系观本质上是一个"引起关系论"：将载体和解释项间的关系解释为"引起"关系。

引起关系论存在诸多问题。首先，这无异于将所有使用和产生符号的过程排除在"符号"概念之外，将"符号"现象局限于接受符号的过程。如果是符号载体引起符号它者，那么符号载体必先于符号它者而出现，这只与接受符号的过程相关；而在使用和产生符号的过程中，是将某心理事物表达或命名为某事物，符号它者必先于符号载体而出现。其次，即便在接受符号的过程中，符号载体也不一定"引起"符号它者。对于莫里斯而言，"引起"根源于刺激反应过程，应是一种比较直接、客观、必然的生理上的联系。如果这样，该如何解释如下现象：符号不为人理解，或符号在不同情境下对不同人而言有不同理解。难道要说不同情境下不同人的生理结构如此不同，以至于造成不同的反应倾向吗？显然，正常情况下，人与人的生理结构并没有本质区别，生理结构也并不因情境而变化。再次，即便在接受符号的过程中，说"符号载体引起符号它者"，也是一种简单化的、不准确的说法。莫里斯之所以如是说，其唯一论据是在某些情况下，依据行为主义心理学的方法，可以观察到如下现象：某人接触到某符号载体，尔后很快作出某种反应。然而，

---

① Charles Hartshorne, Paul Weiss. eds., *Collected Papers of Charles Sanders Peirce*, vol. 5. Bristol: Thoemmes Press, 1998, p. 326.

② C. E. Osgood, "On Understanding and Creating Sentneces", *American Psychology*, 18 (1963): 735—51.

这并不能证明前者引起后者。

先来看看条件反射实验。狗听到铃声后确实可能分泌唾液，但并不能说铃声引起分泌唾液。一个简单的后续实验就能证明这点：响铃后，不给狗提供食物，如此反复多次，再响铃，观察狗是否还分泌唾液。答案往往是否定的。可见，并不是响铃本身引起了唾液分泌。那么，如何解释铃声与分泌唾液紧邻着先后出现这一现象呢？这个现象事实上至少预设了两个阶段：无条件刺激阶段和条件刺激形成阶段。在前一阶段中，食物刺激狗的感知神经，狗分泌唾液；在后一阶段中，在食物刺激狗的感知神经时，铃声也总是刺激狗的神经，久而久之，狗将铃声带来的神经刺激、食物带来的神经刺激与分泌唾液记忆为一个单元。真正的条件刺激阶段，即听到铃声便分泌唾液，事实上是一个复杂的过程：铃声刺激狗的神经，唤起了狗对食物的刺激的记忆，该记忆如同真实的食物带来的神经刺激一般，使狗分泌唾液。换句话说，从听到铃声到分泌唾液至少涉及三个过程：对铃声的感知，上对铃声的感知而回忆并联想起对食物的感知，由对食物的感知的回忆而导致分泌唾液。第一步和第三步都相当客观，几近必然联系，或许还可以被视为“引起”关系，但基于回忆的联想却不是必然的，而是可以出错或改变的——如同上述后续试验一样，显然，无法将其说成是“引起”关系。不属于严格的条件反射现象的符号现象，就更不能简单地说成“引起”关系了。比如，我们稍为扩展一下上述条件反射的例子，即将反应从“分泌唾液”延伸至“跑到食槽吃食物”，形成如下符号现象：食物往往会使狗跑到食槽处吃食物；每次给食物时都响铃；久而久之，即便狗没有看到食物本身，响铃就会使狗跑到食槽处吃食物。这个现象也可以分为两个阶段：食物使狗跑到食槽处吃食物和铃声使狗跑到食槽处吃食物。在第一阶段中，食物刺激狗的感知神经，狗分泌唾液，产生跑到食槽吃食物的驱动力，形成跑到食槽吃食物的意愿，最终造成跑到食槽吃食物的反应。显然，要说该阶段中食物“引起”狗跑到食槽处吃食物，显然是过于简单化的、不准确的说法。该阶段的前三个步骤或许是必然的，还可以说成是“引起”关系；但是，后两个步骤却不是必然的，譬如，在狗已经吃饱的情况下或在狗行动不便的情况下，这一关系是可以改变的。在第二阶段中，在食物刺激狗的感知神经时，铃声也总是刺激狗的神经；久而久之，狗将铃声带来的神经刺激、食物带来的神经刺激、分泌唾液、产生跑到食槽吃食物的驱动力，甚至是跑到食槽吃食物的意愿和跑到食槽吃食物的动作记忆为一个单元，在这个记忆单元中，前四个步骤间的联系更为紧密，如同本能反应，后两个步骤间的联系相对松散，如同半本能反应。因此，在该例子中，从听到铃声到跑到食槽吃食物也涉及三个过程：对铃声的感知，因对铃声的感知而回忆并联想起对食物的感知，由回忆对食物的感知而跑到食槽吃食物。在该过程中，只有第一步是客观的、几近必然的关系，而第二和第三步都是可以改变的，整个过程比一般的条件刺激过程更不宜称为“引起”关系。而在其他与刺激-反应无关的符号现象（例如一般的自然符号与惯例符号）中，就更不能将符内联系说成“引起”关系了。

就这个问题而言，同样受行为主义心理学影响的奥格登和瑞查兹的认识就远比莫里斯深刻。他们注意到了“引起”（cause）一词的误导性，认为所谓的“引起”，其实是一种经验的重现。[①] 当奥格登和瑞查兹说“符号是这样的一个刺激物，它类似于某个原刺激的一部分，且足以唤起由原刺激所引起的心理印迹”[②] 时，他们事实上将符号解释为如下过程：原刺激 A’ 引起某心理事物 B’；符号载体 A 与 A’ 是同一情境下的两个成员，总是一起出现，解释者记住了两者间的联系；当解释者看到 A 时，唤起了对 A’ 的记忆，唤起了对“A’ 引起 B’”的回忆，并因此产生 B’ 的残余痕迹 B。胡塞尔的“观念联想”或许最能揭示这个过程的本质。在论及“标号”时——胡塞尔认为，符号可以分为两种，“标号”和“表述”——“标号”这一观念源于某些心理事实，这些心理事实隶属于我们历史上所谓“观念联想”的更大的心理事实群，而“观念联想”涉及与联想律中观念的“共现”、观念的“重新唤起”相关的事实。[③] 简而言之，标号涉及这样的一个过程：某人现时地知晓某物体或事态存在；尔后，他将该物体或事态的存在体验为一种动机；该动机使他产生联想；通过联想，他重新唤起了某个观念群，在该观念群中，该物体或事态与另一物体或事态相联系在一起；这样，他就从原物体或事态联想到了另一物体或事态。“引起说”的不合理性，也可以在心理学上得到佐证。一般来说，符号载体是物理性的，而符号它者是心理性的——这至少适用于莫里斯、奥格登和瑞查兹等人。物理性的事物能直接引起心理性的事物吗？能，通过感知。然而，感知过程的结果只能是有关符号载体的表象，有时还伴随着一些内分泌的反应。无论是皮尔斯的“解释项”，还是莫里斯的“解释项”

---

① C. K. Ogden, I. A. Richards, *The Meaning of Meaning*. New York: Routledge & Kegan Paul, 1923, p. 55.

② C. K. Ogden, I. A. Richards, *The Meaning of Meaning*. New York: Routledge & Kegan Paul, 1923, p. 53.

③ Edmund Husserl, *Logical Investigations* Ⅰ, trans. J. N. Findlay. London: Routledge, 2001, p. 186.

（或说“反应倾向”），都是异于符号载体的表象的事物，都超出了感知过程中“引起”的效果范围。可以说符号载体引起关于它本身的表象，但却不能说有关符号载体的表象引起符号它者。因此，也就不能说符号载体引起符号对象了。

（三）两个“它者”的共现性

莫里斯符内联系观的第三个问题在于：莫里斯所主张的两个它者并不总会同时出现于符号过程中。

在莫里斯提出的狗的例子中，铃声是符号载体，狗是解释者，某处有食物这个情况是意指，狗去某处找食物的倾向是解释项；在司机的例子中，那句话是符号载体，司机是解释者，某处有山体滑坡这个情况是意指，司机绕开山体滑坡处的倾向是解释项。细加分析，我们就会发现其中的问题。我们知道，莫里斯将意指和指称区分开来了；换句话说，上述两例中的意指，其实都是心理现象。在第一个例子中，对于狗来说，铃声真的一方面在心里代表着“某处有食物”，另一方面在心里引起“去某处找食物的倾向”吗？狗的心里或许真的有这两个心理运动；然而，如前分析，这个过程实际上应该是由这样的三个环节构成的：对铃声的感知，因回忆起对铃声的感知而回忆并联想起对某处的食物的感知，因回忆起对某处的食物的感知而去某处找食物。显然“某处有食物”和“去某处找食物的倾向”这两个心理现象是先后关系，而不是共存关系。那么，真正和载体“铃声”直接发生联系的是“某处有食物”这一心理现象；这个联系才是真正的符号过程，而“某处有食物”和“去某处找食物的倾向”之间的联系，是可以用心理学的联想率作出充分解释的心理现象，没有必要将其纳入符号现象之内。同理，在司机一例中，“某处有山体滑坡”这个心理现象可以纳入符号学的范畴，而“司机绕开山体滑坡处的倾向”则不必纳入符号学范畴。上述两例都涉及“指称”，其中的“意指”都是与指称相对应的心理现象，那么，在不涉及指称的例子中，情况如何呢？比如，用“三颗信号弹”表示“进攻”；用“奖状”表示“荣誉”。这些情况中，它者都只有一个，即“进攻”或“荣誉”这个心理观念。问题是，这个观念是意指还是解释项呢？“进攻”可以说是心理倾向，应该视为解释项；“荣誉”显然不是心理倾向，那就只能视为意指，而且是没有与之对应的指称的意指。显然，要统一地解释这些例子，必先做到如下三点：首先，要将解释项从“反应倾向”还原为“影响”，从而退归到皮尔斯的“直接解释项”；其次，要明确意指并不一定有相应的指称；再次，把解释项限定为“直接解释项”，将皮尔斯的“动态解释项”和“最终解释项”视为符号过程之后的心理过程；最后，要明确符号过程中不会同时存在两个它者。如果我们要坚持说意指是符号载体所指涉的内容，解释项是符号载体对解释者的影响，那么，我们只能把解释项视为限于符号接受过程中的意指，或者认为意指和解释项是两个并列的术语：在符号使用过程中，符号载体代表“意指”，而在符号接受过程中，符号载体造成“解释项”。

三、结语

莫里斯的“符号载体”“预备刺激”“符号”，相当于皮尔斯的“代表物”或“符号”；莫里斯的“意指”（designatum 或 signification）或“刺激物”类似于皮尔斯的“直接对象”；莫里斯的另一个概念“指涉”（denotatum），相当于皮尔斯的“动态对象”；莫里斯的“解释项”直接源自皮尔斯的“解释项”。显然，莫里斯的符号观实际上是皮尔斯的三元关系符号论和行为主义心理学的结合。因此，正如皮尔斯一样，莫里斯过于侧重符号接受过程，甚至将符号使用过程和符号接受过程混为一谈，将符号过程本身和符号过程之后的心理过程混为一谈；正如行为主义心理学一样，莫里斯的符号论过于简单化，过于机械化地看待心理过程，未能揭示符号过程的本质。

当然，莫里斯的符号论也为符号学发展作出了重要贡献。他比前人都更明确地将符号过程视为符号学的基本对象，最早明确地提出将符号学奠基于行为学，明确地将解释者与环境作为符号过程的元素。他试图建立符号科学的努力，较高程度地促进了符号学在科学性方面的进步。只可惜，他所依赖的实用主义符号观和行为主义心理学有其固有的缺陷，削弱了他苦心建立的符号理论的效力。

作者简介：

金毅强，浙江师范大学行知学院讲师，研究方向为翻译理论与实践、语言哲学、行动理论。

Author:

Jin Yiqiang, lecturer in Xingzhi College of Zhejiang Normal University. His research fields include translation studies, philosophy of language, and action theory.

E-mail: Jinyiqiang2005@aliyun.com

Social Semiotic Multimodal Research: A Meaning-based Approach*

Liu Yu

Abstract: Multimodal research has attracted increasing interest and set up dialogues with many different disciplines. Based on social semiotic theories of communication, this research examines multimodal representations in scientific discourse with a meaning-based approach to explore the functional specialization of non-verbal modes such as scientific diagrams, the relationships between different semiotic resources in the same text, and the transformation from one mode to another. The present study also responds to several theoretical and methodological issues made of social semiotic multimodal research and discusses the implications of multimodal studies for teaching and learning science.

Key words: multimodality, social semiotics, meaning, science education

社会符号学视角下的多模态研究：一项基于意义的研究方法

刘　宇

摘要：多模态研究已经成为当今人文及社会科学领域中的热点问题，并且同多个学科建立起对话关系。本文从社会符号学的视角出发，采用基于意义的研究方法，对科学语篇中的多模态表征进行系统分析。分析范围包括诸如科学图像等非语言表征的功能特性，同一语篇中不同符号系统之间的关系，以及不同模态之间的转化过

* This research is supported by "Research on Scientific Texts from a Multimodal Perspective" (SISU201207) granted by Sichuan International Studies University.

程。针对外界对多模态分析的理论和研究方法提出的问题和质疑，本文也将作出回应，并讨论多模态研究给科学教育带来的启示。

关键词：多模态，社会符号学，意义，科学教育

Ⅰ. Introduction

The multimodal landscape of communication has attracted a growing attention from scholarship in the past decade. On one hand, new academic publications (e. g., the journal of *Multimodal Communication*) emerged as a regular forum for exploring different representational forms; on the other hand, multimodal studies were increasingly published in reputable linguistics journals (e. g., *Language Sciences*), which used to accept researches on language only.

One problem with existing multimodal research, however, lies in its underdeveloped theories. As Jewitt cautioned, multimodality at the current stage is far from a full-fledged theory but a domain of inquiry influenced by a wide range of disciplines such as sociology, art history, and cultural studies (2009a, p. 2). While these theories are useful to examine some aspects of multimodality, they do not provide research tools for analyzing the full range of representations and thus have limitations to develop a comprehensive theory of multimodality.

In contrast, social semiotics conceptualizes all forms of semiosis with a meaning base. Namely, language along with painting, sculpture and so on is considered one of many modes of meaning, all of which interrelate to constitute human culture (Halliday & Hasan, 1985, p. 4). The meaning-based approach has been strongly linked with multidal studies since the 1990s, as evidenced by the steadily increased social semiotic research on displayed art (O'Toole, 1994), visual design (Kress & van Leeuwen, 1996), music (van Leeuwen, 1999), and mathematical discourse (O'Halloran, 2005), to name just a few.

This paper aims to further develop multimodal theories from a social semiotic perspective. The next section briefly introduces the meaning-based approach and its key theoretical underpinnings for multimodality. Then two main areas of meaning-based multimodal research are described: meaning making within the same mode and meaning making across different modes. Given that multimodal research has attracted much attention from science education scholars, the analysis of meaning in multimodality is demonstrated through a reference to scientific discourse. This research also responds to several recent criticisms of social semiotic multimodal research. Finally, the present study discusses the pedagogical implications of multimodality.

Ⅱ. Key Tenets of A Meaning-based Approach

Social semiotics is the study of sign systems wherein each choice of sign acquires its meaning against the background of other sign choices not within the sign system itself but in the context of specific social situations (Halliday & Hasan, 1985, p. 4). The meaning-based approach to multimodality has three key theoretical assumptions, which are briefly explained below.

First, meaning is both a social and representational phenomenon, which implies stratification of semiotic systems at different levels of abstraction (Halliday & Matthiessen, 1999, pp. 3－7). For instance, when human beings make a speech to communicate, the meaning is shaped by social norms and the moment by moment situation at the more abstract level (the context stratum), organized in specific language forms and structures, and ultimately expressed in certain sound patterns at the more concrete levels (the lexicogrammar stratum and the expression stratum respectively). A meaning-based interpretation adopts a bottom-up approach and highlights the grammatical construction of meaning, especially in the analysis of language.

Secondly, every communicative practice, in which one or multiple semiotic resources may be deployed, has three kinds of meaning or serves three generalized semiotic functions (metafunctions) simultaneously: to construct "doings" or "state of affairs" in the world as ideational meaning, to take a stance towards the presentation and to the reader/viewer as interpersonal meaning, and to organize related elements into a coherent message as textual meaning (Halliday & Matthiessen, 2004, pp. 29—31). In fact, the shared metafunctional principle has been identified by O'Halloran as the major strength of social semiotic theories for multimodal discourse analysis (2008, p. 444), for it not only provides analytical tools to explore how modalities other than language make meaning, but also enables semantic integration between different semiotic choices.

Thirdly, meaning operates through time in an ever-changing process called semogenesis (Halliday & Matthiessen, 1999, pp. 17－18). The semogenetic view has been recently extended beyond language to explore the change across different semiotic choices. In the pioneering research on mathematical discourse, O'Halloran adopts a historical perspective and convincingly argues that modern mathematical symbolism grew out of written language and developed a range of specialized lexicogrammatical devices to realize semantic expansions, thereby explaining the complexities of mathematical reality outstripping the meaning potential of language (2005, pp. 94－97).

Ⅲ. Two Main Areas of Meaning-based Multimodal Research

There are two main areas of meaning-based multimodal research considering the number of modes under investigation. Multimodal studies have been undertaken to explore the functionality of individual modes other than language and the semantic interaction between two or more semiotic resources in communication. The present section does not intend to make an exhaustive list of multimodal research, but only discusses those studies which have been adopted to inform science teaching and learning.

1. Meaning Making within the Same Mode

As mentioned earlier in Section Ⅱ, the shared metafunctions actually provide a common platform to conceptualize all forms of semiosis. Due to the space constraints, this paper only focuses on the ideational metafunction of representations.

From a multimodal perspective, non-verbal modalities can be modeled as systems of interrelated options to make meaning, thereby offering a degree of prediction in how semiotic resources will be designed for communication in specific situations. For example, the ideational meaning options of visual representations can be mapped out through the mechanism of system networks as follows:

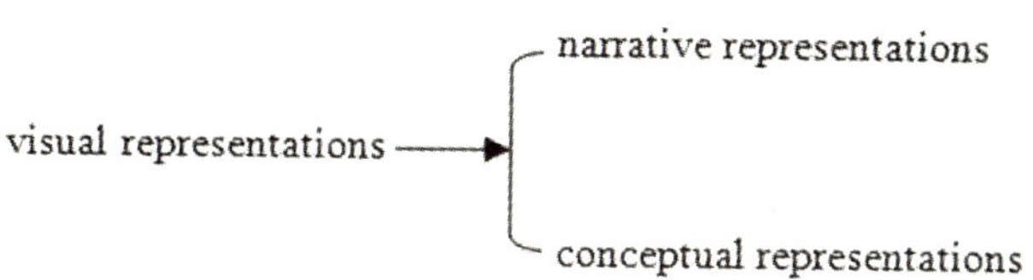

Figure 1 Basic System of Visual Representations

Figure 1 presents a basic network of visual structures. Reading from left to right, visual representations (the entry condition to this system) fall under either the category of narrative representations or the category of conceptual representations. The left-to-right direction of the network also indicates an increasing scale of delicacy. Formulation of systemic networks such as Figure 1 is intended to explicitly account for the meaning potential of semiotic resources, which raises an issue for some researchers nevertheless. This issue will be responded to in Section Ⅳ, I.

According to Halliday and Matthiessen, a linguistic systemic choice is realized by the presence of structural elements (2004, pp. 20－24). For instance, *transitivity* is the grammatical system to model experience as "a manageable set of process types" to represent some kind of the complex "goings-on" in the world (Halliday & Matthiessen, 2004, pp. 170－178). One systemic choice of *transitivity* is a material process, which construes the meaning of "doing" or "happening". A material process (e. g. *Particles move at a high speed*) can be organized through a simplified structure "participant ^ process^ circumstance" ("^" means *followed by*).

Likewise, the systemic option of visual *transitivity* is manifested in visual structures (Kress & van Leeuwen, 1996, pp. 43－45). For example, the choice of narrative representation in Figure 2 shares similar structural configurations with the material process (*Particles move at a high speed*). However, it is important to note that the same semantic categories have different forms of realization in language and visual images. They also operate at different grammatical ranks.

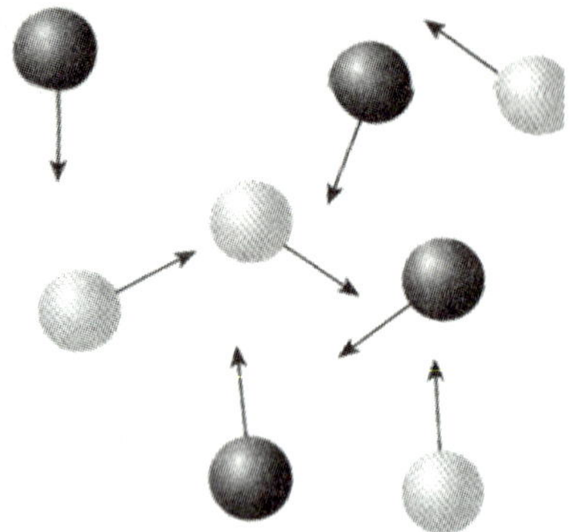

Figure 2 Visual Representation of Particle Movement[①]

To illustrate, the material process (*Particles move at a high speed*) operates at the rank of clause in language whereas the visual representation in Figure 2 does at the rank of figure[②]. Furthermore, the semantic categories of participant and process operate at the grammatical rank of word in the form of a noun (*particles*) and of a verb (*move*) respectively. The meaning roles of participant and process are visualized as small circles and arrows at the rank of member in Figure 2.

Also noteworthy is that language and images do not make exactly the same meaning. For example, the colors of the circles (in the original) in Figure 2 indicate that there are two different kinds of particles under investigation. This meaning cannot be found in the corresponding clause (*Particles move at a high speed*).

Kress explains that different modes have unique meaning-making resources and thus have specific "epistemological commitments" (unavoidable affordances) (2003, p. 3). Lemke (1998) further distinguishes between two aspects of the ideational meaning: meaning by kind and meaning by degree, and contends that although all semiotic resources can construe both typological meaning and topological meaning, they are good at one of the two types of meaning only.

---

① Figure 2 is reproduced from Onn, H. L., Ang, E. J. A., and Khoo, L. E. (2006, p. 199).

② In O'Toole's analytical framework, a figure is a visual rank construing simple "goings-on" in the world. The rank of figure is made up of members at the lowest level (1994, p. 11).

Language, as a typologically oriented semiotic resource, is unsurpassed as a tool for the formulation of difference and relationship, for the making of categorical distinctions. It is much poorer (though hardly bankrupt) in resources for formulating degree, quantity, gradation, continuous change, continuous co-variation, non-integer ratios, varying proportionality, complex topological relations of relative nearness or connectedness, or nonlinear relationships and dynamical emergence (1998, p. 87).

While Lemke's distinction between typological meaning and topological meaning is programmatic, the representational resources provide concrete tools for analyzing the meaning potential of different modes. For instance, it seems that in Figure 2 the resource of color in visuals imposes the commitment to classification. Furthermore, the image of arrows employs the resource of length to indicate the speed of particle movement as the semantic category of circumstance. The two resources enable the visual representation of Figure 2 to make topological meaning, which is not possible by language.

2. Meaning Making across Different Modes

The functional specialization principle is also useful to justify the multimodal nature of human communication because any single modality is partial in relation to the whole meaning repertoire. For example, despite being a most powerful and comprehensive mode of meaning, language alone is less effective to represent the topological complexities of scientific communication, and has to mingle with other semiotic choices to expand the meaning potential. The semantic orchestration across different modes can be explored from two perspectives: the synoptic perspective and the dynamic perspective.

(1) The synoptic view.

The synoptic view of meaning making across modes mainly derives from Halliday and Hasan's (1976) research on linguistic cohesion (i. e. meaning relations between linguistic expressions). Multimodal representations are therefore regarded as one single textual phenomenon in which cohesive devices function to integrate verbal and other semiotic forms as a coherent whole. For example, drawing on the representational grammar system of visual design and the categories of lexical cohesion, Royce suggests a range of multimodal cohesion such as inter-semiotic repetition, hyponymy and collocation to analyze text-image relations (1998, p. 29), which is useful to reveal students' conceptual difficulties in understanding academic discourse.

For instance, Crisp and Sweiry (2006) investigated multimodal phenomena in chemistry examination questions. In one of their collected sample questions, Figure 3 was accompanied by the verbal part ([...] *some brands of toothpaste contain sodium carbonate. Three products are made when sodium carbonate reacts with hydrochloric acid. What are they?*) It was reported that an extraordinarily high proportion of the young test takers gave wrong answers such as *shampoo* and *soap*.

Figure 3 Photograph in a Science Exam Question①

According to Crisp and Sweiry, the included photograph was to blame for students' mistakes (2006, pp. 149−151): Given that the word *products* can mean something made in a factory to be sold or something produced through a chemical process, the image showing toothpaste, shampoo and soap triggered in young learners' mind the former meaning as in *household products*. It is therefore claimed that visual images negatively affected students' understanding of scientific concepts on some occasions.

From a multimodal view, pictorial representations constitute an important modal resource to construct scientific concepts nonetheless, and

① Figure 3 is reproduced from Crisp and Sweiry (2006, p. 149).

should be an integral part of scientific discourse. It seems that the novice students' wrong answers may have stemmed from their lack of sufficient knowledge on multimodal cohesion.

To illustrate, when young learners strongly associated the photograph with the word "products", they actually attempted to find the image-text meaning relation in the examination question. Considering that shampoo, soap and toothpaste were three kinds of household products, novice students thus assumed that the photograph was interrelated to the word *products* through the semantic link of hyponymy.

In contrast, the examination designer was likely to link the photograph with the word "toothpaste" through the cohesive resource of intersemiotic repetition, as the concept of toothpaste was visually represented in Figure 3, and through the cohesive device of intersemiotic collocation, for toothpaste was often put in the same place with other household products such as shampoo, soap and hand wash.

The meaning-based examination indicates that the inclusion of photographs in Figure 3 did not necessarily give rise to students' misunderstanding of the examination question. Rather, young test takers obviously realized that there existed semantic links between the visual and verbal components in a multimodal representation. The challenge for them was how to identify the type of image-text cohesion intended by the examination designer. This problem can be resolved when students learn basic knowledge about intersemiotic cohesion.

(2) The dynamic view.

While a synoptic account is useful to explore multimodal communication from a spatial perspective and effectively reveals semantic convergence between various modes, it is limited in its ability to demonstrate how meaning changes and expands in multisemiotic discourse. Complementarily, a dynamic view is needed to examine how crossmodal processes unfold through time.

Pioneering dynamic analysis of semiosis might be best represented by Iedema's (2001) *resemioticization* research, which focused on how organizational discourse progressed across different modalities in its real-time unfolding process. For example, a project of renovating and expanding a mental hospital started with embodied semiotic resources such as spoken language, gestures, and facial expressions at planning meetings. Then it moved to disembodied resources including written planning reports and the visual architectural design, and ultimately changed into the most durable sign: the buildings.

Iedema noted that in the semiosis process, meaning was under constant changes (2001, p. 30). For instance, the architect-planner's written summary was far from a mere reflection of what was said by the medical staff at earlier stages; instead, the architect-planner selected particular lexicogrammatical resources to semantically metonymize the stakeholders so that others would find it very difficult to challenge his utterance. In addition, when the written report was later visualized as a design, individual stakeholders' opinions and expectations were further compromised.

Likewise, Thibault re-interpreted multimodal communication from a semogenetic perspective as the ongoing contextualization of meanings arising from different modalities (2000, p. 362). Lim classified contextualizing relations as two sub-types: co-contextualizing or convergence where the meaning of one semiotic resource shares similarity with the meaning of another, and re-contextualizing or divergence where the meaning of one modality seems to be odd with the meaning of another (2004, p. 239).

While these pioneering studies provide programmatic accounts of general meaning making patterns in the process of resemioticization, analytical frameworks are needed to demonstrate what semantic changes take place and how the changes are realized through cross-modal modulations.

Taking a meaning-based approach, Liu and Owyong examined how the subject of chemistry was historically resemioticized from language to symbolic expressions (2011, pp. 829 – 832). Based on the grammatical analysis of language and chemical symbolism, the two authors proposed several mechanisms to describe the semantic changes of resemioticization. For example, when the technical term *copper oxide* evolved as $Cu + O$ in the early 1800s, the mechanism of intersemiotic transcategorization was found to operate to expand the meaning potential of chemistry.

Grammatically, *copper oxide* is a noun and thus construes the meaning of a thing. In contrast, *Cu* + *O* is a symbolic clause in which both *Cu* and *O* function as co-equal participants to activate the process. It therefore follows that symbolic expressions of chemicals, far from a fanciful way of representing their names. On the contrary, the symbolic form implies that chemical compounds were no longer regarded as a stable entity but as a dynamic interaction between different particles at the atomic level. Such a semantic shift was crucial to support and develop the submicroscopic view of chemistry as a new theory in the early 19th century. In this sense, resemioticization enables scientists to effectively explore chemical phenomena with new research tools.

Ⅳ. Issues in Social Semiotic Multimodal Research

Taking Halliday's (1978) social interpretation of communication as the point of departure, social semiotics has been usefully adopted to theorize multimodal research and has effectively addressed a number of research questions. Despite the increasing interest in social semiotic multimodal research, some of its theoretical assumptions and analytical approaches were questioned and criticized even by social semiotic scholars in recent years. The present section comments on several raised issues and aims to clarify important points of multimodality.

1. Formulation of Modal Systems

Social semiotic multimodal research is claimed to be primarily interested in formulating inventories of the semiotic potentials as exemplified by O'Toole's (1994) articulation of systems of choice in displayed art and O'Halloran's (2005) grammatical systems for analyzing mathematical discourse. This method is questioned for its alleged partiality, because any suggested modal system cannot "map all the complex ways in which people make meaning [...] given the dynamic and changing character of meaning making" (Jewitt, 2006, p. 19). It is also argued that the modal systems consist of pre-determined categories and are conceived as prescriptive rather than descriptive (Jewitt, 2009b, p. 30).

The issue of partiality in the account of modal systems can be addressed by applying the key notion of "instantiation" in social semiotics that system and text lie at the poles of the same cline. As Knox aptly states, the foundational work of O'Toole (1994) attempts to map out the meaning potential of displayed art and is located near the axis of system (2009, p. 130). Since a system is essentially characterized by abstraction and generalizability, it need not "*fit the instance in its specificity as it occurs in nature*" (Cartwright, as cited in Hasan, 1995, p. 188, italics in original).

However, this does not entail that social semiotic multimodal studies pay little attention to the "instance" pole of the cline. For example, O'Toole's (1994) systemic grammars of buildings have inspired multimodal research including the semiotic make up of an exhibition at the Singapore History Museum (Pang, 2004) and of Singapore's Orchard Road and Marriot Hotel (Alias, 2004). Analysis of these specific instances not only provides a testimony to the applicability of O'Toole's (1994) grammatical framework, it also provides feedback for the original systems. ①

Furthermore, the networks and categories of the modal systems do not make prescriptions, but offer meta-knowledge to conceptualize semiotic artifacts and activities and make an explicit account of their meaning potential. For instance, the system of *transitivity* in language has been extended to investigate multimodal discourse (see Figure 1). As Kress and van Leeuwen note, they do not simply impose linguistic terms on visual design (1996, p. 76), for instance, to identify a "visual material process" (though there are parallels when language and images construe the experience of "doing"). Rather, the *transitivity* system provides a productive analytical tool to model meaning-making patterns in visual images and other semiotic resources.

Admittedly, the validity of the proposed modal systems even in the foundational work of Kress and van Leeuwen (1996) and O'Toole (1994) need to be further testified and recent multimodal research exercises more caution when adopting these analytical frameworks. For example, when

---

① For example, Alias (2004) discusses how the grammar of buildings contributes to the construction of capitalism and consumerism and thus extends O'Toole's (1994) grammatical analysis of displayed art to the more abstract semiotic level of ideology.

analyzing multisemiotic print documents, Bateman questions the feasibility of Kress and van Leeuwen's (1996) ideological interpretation of the compositional system of *information value* (2008, pp. 40—53).

Likewise, Jones' empirically grounded analysis of science textbooks reveals that images and verbal texts can appear on either the left-hand or right-hand side of the page (2007, pp. 249—250), which provides counter evidence of Kress and van Leeuwen's (1996) claim that the horizontal axis of a page carries the *information value* of Given-New where linguistic components frequently occupy the left-hand side to present something the reader is familiar with while the right-hand side is often taken by visual displays to convey contestable information. However, the new strand of empirical research does not invalidate the whole proposed modal systems, but provides revisions to the model.

2. Stratification of the Content Plane of Multimodal Discourse

From a meaning-based view, language is a multistrata semiotic system, which construes, is construed by, and over time re-construes context. In a similar vein, other modalities operate in the semiotic environment of context, and are stratified into the content plane and the expression plane (Matthiessen, 2009, p. 12). However, it remains an issue whether the content plane of non-verbal forms of semiosis can be split into the strata of semantics and grammar.

Firstly, it is found that some modalities (e. g. mathematical symbolism) historically had a linguistic origin, and thus were highly similar to language in terms of the semiotic organization patterns (O'Halloran, 2005, pp. 94—97). Furthermore, while other modes such as visual displays possess quite different meaning potential from language, preliminary stratified models (e. g. O'Halloran, 2005, 2008; Lim, 2004) have been usefully applied to demonstrate multimodal meaning making in mathematical discourse, print advertisements and children's picture books.

Closely related is another question whether the notion of rank, which is originally used to analyze the grammar of language, is also productive to map out the meaning potential of multimodal discourse (Machin, 2009, pp. 186—

188). Martinec explains that it is determined by the size and nature of the analytical data whether images should be modeled according to ranks (2005, pp. 162-163). For instance, O'Toole's (1994) examples such as Botticelli's *Primavera* belong to large-scale narrative events consisting of diverse episodes of more or less equal status. In contrast, Kress and van Leeuwen (1996) select less complex narrative images with one main process in which the notion of rank is less important for analytical purposes.

Taking Martinec's (2005) argument as the point of departure, it seems that the feasibility of internal stratification and ranks of multimodal representations relies on the nature of the contexts in which they are used. For instance, the two notions are crucial in the analysis of scientific discourse. Firstly, mathematical and chemical symbolism grew out of natural language and develops similar patterns of semiotic organization. Also, scientific diagrams historically developed unique grammatical resources, and a rank-based account was productively used to shed light on how sophisticated scientific knowledge is constructed (Liu & DwiNugroho, 2012).

3. Inadequate Emphasis on Context

Social semiotic multimodal research is also criticized for being pre-occupied with building grammatical inventories at the cost of contextual analysis. According to Machin, while O'Toole is firmly against the knowledge "that can be read up in a library", his analysis of *Primavera* actually relies on contextual knowledge rather than the application of the visual grammar (2009, p. 187). However, it should be kept in mind that O'Toole (1994) never emphasizes grammar over contextual knowledge; his argument is that contextual knowledge *alone* is limited in its ability to take the meaning of semiotic artifacts and needs to be implemented with a grammatical analysis.

Despite O'Toole's (1994) focus on building inventories of the semiotic potentials, his main purpose is to lay the foundation for the grammatical approach to multimodal discourse. In fact, from a social semiotic perspective, grammar is the essential resource that construes experience (Halliday & Matthiessen, 1999, p. 17). So it might not be appropriate to conclude that O'Toole (1994) pays little attention to context just because of his account of grammaticality.

A comparable example is Halliday and Matthiessen's (2004) *An Introduction to Functional Grammar*, which makes a comprehensive account of grammatical resources in language rather than of social context. Obviously, this book does not count as evidence that Halliday and Matthiessen tend to ignore the notion of social context. It is worth mentioning that the proposed grammatical frameworks are not the whole story of multimodal research, but a starting point to analyze multimodal discourse and allow readers/viewers to relate the analysis to "the social, intellectual, and economic world within the artist and his patrons worked" (O'Toole, 1994, p. 4).

In fact, much of existing social semiotic multimodal research makes in-depth analysis of social context. To take an example, O'Halloran (2009) investigates the historical evolution of mathematical discourse and explores how social and technological changes shape the semiotic landscape of mathematics. Furthermore, taking Bernstein's sociology of education, O'Halloran's (2005) analysis of mathematics classroom discourse is not limited to the situated interaction between teacher and students under observation, but takes into account the curriculum and the underlying socio-cultural relations.

4. Redundant Terminology

In order to map out the meaning-making systems of different semiotic resources and cross-modal interaction, social semiotic research develops a meta-language to describe grammars and functionality of multimodal discourse. The meta-language entails the use of terminology, which has incurred criticisms that social semiotics tends to multiply the terms in use and create semiotic entities (Machin, 2009, p. 189).

The first point to be clarified is that multimodal social semiotic approaches do borrow existing technical terms from other fields of research. One example is the crucial notion *modal affordance* in multimodality. As Jewitt points out, the term *affordance* originated in Gibson's cognitive theory and was interpreted as a matter of perception (2006, pp. 25－26). However, when applied in multimodal studies, *affordance* is no longer a psychological concept but a complex one involving the material and the socio-cultural aspects of semiotic resources (Jewitt, 2009b, p. 24).

Secondly, given that social semiotics is a specialized field and its experiential meaning is realized in the patterns of lexis, it is not only necessary but also important for multimodal research to develop its own terminology (Wignell, Martin, & Eggins, 1993, p. 162). For instance, when analyzing the generic structure potential of print advertisements, Cheong (2004) coins the technical lexis *lead* to describe the most outstanding visual component. It should be kept in mind that *lead* is far from redundant or a fanciful way of saying the image. Instead, this notion is meaning-oriented and emphasizes the interpersonal metafunction of visual displays in the advertisement.

In the mean time, social semiotic scholars (e. g. , Bezemer & Kress, 2008; Jewitt, 2009a, 2009b; O'Halloran, 2005) have made preliminary efforts to clarify crucial terminology in multimodal studies such as *semiotic resource*, *mode*, *modality*, *multimodal* and *multisemiotic* to avoid potential misunderstanding.

Ⅴ. Pedagogical Implications and Concluding Remarks

In the past few years, the meaning-based approach to multimodality has well informed research in a wide range of disciplines, notably in the field of science teaching and learning.

Firstly, social semiotic multimodal research is epistemologically significant for science education. The semantic analysis of multisemiotic phenomena in scientific discourse reveals that scientific concepts are constructed in representational forms and constantly shaped and re-shaped by lingual, visual, symbolic and many other modal resources. It therefore provides further evidence to support the view that "knowledge is seen, not as a resolved set of declarative concepts, but as a network of interlocking representations that are to some extent negotiable and 'in process'" (Hubber, Tytler, & Haslam, 2010, p. 19).

Secondly, social semiotic theories also provide a meta-language for teachers and learners to negotiate the meaning of scientific representations. While the use of a meta-language is sometimes criticized as a weak point of multimodal research, the New London Group argues that an accessible social semiotic meta-language is much needed to facilitate a rise in literacy, because the meta-language can provide an explicit account of the link between the modal systems and their use in social contexts (1996, p. 77).

Despite the concern over the technical aspects of the meta-language, recent studies in primary and secondary schools provide preliminary evidence that even young pupils can learn the basics of social semiotics, and the meta-language does not lesson students' enjoyment, but enhances the their engagement with the pedagogical discourse, develops their critical orientation, and improves their learning outcomes (Unsworth, 2008).

As may be clear from the preceding discussion, this research aims to contribute to two different communities. By describing the research scope of multimodality, the present study calls for educational researchers and practitioners' attention to semiotic complexity in scientific discourse and offers them a meaning-based approach to examine how scientific knowledge is constructed in the form of single and multiple modes. Also, this study responds to several criticisms semiotics scholars made of social semiotic multimodal research and attempts to clarify some of the theoretical and methodological issues. However, further research is needed to theorize multimodality and engage with its limitations.

References:

Alias, S., (2004). "A Semiotic Study of Singapore's Orchard and Marriott Hotel", in K. L. O'Halloran, ed., *Multimodal Discourse Analysis: Systemic Functional Perspectives*, (pp. 55—79). London: Continuum.

Ang, A. K. M., (2004). "Making History in *From Colony to Nation*: A Multimodal Analysis of a Museum Exhibition in Singapore", in K. L. O'Halloran, ed., *Multimodal Discourse Analysis: Systemic Functional Perspectives* (pp. 28—54). London: Continuum.

Bateman, J. A., (2008). *Multimodality and Genre: A Foundation for the Systematic Analysis of Multimodal Documents*. Hampshire: Palgrave Macmillan.

Bezemer, J., Kress, G., (2008). "Writing in Multimodal Texts: A Social Semiotic

Account of Designs for Learning", *Written Communication*, 25, pp. 166—195.

Cheong, Y. Y. (2004). "The Construal of Ideational Meaning in Print Advertisements", in K. L. O'Halloran , ed. , *Multimodal Discourse Analysis: Systemic Functional Perspectives* (pp. 163—195). London: Continuum.

Crisp, V. , & Sweiry, E. , (2006). "Can a Picture Ruin a Thousand Words? The Effects of Visual Resources in Exam Questions", *Educational Research*, 48, 139—154.

Halliday, M. A. K. (1978). *Language as Social Semiotic: The Social Interpretation of Language and Meaning*. Baltimore: University Park Press.

Halliday, M. A. K. , Hasan, R. , (1976), *Cohesion in English*. London: Longman.

——, (1985), *Language, Context and Text: Aspects of language in a Social-semiotic Perspective*. Geelong, Victoria: Deakin University Press.

Halliday, M. A. K. , Matthiessen, C. M. I. M. , (1999). *Construing Experience through Meaning: A Language-based Approach to Cognition*. London: Cassell.

——, (2004). *An Introduction to Functional Grammar* (3rd ed.). London: Arnold.

Hasan, R. , (1995). "The Conception of Context in Text", in P. Fries, M. Gregory, eds. , *Discourse in Society: Systemic Functional Perspectives* (pp. 183 — 283). Norwood, N J: Ablex.

Hubber, P. , Tytler, R. & Haslam, F. , (2010). "Teaching and Learning about Force with a Representational Focus: Pedagogy and Teacher Change", *Research in Science Education*, 40, 5—28.

Iedema, R. , (2001). "Resemiotization", *Semiotica*, 137, 23—39.

Jones, J. , (2007). *Multiliteracies for Academic Purposes: A Metafunctional Exploration of Intersemiosis and Multimodality in University Textbook and Computer-based Learning Resources in Science*. Unpublished doctoral dissertation, University of Sydney.

Jewitt, C. , (2006). *Technology, Literacy and Learning: A Multimodal Approach*. London: Routledge.

Jewitt, C. , (2009a). "Introduction: Handbook Rationale, Scope and Structure", in C. Jewitt . ed. , *The Routledge Handbook of Multimodal Analysis* (pp. 1—7). London and New York: Routledge.

Jewitt, C. , (2009b). "Different Approaches to Multimodality", in C. Jewitt, ed. , *The Routledge Handbook of Multimodal Analysis* (pp. 28—39). London: Routledge.

Knox, J. , (2009). *Multimodal Discourse on Online Newspaper Home Pages: A Social-semiotic Perspective*. Unpublished doctoral dissertation, University of Sydney.

Kress, G. , (2003). *Literacy in the New Media Age*. London: Routledge.

Kress, G. , van Leeuwen, T. , (1996). *Reading Images: The Grammar of Visual Design*. London: Routledge.

Lemke, J. L., (1998). "Multiplying Meaning: Visual and Verbal Semiotics in Scientific Text", in J. R. Martin, & R. Veel, eds., *Reading Science: Critical and Functional Perspectives on Discourses of Science* (pp. 87—113). London: Routledge.

Lim, F. V., (2004). "Developing an Integrative Multisemiotic Model", in K. L. O'Halloran, ed., *Multimodal Discourse Analysis: Systemic Functional Perspectives* (pp. 220—246). London: Continuum.

Liu, Y., Owyong, M., (2011). "Metaphor, Multiplicative Meaning and the semiotic Construction of Scientific Knowledge", *Language Sciences*, 33, 822—834.

Liu, Y., DwiNugroho, A., (2012). "The Social Semiotic Construction of Chemical Periodicity: A Multimodal View.", *Semiotica*, 190, 133—151.

Machin, D., (2009). "Multimodality and Theories of the Visual", in C. Jewitt, ed., *The Routledge Handbook of Multimodal Analysis* (pp. 181—190). London: Routledge.

Martinec, R., (2005). "Topics in Multimodality", in R. Hasan, C. M. I. M. Matthiessen, & J. Webster, eds., *Continuing Discourse on Language: A Functional Perspective* (Vol. 1), (pp. 157—181). London: Equinox.

Matthiessen, C. M. I. M., (2009). "Multisemiotic and Context-based Register Typology: Registerial Variation in the Complementarity of Semiotic Systems", in E. Ventola, A. Guijarro, eds., *The World Told and the World Shown: Multisemiotic issues* (pp. 11—38). Basingstoke: Palgrave Macmillan.

New London Group, (1996). "A Pedagogy of Multiliteracies: Designing Social Futures", *Harvard Educational Review*, 66, 60—92.

Onn, H. L., Ang, E. J. A. & Khoo, L. E., (2006). *Chemistry Expression: An Inquiry Approach*. Singapore: Panpac Education.

O'Halloran, K. L., (2005). *Mathematical Discourse: Language, Symbolism and visual Image*. London: Continuum.

O'Halloran, K. L., (2008). "Systemic Functional-multimodal Discourse Analysis (SF-MDA): Constructing Ideational Meaning Using Language and Visual Imagery", *Visual Communication*, 7, 443—475.

O'Halloran, K. L., (2009). "Historical Changes in the Semiotic Landscape: From Calculation to Computation", in C. Jewitt, ed., *The Routledge Handbook of Multimodal Analysis* (pp. 98—113). London: Routledge.

O'Toole, M., (1994). *The Language of Displayed Art*. London: Leicester University Press.

Royce, T. D., (1998). "Synergy on the Page: Exploring Intersemiotic Complementarity in Page Based Multimodal Text", *JASFL Occasional Papers*, 1, 25—49.

Thibault, P. J., (2000). "The Multimodal Transcription of a Television Advertisement:

Theory and Practice", in A. Baldry, ed., *Multimodality and Multimediality in the Distance Learning Age* (pp. 311—385). Campobasso, Italy: Palladino Editore.

Unsworth, L., (2008). "Explicating Inter-modal Meaning-making in Media and Literary Texts: Towards a Metalanguage of Image/Language Relations", in A. Burn & C. Durrant, eds., *Media Teaching: Language, Audience, Production* (pp. 48—80). Kent Town, South Australia: Wakefield Press and AATE—NATE.

Van Leeuwen, T., (1999). *Speech, Music, Sound*. London: Macmillan.

Wignell, P., Martin, J. R., & Eggins, S., (1993). "The Discourse of Geography: Ordering and Explaining the Experiential World", in M. A. K. Halliday & J. R. Martin, eds., *Writing Science: Literacy and Discursive Power* (pp. 136—165). London: Falmer Press.

Author:

Liu Yu, an associate professor in the College of International Education at Sichuan International Studies University, China. He received his Ph. D. in language studies and multimodality from National University of Singapore.

作者简介:

刘宇，新加坡国立大学语言学博士，四川外国语大学国际教育学院副教授。

E-mail: liuyunus@gmail. com

论礼物的普遍分类：一个符号学分析

赵星植

摘　要：到目前为止，学术界还未见对人类社会的所有礼物进行分类的努力。本文尝试采用符号学相关原理，从礼物符号文本的意向性与馈赠双方关系的时间性这两个维度，对人类文化中所有的礼物交换类型进行一次系统性的分类。本文想通过分类说明：不同礼物类别之间的差异，其实就是礼物符号文本自身携带的文本意向性导致的符号表意重心的位移；而礼物符号文本又在具体的交换过程中与馈赠双方发生交互关系，由此形成不同的礼物符号表意特性，并据此完成不同的符号表意功能。

关键词：礼物，普遍分类，文本意向性，关系的时间维度，符号学

A General Classification of Gifts: A Semiotic Analysis

Zhao Xingzhi

Abstract: So far, there has not been a general classification embracing all types of gifts and their exchange patterns. Hence, this paper endeavors to fill up this research gap by adopting a semiotic approach. Based on two criteria, namely, the intentionality of the gift-texts and the temporal directionality of the interpersonal relationships, all the patterns of gift exchanges in the human culture could be classified into three domain types with eight subtypes. It is worth noting that different kinds of intentionality carried by gift-texts themselves, interweaving with varying degrees of relationships within specific social contexts, result in the variations of the gifts as well as their exchanging patterns.

Key words: gifts, general classification, intentionality, temporal directionality, semiotics

一、问题的提出

（一）当代社会礼物形式与意义的问题凸显

在当代社会，礼物无论是在形式上还是在其自身意义上都在发生着激烈的变化。首先，礼物的形式正在向“物”与“符号”这两个极端发展，具体表现为：第一，礼物与商品的边界变得模糊不清。据统计，目前在中国奢侈品消费市场中，70％的购买是用来送礼①；礼物越来越贵重，导致“回收礼物”在国内也逐渐发展成为一条产业链。这也就意味着，礼物也如同商品一样可以“买进卖出”，更可以按照市场逻辑进行具体操作。由此导致的严重后果是，传统礼物携带的人情伦理等文化规则居然也可以像商品一样用金钱衡量：礼物作为礼物而存在的文化逻辑在市场规则的操作下落空。第二，在当代，礼物作为“物”的实用意义变得无限小，人们越来越看重礼物的符号价值。由此，我们可以看到大量包装远超实物的“空壳礼物”，或是名流交往中盛行的“头衔礼物”；更别说在当今礼品市场上畅销的各类“定制礼物”“个性礼物”等。它们的共同特征就是礼物的实质形式已经基本被抽空，代替人们行使礼物交际功能的是其符号价值。应当说，在当今社会，礼物的外在形态正在以惊人的速度发生着各种各样的变异。

其次，对礼物意义的分裂式解读。正如费孝通所述，中国的人际关系呈现出一种“差序格局”②，人情、伦理、关系成为维系社会交往的重要模式。而这种以“礼”为中心的传统人际交往模式在当代却与以法律、社会契约为主导的现代交往秩序并存发展，由此导致的是人们对礼物的意义与价值的矛盾性解释。赵毅衡认为，“元元语言集合能够发生冲突，这个时候就会出现更高一层的解释漩涡，可以称之为评价冲突”。③ 即便同一个意识形态体系也会出现评价冲突。当代中国社会对礼物社会价值的评价正处于这种评价漩涡的悖论中：一方面，文化集团主体赞同这种以礼物为中介的人情往来，这既是中华民族注重“礼尚往来”这一传统美德的体现，更是传统文化习俗传承的

---

① 《中国礼品指南》，《新周刊》，2013 年第 1 期。

② 费孝通：《乡土中国》，上海人民出版社，2007 年，第 29 页。

③ 赵毅衡：《符号学》，南京大学出版社，2012 年，第 241 页。

重要组成部分；另一方面，文化主体又在加大力度批判礼物在当代社会中逐渐成为“行贿”“腐败”的主要工具这一事实……由此，我们陷入了对礼物价值“既赞同又批判”的评价漩涡之中。可以说，当代中国社会面临的是一场礼物评价危机，更是一种伦理危机，若不找出这种危机的根源，就无法对礼物在当代的社会价值作出评判。

（二）礼物普遍分类问题呼之欲出

礼物在当代社会形式与意义的变迁，直接导致礼物外延的无限扩展；而作为礼物交换主体的我们，若理不清礼物的实质及其边界，则很有可能会陷入礼物的形态与价值的双重迷失当中。这也就意味着，我们无法在操作层面回答如下三个问题：第一，我们不知道送什么；第二，我们不确定在什么场合可以送礼物；第三，我们无法对送礼行为本身作出一个客观、理性的评价，也即没有一个统一的意义解释标准。

与礼物在当代发生的剧烈变化形成鲜明对比的是，学术界似乎对礼物的研究还存在着一定的惰性。马塞尔·莫斯（Marcel Mauss）一百多年前建立的针对古式社会的礼物交换现象的“人类学-社会学”经典范式[①]，至今还广泛地影响着礼物研究诸领域。从学科领域来看，至今礼物研究的“主力军”还主要集中在人类学、社会学这两个学科。从礼物研究所关注的重点来看，当代中西方礼物研究基本还是遵循上述经典研究范式，将礼物研究的重心放在古式社会或落后社会的礼物交换现象。以中国礼物研究现状为例，根据“中国知网”（CNKI）的数据显示，截至 2013 年 9 月，以“礼物”为主题的论文达到 1476 篇，但接近三分之二的论文存在同质化的倾向，且其研究还是以对农村地区或少数民族地区的礼物交换习俗的民族志考察为主。这些研究涉及的存在于具体区域或具体时代背景下的礼物交换，无论是从形态上还是意义上，都比当代社会中的礼物交换单一了许多。由此带来的问题就是，这类研究无法很好地解释礼物在当代社会中出现的诸种问题，更不可能站在整体的层面，对礼物交换这一人类社会共同存在的文化现象进行更具普适力的研究。

为此，我们不得不郑重地讨论的礼物普遍分类问题。本研究准备把古今中外典型的礼物样式及其交换方式纳入我们视野中，试图从最普遍的层面对其进行一次分类，目的就在于对礼物的内涵与外延进行一次清理。只有这样

① 张旭：《礼物：当代法国思想史的一段谱系》，北京大学出版社，2013 年，第 40～55 页。

才能从实质层面抓住礼物的本质，从而才能系统、客观地评价当代某种具体的礼物交换行为及其影响。

（三）转向礼物的符号学研究

上文已经提及，目前传统礼物研究范式无法很好地解决当代礼物的诸种问题，特别是其形式与意义变迁的问题。因此，本文认为要建构一套足以囊括整个人类社会礼物以及礼物交换的系统性的理论分析框架，则不得不从符号学那里需寻求理论资源。

归根结底，“礼物交换”是一个有关意义的问题，是馈赠双方之间建立、表达以及维护关系意义的过程。而“符号学即意义学”①，其目的就是为当代人文社科各种课题寻找一个共同的方法论；那么，礼物交换现象正是符号学的用武之地。从另一方面说，“文化是社会所有相关表意活动的总集合”②，所有的文化问题，分析到底，都是意义的产生和解释的标准问题，也就是一个符号学的问题。而作为人类社会重要文化现象之一的礼物，若要深究其在不同语境中的变异形态及其方式，也只能依靠符号学：因为只有从根子上弄清礼物符号表意的基本机制，才不至于被当今礼物形态变异与标出的现实所迷惑，才能建立具有可操作性的、系统的礼物交换研究理论，才能够在讨论当今社会礼物交换的社会价值时有一个统一、客观的分析框架与评价标准。

二、普遍分类的前提：礼物的符号学定义

对礼物及其交换类型进行普遍分类的前提是“礼物”自身定义需明确且恰当。实际上，定义与分类是一个问题的两面。现有研究把礼物定义得过于狭窄，基本按照礼物在某个具体社群中的具体表现形式进行定义，由此导致礼物研究范畴的缩小，更造成当今礼物研究中许多重要礼物类型的缺场。因此，恐怕只有从礼物表意的根源以及所蕴含的共同特征入手，对其进行足够抽象的定义，才能够适应当下礼物研究的需求。

我们认为，礼物交换从本质上说就是一种符号表意实践活动，它是馈赠者为了达到向受赠者传递“关系意义”的目的而进行的礼物-符号载体的赠予过程。而礼物就是馈赠者为向受赠者传递“关系意义”而采用的符号载体，馈赠者认为此种符号载体有益于对方，并且期待通过馈赠获得某种回报。

---

① 赵毅衡：《符号学》，南京大学出版社，2012年，第3页。

② 赵毅衡：《符号学文化研究：现状与未来趋势》，《西南民族大学学报》（人文社科版），2009年12期。

上述定义首先强调礼物是一种“关系符号”（Tie-sign）的载体，其目的是用来承载馈赠双方之间的“关系意义”。这里所谓的“关系意义”是一个泛指概念，它是馈赠者通过礼物符号与受赠者建立起来的内在意义联系。具体来说，主要有两种关系意义。首先是“人际关系”，馈赠方可以通过礼物传递如下三类人际关系意义：（1）双方建立一段新的关系与纽带；（2）证明与维持双方已建立的关系；（3）加深彼此的关系程度，基于双方关系程度进行情感性表达。其次是人与自然、神明世界的拟人主体之间的关系。礼物表达此类关系意义常见于古式社会的传统礼物交换仪式：馈赠者往往期望通过向上述拟人主体献祭而获得“庇护”“恩惠”，或获取“心理慰藉”，如中国古式社会的“祭品”，又如杨炎在《大唐燕支山神宁济公祠堂碑》中所记：“其封神为宁济公，锡之肇带，备厥礼物。”[①] 再如西方古式社会的“夸富宴”（potlatch）对礼物的大量耗费，以期祈求大自然的回馈。也就是说，无论礼物符号所指的对象是谁，它都始终传达着馈赠双方之间的关系意义，以及由此引出的对关系情感的表达、关系需求的满足、工具性关系链条的建构诸问题。因此，“传递关系意义”应当作为礼物符号表意的主导功能而得到解释。

正如没有不表达意义的符号一样，也没有不表达关系意义的礼物。“符号是被认为携带意义的感知”[②]，而符号依托于一定的物质载体才能被人感知。在礼物交换的表意活动中，馈赠者对馈赠双方间关系意义之传达，必须借助礼物这个载体，它作为一种“关系符号”的载体而存在；反过来，受赠方也只能根据礼物这种符号载体对双方的关系意义进行解释。也就是说，礼物之所以区分于其他物品，是因为它具备后者所不具备的符号表意功能。因此，阎云翔所谓“无礼之物就是物品而不是礼物”[③] 正表达了这层意思：“无礼之物”就是没有被符号化，也就是没有携带关系意义的物品，因而它不是礼物。反之，一般使用物若要上升为“礼物”，必然会通过种种符号化的过程超越其“物性”，变成一种可以承载馈赠双方关系意义的符号载体。

在此需要特别指出的是，礼物符号载体在多数情况下并不单独存在，它往往与其他符号组合，并主要以“符号文本”的形式出现。赵毅衡认为：只要满足以下两个条件，就是符号文本：

---

① 《古代汉语词典》，商务印书馆，1998 年，第 958～959 页。

② 赵毅衡：《符号学》，南京大学出版社，第 1 页。

③ 阎云翔：《礼物的流动——一个中国村庄中的互惠原则与社会网络》，李放春、刘瑜译，上海人民出版社，2000 年，第 96 页。

(1) 一些符号被组织进一个符号组合中；

(2) 此符号组合可以被接受者理解为具有合一的事件和意义的向度。[①]

日常馈赠中的礼物需要包装这种伴随文本的衬托，而且礼物包装还包括物品自身的包装，以及馈赠者为送礼而特意进行的包装等；仪式性场合的礼物，更需要与仪式中的行为符号（仪式姿势语）、语言符号（仪式语言）等结合，才能行使礼物在此场合中的功能。再次，从接受者的角度说，受赠者在接收到馈赠者的礼物时，往往要先把受赠者的身份、与对方的关系程度等型文本组合到一个礼物符号文本中，才能对礼物的意义进行综合判断。因此，礼物自身是一种符号载体，但是礼物表意的过程总是以礼物符号文本的形式出现。

通过上文对礼物的符号学定义的讨论，我们已经可以看出礼物符号学与传统礼物研究的差异与优势。以人类学－社会学为代表的传统礼物研究重在对某种具体礼物交换类型的研究及深描，它为我们呈现的是一个个具体的礼物交换场景及其文化规约机制。但这些研究结论往往凸显不同礼物类型的具体性与特殊性，因此不便于对礼物进行纵向与横向的比较。这也就使我们很难在不同的社会语境中就同一类礼物进行定位与归纳，也很难从不同的礼物类型中提炼出共同的表意特征及演变规律。这也就是为什么至今为止还没有相关研究试图对礼物进行普遍分类的原因。而礼物符号学则试图在这些庞杂繁多的礼物类型中提炼出它们共同的表意机制与特征，因此它可以在总体规则层面理清礼物的本质及诸种变迁方式。这也就从根本上走出了礼物研究的传统范式，使得礼物的普遍分类成为可能，也使得我们可以在一个较为完整的系统中对某种具体礼物的价值及功能有个较为准确的定位，并且可以在同一个解释标准中对不同礼物类型进行比较。

下文，我们将试图在符号学视域中对人类社会所有的礼物表意类型进行分类；试图理清礼物的边界与外延，并说明不同礼物交换模式的不同符号表意特征。

三、现有礼物研究中的两种主要分类方式及其问题

现有研究对礼物的分类主要按照两种路径进行，第一种是按照馈赠者的动机分类。哈路弥·贝夫（Harumi Befu）是第一位按照“动机”对礼物进行

---

① 赵毅衡：《符号学》，南京大学出版社，第43页。

分类的学者。在对日本社会中的礼物交换现象进行田野调查后，他试图把礼物分为如下两类："表达性礼物"和"工具性礼物"。"表达性功能即赠者和受者之间既有的地位关系决定了礼物交换的情境，如要送礼物的种类与价值，而馈赠支持了该地位的关系；工具性功能则为交换状况（礼物的特点与价值）决定了地位关系，即一个人通过送礼操纵了地位关系。"①

第二种是将送礼者的动机与赠受双方的社会关系进行交互，并据此对礼物进行分类。阎云翔根据贝夫二分法，再结合两种基本社会关系——纵向的和横向的，将礼物交换分为如下四类：横向情境中的表达性馈赠、横向情境中的工具性送礼、纵向情境中的表达性馈赠、纵向情境中的工具性送礼。②类似的还有乐晶对转型期中国城市居民礼物交换模式的分类。他将城市居民间的礼物分为四种类型：情感表达型礼物、情感工具型礼物、情感投资型礼物和交易型礼物。③ 而黄光国则从中国社会关系运作的手段将关系分作三种：工具型关系、混合型关系、情感型关系。④

大概是受传统礼物研究范式的影响过于深刻，我们只能在上述这些分类中看到部分社群中的礼物交换模式及其特征。而礼物交换是贯穿整个人类文化的一种重要表意活动与机制；更为重要的是，礼物交换并不仅局限于人与人之间，还有社群与社群之间、国与国之间的礼物交换，比如国礼、朝贡等，显然上述分类将礼物的范畴缩小了。其次，动机是馈赠者在建立一段馈赠关系前，对馈赠双方的相互关系、地位等级、互惠期待等方面所进行的一系列心理评估；从符号学层面上来说，所谓动机就是符号发送者的"意图意义"，但是从普遍层面考察，"意图意义"无法从馈赠主体那里理清，个体的主观意图过于多变，并且常常伴随着多层含义。因此，仅通过田野调查的方法对馈赠主体"意图意义"进行考察，只能代表某种意义社群的观点，并不能代表整体。

其次，许多学者考虑到了礼物馈赠主体间的社会关系的维度。这点本研究赞成，因为礼物交换离不开社会语境以及社群中的诸种关系成分，这也在

---

① Harumi Befu, "Gift-giving and Social Reciprcocity in Japan", *France-Asiea*, 1966, (21): 166－177.

② 阎云翔：《礼物的流动——一个中国村庄中的互惠原则与社会网络》，李放春、刘瑜译，上海人民出版社，2000 年，第 219～221 页。

③ 乐晶：《转型期中国城市居民礼物交换模式及其特征初探》，《江西师范大学学报》，2006 年第 1 期。

④ 黄光国、胡先缙：《人情与面子：中国人的权力游戏》，中国人民大学出版社，2010 年，第 35～45 页。

很大程度上决定了馈赠主体对礼物及其馈赠方式的选择。但是，传统研究对关系的划分是以具体社会语境中的人际关系距离为依据的，这又再次回到上文所提及的问题：关系并不仅仅是微观人际关系，还有更为宏观的社群关系、国际关系，并且，关系模式与距离因为社群的不同而不同。由此，无法据此对礼物作出普遍性的分类。

四、符号文本“意向性”与关系的时间维度：一种礼物普遍分类的尝试

基于馈赠主体的分类研究其方法注定是社会学－人类学田野调查式的，这实际上申明了此方法站在全域的视角对礼物进行分类的不可行。由此，我们认为跳出对馈赠主体的单方关注，将视角转向礼物符号文本与文本中的主体间关系，可能是解决解决礼物普遍分类的出口。赵毅衡在《广义叙述分类的一个尝试》一文中提出了一套按照“文本意向性”来对所有叙述体裁进行分类的方案。[①] 他指出：“文本是体现了主体间关系的符号组合，在叙述主体与接受主体之间，有一定的意向关系，这种意向体现为文本的意义和时间的方向性：所有的叙述文本，都靠意向性才能执行最基本的意义表达和接收功能”……因此，“似乎是讲的同样故事，在主导意向性不同的叙述体裁文本中，就会有完全不同的意义”。[②]

因当说，“意向性”是任何符号表意文本的普遍问题。我们认为礼物符号文本同样包含着不同“意向性”文本品质，而这种文本品质导致同一种礼物形态在不同礼物符号文本中表达完全不同的意义，发挥完全不同的交际作用与功能。按文本意向性对礼物进行分类也就解决了礼物形态众多，无法说清的难题。本研究拟讨论的礼物符号文本的意向性问题受奥斯汀（J. L. Austin）的“言语行为”（Speech Acts）三类型说的启发，不同的是奥斯汀所讨论的是语句的品质，而本研究则重在讨论礼物表意过程中，以“物－符号”为主体的符号文本中所呈现出的独特表意品质与交际功能。奥斯汀提出的言语行为三类型是：

（1）以言言事（locutionary acts），中文又译“说话行为”“语谓行

---

① 赵毅衡：《广义叙述分类的一个尝试》，第四届叙事学国际会议暨第六届全国叙事学研讨会大会主题发言稿，广州，2013 年 11 月，< http://www. semiotics. net. cn/upload/pdf/20131112143614065. pdf >。

② 请参见赵毅衡：2013 年叙述学课程第二讲课件《意向性与媒介分类》。

为"，或"言内行为"，即说出一句有意义的话，表达一种意义；

(2) 以言行事 (illocutionary acts)，中文又译"施事行为""语用行为"，或"言外行为"，它完成交际的任务，是说事、做事、起效的节点；

(3) 以言成事 (perlocutionary acts)，中文又译"取效行为""语效行为"，或"言后行为"，是通过说某事而造成或获得某种结果，例如说服、劝说、吓唬等。[①]

奥斯汀想通过"言语行为"理论表达是，言语主体通过话语交流可以实现具体交际功能并且重在强调"以言行事语力"(illocutionary force)。也就是说，语言不仅可以传达"含义"，重要的是语言具有独立的"语力"(force)，即用语言促使事件发生的能力，也即，语力能够在"语言之外"的听者身上产生意动效果，产生采取某种相应的心理冲动，甚至真的去做言语劝说或要求他去做的事。[②]

致力于研究基于社会语境中的交流及其符号表意行为的社会符号学理论也非常重视"言语行为"理论。社会符号学家韩礼德 (M. A. K. Halliday) 强调言语行为的"对话性"(dialogic)："言语的'行为'可能被称为'互动行为'(interact) 更为适合：它是一种交换行为 (exchange) ——言语中给予信息暗示着要求接受信息；同理要求 (demand) 某事暗示着必须回应的义务。"[③] 由此他将"言语互动行为"扩展为四类：(1) 提供信息 (offering information)，句子以陈述语气为主；(2) 要求信息 (demanding information)，句子以疑问语气为主；(3) 提供物资与服务 (offering goods and service)；(4) 要求物资与服务 (demanding goods and service)，句子以祈使语气为主。韩礼德的贡献在于将言语交际看成一种互动行为，交际文本自身携带着的语法标记，促使着交际双方对此采取相应的互动行为。

礼物交换是一个典型的交际符号文本；礼物符号文本自身携带着馈赠者期待与对方交际的信息。交际文本这一体裁就规定了礼物符号文本必须携带交际与互动的"文本意向性"。我们在前文对"礼物交换"的定义中，就说明了馈赠者期望通过礼物符号文本向受赠表意，并且由此期待从对方那里获取"某些回报"。而"期待某些回报"这一交际前提决定了礼物符号文本必须具

---

① 邱惠丽，《奥斯汀言语行为论的当代哲学意义》，《自然辩证法研究》，2006 年 7 月号，第 37～42 页。转引自赵毅衡：2013 年叙述学课程第二讲课件《意向性与媒介分类》。

② 赵毅衡：2013 年叙述学课程第二讲课件《意向性与媒介分类》。

③ Halliday, M. A. K. *Language as Social Semiotics: The Social Interpretation of Language and Medaning*. Maryland: Maryland University Press, 1978, p. 68.

备言语行为理论所提及这种“语力”或韩礼德所谓的“互动行为”能力；它能够促进礼物交际事件的完成，并且发挥着相应的功能。为此，我们认为礼物符号文本与言语行为一样具备如下三种“意向性”文本品质：

(1) 以物[①]言事：即通过礼物向对方表达意义，表达情绪（对应于贝夫礼物二分法的“表达功能”）；

(2) 以物行事：在礼物交换中主要是通过礼物完成仪式性交际任务，礼物成为某种仪式、事件的重要组成部分；

(3) 以物成事：通过礼物交交换，与对方达成某种“功利性结果”（对应于贝夫的“工具性礼物”）。

从上述有关礼物的文本意向性分类中，我们可以看到（1）类和（3）类与贝夫的馈赠者动机分类相类似，但这两类是礼物符号文本在理论上因当具备的三种意向性因素，也即从文本试推馈赠者“动机”；而贝夫则主要从馈赠者自身出发来分类。而（2）类是以往分类中被忽略的维度，仪式性礼物交际从莫斯开始一直都是礼物研究的重点，但却往往在礼物分类研究中被忽略，因为许多研究者认为“语境”并不足以构成礼物交换的主要模式，个体间的礼物交换可以在仪式性与非仪式性语境中进行。但是，礼物交换并不仅仅在个体间进行，它们很有可能是一个文化群体的集体行为并且发挥着一种文化整合的作用，例如中国传统社会中的国家祭典，西方后进社会的“夸富宴”，献祭仪式中的礼物馈赠行为等。这些行为中，“完成仪式”才是礼物表意的核心，也就是我们所谓的“以物行事”，如同奥斯汀所谓的言语交际中的“以言行事”功能一样，礼物交换主要是为了完成仪式任务。

其次，礼物交际毕竟是在具体的社会语境中进行的，而礼物符号载体又以表达关系意义为主导功能；因此，礼物的普遍分类则不得不考虑馈赠主体之间的关系问题。但是现有研究基于馈赠主体之间关系的测量往往以空间为主导因素，也即以馈赠者为圆心，根据其与受赠者主体之间的距离远近而进行分类。应当说，以为空间来划分关系程度在某种具体社会语境中讨论比较适合，但本研究的分类倾向于礼物交换的宏观结构类型，将馈赠者与受赠者之间的关系按空间来划分就会出现分类的困难。以同心圆或上下等级关系的方式分类并不能避免分类交叉的现象：比如距离较远，但关系却异常紧密，反之亦然。因此，这种划分在很大程度上与馈赠者自身的交际能力、关系复

---

① 在这里“物”是一个广义的概念，应当作“礼物”理解；再次重申，礼物可能是实物，也可能是一种按照礼物模式表意的纯符号。

杂度以及所处的社群文化紧密相关，因而并不具备普适性。其次，此种分类方式并不能处理国与国之间、个人与社群之间、人与拟人主体之间的关系，因为我们无法判断此类馈赠行为中主体间关系距离的远近。

但是，对于馈赠者主体而言，二者的关系必然是具备时间向度的。我们认为任何关系都具有过去、现在与未来三种时间向度。这里的三种时间向度并不是在描述关系的客观状况，而是馈赠主体对赠受双方的关系的一种判断与期待，而这种期待决定了赠受双方对礼物馈赠与接受的选择。社会学家翟学伟在《中国人的关系向度及其在互联网中的可能性转变》一文中也提到当今关系学研究中“重空间、轻时间”的特征，他认为“人们对关系/交往时间预期的不同会导致人们行为模式上的巨大差异”。[①] 他的观点，应当说与本文的研究不谋而合。因此，我们基于时间的维度对于赠受双方的关系作出如下分类：

（1）过去：赠受双方的关系以时间的积累为衡量标准。

（2）现在：赠受双方在礼物交换之前并无直接关系（可能有间接关系），馈赠者着眼现在看待彼此的关系，并期待建立或临时开始一段关系。

（3）未来：馈赠者立足未来看待赠受双方的关系，期待建立一种长期的互惠关系。

我们将礼物符号文本的意向性与赠受双方关系进行交互，可以得出 3 种礼物交换主型；并且根据这 3 种交换主型又可以得出 8 种礼物类型。请见下表：

表 1　礼物交换普遍分类表

文本意向性/关系	过去	现在	未来
以物言事（表达）	关系表达型	关系建构型	关系投资型
以物行事（仪式）	社群整合仪式型	人生过渡仪式型	祈祷仪式型
以物成事（工具）	关系强化型	关系工具型	无

① 翟学伟：《中国人的关系向度及其在互联网中的可能性转变》，《中国人的关系原理：时空秩序、生活欲念及其流变》，北京大学出版社，2011 年，第 289～310 页。

五、3种礼物交换主型以及8种礼物类型

（一）“以物言事”类的礼物交换主型

这类礼物交换主型的重要特征在于馈赠者将礼物符号文本的情感表达功能作为该类礼物表意的主导功能，将向受赠者表达“回报”的愿望变成一种交际策略而暗藏在情绪表达功能的序列之中。为行文方便，我们可将此类交换主型简称为“表达型礼物交换”。需要注意的是，这里所谓“表达型”是基于礼物符号文本的意向特性而得出的，而非贝夫基于馈赠者动机而进行的分类；以下两类同理。该主型又可以根据赠受双方的关系分为关系表达型、关系建构型、关系投资型三个类型。三种类型对“回报”的期待程度呈现递增趋势，礼物符号载体的实用价值与符号价值的比率也呈递增趋势。

（1）关系表达型。该类礼物着重维护双方长期积累的相互关系，礼物符号文本重在表达情感意义。代表礼物类型主要有：亲属、朋友等之间日常生活中的礼物馈赠，中国古代名流间的“书画雅赠”，国与国之间互赠的国礼等。该类礼物符号文本的特点是其符号表意性大于符号实用性。

（2）关系建构型。它是馈赠者为了与受赠者开启一段新的相互关系而采用的主要礼物馈赠类型。如初次见面双方的“见面礼”，或馈赠者为建构新的业缘关系（新同事）、社群关系（新邻居）、组织关系（新社团）而进行的横向性送礼。这类礼物在实用价值与符号价值的比例搭配上比较微妙：如果该类礼物符号文本过于偏向实用价值，则会越出该类型礼物交换的边界，向关系-工具型发展，这可能对受赠者来说是一种冒犯。这就意味着，此类礼物交换亚型需要更多的符号表意策略。

（3）关系投资型。该类礼物的馈赠者期待与受赠者建立一种基于未来的长久的持续性互惠模式，因此馈赠者在某次或多次具体的馈赠场合中并不求回报，并着重表达对受赠者的感情。但馈赠者对受赠者长期的“回报”期待程度是最高的，因为他把这种馈赠关系当作类似于金融学所谓的“长期投资关系”。它主要体现在具有社会等级的纵向社会关系中，例如当代社会中下级向上级礼节性地送礼，再如中国古代皇权社会附属国向宗主国朝贡，以及臣子向皇帝进贡，都是祈求获得上一级的庇护，以期建立一种长久的互惠关系。

（二）“以物行事”的礼物交换主型

该类礼物交换主型把礼物当作仪式的一部分，也即礼物也是仪式成为仪

式的原因。我们可以将此类型简称为“仪式型”礼物交换。总体来说，此类礼物交换主型中的礼物成为仪式的纽带，它连接了个人、社群与文化，因此，此类型中的礼物符号文本呈现出来的是强烈的“以物行事”的意动性，该类符号文本的目的在于完成各种仪式性交际任务。根据赠受双方的关系，这类主型下的礼物又可以分为三种类型：社群整合仪式型、人生过渡仪式型、祈祷仪式型。三类礼物符号文本的选择与解释在很大成程度上受到不同解释社群的文化元语言的压力，因此三种亚型中的礼物也承担着不同的功能，故而礼物符号形态本身也呈现出显著差异。

（1）社群整合仪式型。馈赠主体主要是赠受双方与其共同归属的文化社群，三者之间的关系是一种典型的基于过去的文化传承关系。该类礼物的特点在于赠受双方通过文化社群的特有仪式，来满足自己的文化社群归属需求，因此，礼物符号文本是仪式的一部分。此类礼物交换类型的代表有：中国传统习俗“祭祖”仪式中的礼物馈赠，各文化社群传统节庆中（如春节、中秋节、圣诞节等）的礼物交换，西方古式社会“夸富宴”中的礼物交换。

（2）人生过渡仪式型。“过渡仪式”（rites of passage）在任何文化群体中都普遍存在，它是基于人在自然生长过程中所必须经历的一些节点性事件而举行的仪式，例如成人礼、婚礼、葬礼等，人们在这些过渡性仪式中被给予新的社会身份并且被社会成员所接受。过渡仪式必然伴随着礼物交换，并且礼物成为过渡仪式的一个部分，承担着某种具体的文化功能。受赠者新的社会身份与社会关系需要由馈赠者在过渡仪式中通过礼物馈赠的方式来重新确认，因此，赠受双方在此类礼物馈赠中的关系是基于“现在”维度的。

（3）祈祷仪式型。该类礼物的馈赠主体主要是人与想象世界的拟人主体。人们往往在每年或每个季节通过馈赠礼物向其想象的“自然造物主”祈求能与在其在来年或下个季节保持“友好”关系，并且祈求其能够得到其“保佑”。应当说，这种想象式的馈赠关系从本质上就是面向将来的，因为馈赠者无法基于现在或过去来判断与受赠者的关系，他只能通过礼物的形式向对方祈求在礼物交换仪式结束之后的一段时间内，保持良好的“互惠关系”。这种礼物交换类型常见于中西方古代社会、原始社会中的献祭仪式，用贝尔金（Helmuth Berking）教授的话来说，应当将这种献祭活动看作礼物交换的最原始形态之一。①

---

① Helmtuh Berking, *Sociology of Giving*. London: Sage, 1999, pp. 75—80.

（三）"以物成事"的礼物交换模式

该类礼物交换主型显著区别于上述两种主型，其礼物符号文的呈现出强烈的"以物成事"的意动性因素，也就是说，该类礼物交换的目的是在短时间内从受赠者那里获得所需的功利性回报。我们可以将此类型简称为"工具型"礼物交换。另外，此类礼物符号文本与"以物言事"主型相比，更重视礼物符号的实际或实用价值。馈赠主体并不期待双方会维持长期的互惠关系，因此，在这一主型中，基于未来关系的礼物馈赠类型缺失。由此，在此交换主型下只有两种亚型：关系强化型与关系工具型；二者的差异主要在于赠受双方是否有关系积累，这种差异显著地表现在礼物实用价值上面。

（1）关系强化型。此类礼物与关系工具型一样，均强调馈赠者进行礼物馈赠的功利性目的，以期通过礼物交换在短期内得到某功利性结果。不过，与后者不同的是，关系强化型礼物交换中的馈赠主体关系是基于过去的，也就是说馈赠主体之间具有一定的关系基础；而关系工具型礼物交换中的赠受双方在馈赠行为发生之前几乎没有任何关系。因此，该亚型的礼物符号文本的作用在于强化馈赠双方原有的关系基础，并且促成礼物交换后的某种实质性后果，但在礼物的实用价值与符号价值在比率上没有"关系工具型"那么高。

（8）关系工具型。在此亚型中，馈赠者试图通过礼物建立一段临时工具性馈赠关系。馈赠前，礼物交换主体并没有任何关系积累的过程，更不在乎未来是否能够保持相互关系，他们仅仅立足于当下，双方均注重在这种短期的礼物交换过程中各自能够获得的"利己性"实际成果。应当说，此亚型中的馈赠客体已经落到了"礼物"的门槛上，再往前一步就是"行贿"，而"行贿"实际上已经越出了礼物交换的边界，它不再是一种礼物馈赠行为，因为它的主导功能已经不是表达"关系意义"，而仅仅是一种社会交易。因此，"关系工具型"礼物应当作为礼物分类的边界。

五、结论

本文是礼物符号学的基础研究，试图理清礼物的定义及其边界，从而为下一步的深入研究打下基础。礼物交换从实质上来说是一种表意实践活动，而礼物则是馈赠者表达双方关系意义的符号载体。这个定义使得人类学－社会学讨论了多年的礼物问题“祛魅化”：使礼物成为礼物的不是“礼物之灵”[①]；而是人们表达关系意义的需求，馈赠者希望借助这种关系符号获得对方的某种“回报”。

在此基础上，笔者基于礼物符号文本的意向性与馈赠双方关系的时间性，尝试着对礼物进行一次全面、系统的分类。本文想通过分类说明：礼物与礼物之间的类别差异，是礼物符号文本自身携带的文本意向性导致的符号表意重心的位移；而携带着不同文本意向性的礼物符号文本又在不同语境的传递过程中与馈赠双方发生交互关系，由此形成不同的礼物符号表意特性，并且完成不同的表意功能。这种礼物交换普遍的分类讨论给我们启示在于，无论在古代还是在当代，无论是在后进社会还是在发达社会，礼物的本质都是馈赠者用来表达关系意义的符号载体，因此，礼物在当代社会中形式与意义的变迁，实质就是当代礼物符号文本的意向性或者表意的主导因素发生了转变，而这种转变又与当今社会馈赠主体间的关系存在着显著相关性。换句话说，这种变迁并非是一种质变，而是整个礼物交换全域中符号表意重心的位移。所以，只要我们通过分类，看清礼物的形式与意义在当代发生改变的实质，那么，与之相关的社会与文化问题的分析方向也就变得清晰、明确了。

作者简介：

赵星植，四川大学文学与新闻学院博士研究生，四川大学符号学—传媒学研究所驻所研究员，研究方向为礼物符号学、皮尔斯符号学理论。

Author:

Zhao Xingzhi, Ph. D. candidate in Semiotics and Communication Studies, member of ISMS Research Team. His research fields mainly cover semiotics of gift-giving and C. S. Peirce's theories of semiotics.

E-mail: snnjkk@163. com

---

① [法] 马塞尔·莫斯：《礼物：古式社会中的交换的形式与理由》，汲喆译，上海人民出版社，2005 年，第 18～20 页。

"Open Ended" Interactions?

Exploring Similarities in Minimalist Music, Plastic Art and New Media*

Tristian Evans

Abstract: This article examines shared characteristics in minimalist music, the plastic arts and new media. With references to existential semiotics and other analytical techniques, a selection of case studies will be studied, in particular Philip Glass's *Glassworks* (1981) and *Symphony No*. 4 (1996); Richard Serra's "Open Ended" installation (2007—2008), and Chuck Close's artistic techniques as evinced in his portraits of Glass. The study will demonstrate how certain approaches, significations and perceptions are common across various media. The article will examine how minimalist music has been employed in new contexts, namely in the form of television commercials and, more recently, as applications for smartphones and tablet computers, for instance Glass and Beck's REWORK project (2012).

Key words: Minimalist music, art, sculpture, new media, Philip Glass, Richard Serra, Chuck Close

---

* This essay is developed out of papers delivered at the Noises of Art Conference co-organised by Aberystwyth University, the Courtauld Institute of Art, London and Aberystwyth Arts Centre in September 2013, and the Fourth International Conference on Music and Minimalism co-organised by California. State University, Long Beach and UCLA during October 2013.

"开放"的互动？

对极简主义音乐、造型艺术和新媒体的探讨

崔斯坦·埃文斯

摘要：本文讨论了极简主义音乐、造型艺术和新媒体的共同特征，用存在符号学等分析工具，选取艺术个案进行讨论，如菲利普·葛拉斯的音乐作品《玻璃》(1981) 和《四号交响乐》(1996)、理查·塞拉的"开放"装置艺术和查克·克洛斯在葛拉斯肖像中展示出的艺术手法。研究旨在论证在不同的媒介中，艺术家所使用的方法、意味和引起的感知是共同的。本文同时检视了在新的语境之中，也就是在电视商业节目中，以及更为新近的，如智能手机和平板电脑的应用软件中（如葛拉斯和贝克的 REWORK 项目），极简主义音乐是如何被使用的。

关键词：极简主义音乐，艺术，雕塑，新媒体，菲利普·葛拉斯，理查·塞拉，查克·克洛斯

Introduction

The aim of this article is to examine intersections and interactions within the domains of minimalist music, the plastic arts and new media. The focus of the investigation will initially be placed on the relationships between the music of Philip Glass and the artistic outputs of Richard Serra and Chuck Close, before examining recent examples of new media in relation to minimalist and ambient music. The meanings formed in and between specific musical and visual texts will be unpacked with the aid of theories from the area of existential semiotics and music analysis. Firstly, however, it seems logical to begin by mapping out some significant points relating to the origins of minimalism in various contexts before delving into the semiological investigation that will subsequently ensue.

Minimalist music emerged in the mid-1960s when artists, dancers, filmmakers, composers and musicians, including Philip Glass, Steve Reich, Richard Serra, Chuck Close, Michael Snow, Yvonne Rainer and Meredith

Monk, were developing their styles and approaches, and they supported each other by interdisciplinary collaboration mainly in downtown New York. As Jonathan Bernard points out in his article on the aesthetics of minimalist music and the plastic arts, minimalism developed as an alternative to the earlier trends, including the abstract expressionism of Rauschenberg and Pollock, Higgins's intermedia, Brecht's Fluxus and Cage's musical happenings of the 1950s (Bernard, 1993, pp. 86 – 96). General commonalities between minimalist art and music included the repetition of material, the reduction the material, use of audible/visual process, and "an emphasis upon the surface of the work" (Bernard, 1993, p. 95).① Both in musical and visual terms, the term "minimalism" therefore maintains certain similarities. What is further apparent is the fact that the venues used for exhibition and/or performances were akin: Bernard notes that early performances of minimalist music often took place in art galleries (ibid., pp. 86—7), which consequently provided a natural environment for the cross-fertilisation of styles and ideas.

Glass and Serra

During the late 1960s, Glass and Serra worked together on various artistic projects—one of them was a silent film entitled *Hands Scraping* (1968), which featured the hands of both the sculptor and composer gathering steel filings—a gradual and laborious process of dissipating the raw material is depicted in the four-minute silent film.② Also in 1968, Serra dedicated a sculptural piece for Glass entitled "Slow Roll", which exhibited the pliable nature of the materials employed in the artwork. Despite the close collaboration between sculptor and composer, Keith Potter refers to Glass's interview of 1972 in which he stated that references to minimal art were seldom made directly in his musical works (Potter, 2000, p 266). What is seemingly apparent, however, is a common interest by Serra and himself in

---

① Edward Strickland defines minimalism in its simplest form as "a style distinguished by severity of means, clarity of form, and simplicity of structure and texture" (Strickland, 2000, p. 4).

② Dean Suzuki draws attention to the fact that *Hands Scraping* is "a work singularly and obsessively concerned with materials (steel shavings) and procedures ('hands scraping')" (Suzuki, 2013, p. 122).

the concept of "structure and content becoming identical", as found in Serra's sculptures and Glass' own approach to musical form. ①

We can also observe how the magnitude of Serra's sculptures characterising so-called "scale as content" (Battcock, 1995, p. 20) bears similarity to the length of minimalist musical works, which are generally performed over an extended period of time. A performance of Glass' seminal opera *Einstein on the Beach* (1976), for instance, can be of five hours' duration, and the audience are given the freedom to enter and depart from a performance at will, which could result in only a partial hearing of the work. With reference to Serra's large-scale *Circuit* sculpture (1972), Bernard notes that all aspects of such works cannot be fully observed due to their size, therefore the perceiver would have to make decisions on which part of the artwork they studied; moreover, Bernard notes that the scale of the works could induce a sense of "menace" for the perceiver, who could potentially be daunted by the imposing characteristic of such an installation (Bernard, 1993, p. 118). Citing references to "working class heroism" in Serra's works, Casey Nelson Blake writes that "the austere neo-Minimalism of Serra's steel sculptures may in fact heighten viewers' sense that they are confronting an aggressive work that orders their experience according to a hierarchy of social distinction" (Blake, 1993, p. 259). ② In her article entitled "Minimalism and the Rhetoric of Power", Anna C. Chave argues that Serra's work from the late 1970s and early 1980s presents "bully and victim" relationships between the artwork and the perceiver, and that such works as *Tilted Arc* (1981) (which caused a considerable amount of controversy that led to its ultimate demolition) can provoke feelings of "oppression" (Chave 1990, p. 135). While Serra's works at that time maintained potent psychological and socio-

---

① See Maria Anna Tappeiner's documentary programme on the artist, which also features interview material with Glass, for further comments on their working practices. *Richard Serra—Sehen ist Denken* [*Richard Serra—Thinking on your Feet*]. DVD. Dir., Maria Anna Tappeiner, 2005—2007. WDR Mediagroup.

② From Serra's early works onwards, a clear working class aesthetic emerges: Benjamin Buchloh highlights the importance of industry and production in his work. *Hands Scraping* (which features the hands of Serra and Glass) for example represents "the hands of the labouring subject, unknown and invisible, occluded from the perception of the designing subject" (Buchloh, 2007, p. 57).

political meanings, more recent reactions to his work are ostensibly more placid, with certain installations being used to hold weddings and yoga sessions—events that are clearly of a happier and relaxing nature (Crow, 2013, unpag.).

Industry and Materials

With reference to his early works, Steve Reich once noted that both Serra's sculptures and his own music were "more about the materials and process than [...] about psychology" (Buchloh 2000, p. 5). Indeed, aspects of temporality and listeners' perception were equally at the heart of Glass and Reich's early manifestos, and also the minimalist artists—Serra recalled a common "belief in process and extended time and a relation to material" (Tusa, 2002, unpag.). In a documentary on Serra, Glass also recalled how "the content of [Serra's works] was a reflection of the process by which the piece was made, and [he] was doing a very similar thing in music [...] the structure of the piece was the unfolding of that process" (Tappeiner, 2005—2007). In terms of materials, unlike the so-called "high minimalists" who used plastics and stainless steels in their artworks, Serra chose to work with less refined resources such as rubber and lead—such material could "change or augment itself by its manipulation" and "did not have the pretention of the commodity" (ibid.). More recently, Serra employs sheets of oxidised steel, otherwise known as Cor-ten steel, which develops rust of a terracotta hue when subjected to the natural environment.

Glass' workmanlike adaptation of established musical forms and tonalities also associates aesthetically with Serra's choice of materials—crude steel with rust and patina, for instance, that forms a direct link the industrial past—as opposed to the sterility of stainless steel materials. Glass' employment of established harmonic progressions and recognised musical forms (such as the symphony, string quartet or theétude for piano) might again be regarded as references to the musical past, or what Bernard calls the "resurgence of tonality" (Bernard, 2003). In her analysis of "Opening" from *Glassworks* (1982), Susan McClary observes how the work presents an "old-fashioned version of subjective interiority", feelings of "melancholy" and "impossible hope" that are reminiscent of Schubertian oeuvres (McClary 2001, p. 142), thereby demonstrating Glass' ability to reuse forms and tonalities within a postmodern context.

Glass and Bowie— "Heroes" and the Eurostar Commercial

While McClary's comments above reveal Glass' recycling of past traditions, we can also cite examples of Glass' postmodern music being used in new situations. Industry and tradition are both manifest topics in a re-contextualised use of the Symphony No. 4 ("Heroes", 1996), as heard in Eurostar's television commercial (2007) to publicise the launch of the modernised London St. Pancras railway station and the high-speed connection it offers between the UK and Europe. ① Glass' music conveys several different meanings here. Firstly, the music's repetitive element assimilates the motion of a train. Secondly, the grandeur of its symphonic form is compatible with the 19th century industrial productivity, neo-Gothic architectural splendour and industrial triumph. In terms of tonality, Glass' use of major chords reflects the brightness of the visual footage and the overall message of the commercial (promoting a sense of welcome and reflecting the magnificence of the rejuvenated Victorian railway station), which is in clear contrast to his often-employed minor tonalities that create a sense of greyness and bleakness, as in the case of "Façades" from *Glassworks*, as discussed later in this essay.

Significant also is the integration of the "old" and the "new" depicted in the visual narrative (the station's original architecture versus the technological achievement of the modern and rapid train), which is again somehow symbolic when we consider the fact that the music we hear is not only based on Glass' pre-existing symphony, but that the symphony itself is a reworked version of a song entitled "Heroes" written by art rock musicians David Bowie and Brian Eno for their eponymous album (1977). ② Even the

---

① Music by yet another minimalist composer, Michael Nyman, had also been written to commemorate the launch of another high-speed train service; the TGV in France-Nyman's *MGV* (*Musique à Grande Vitesse*) was first performed in 1993.

② See also Jeremy Grimshaw's article for a further discussion on Glass' collaborations with Bowie and Eno (Grimshaw, 2002).

title "Heroes" of Bowie and Eno's song is in itself a quotation, being a reference to the title of a track by the German rock band "Neu!", released two years earlier.① Within the context of popular music, Bowie and Eno's song suggests Romantic notions and ideals of love, heroism and yearnings for utopia. Moreover, the song alludes to the Berlin Wall, and is thus a reference to a socio-political revolution. If Bowie and Eno's song is discussed with regard to Glass' work, we can find further associations: Glass' music is used in a context that reflects other Romantic aesthetics and the 19th century developments, namely the construction of an grand railway station during the Victorian era, neo-Gothic architecture, the development of the symphony, and so on.

In short, by examining Glass' music both in relation to its precursors (Bowie and Eno's song), its original context (Symphony No. 4) and its recontextualised form (the Eurostar commercial), an intricate web of interconnections can thereby be delineated. Even Serra's "working class heroism" resonates in this context. Glass, Bowie and Serra all emerged from relatively humble backgrounds: in his formative years, Glass worked as a taxi driver, as a plumber and together with Richard Serra, as a furniture mover; moreover, Serra had experience of working in steel mills.

Experience and Existentialism

The accessibility of Glass's tonality and the use of a recognised musical form presents yet another parallelism with the accessibility of Serra's sculptures, most notably the recent walkthrough sculptures.② By exploring perceptions of temporality, relatively recent works including "The Matter of Time" (2005) and "Open Ended" (2007—2008) involves a potent psychological effect upon the perceiver, who journeys right through the middle of the work—a process that involves an "intensification of anticipation", as Serra once noted.

① "Neu!" was formed by former members of post-minimal electronic music band Kraftwerk, Klaus Dinger and Michael Rother.

② In an interview with Klaus Ottmann, Serra refers to the accessibility of the "Maillart" work in Switzerland, which "is accessible to anyone, whether you know anything about sculpture or not" (Ottmann, 1989, p. 1).

Some years ago, I visited the Gagosian Gallery in London to view Serra's "Open Ended" exhibition; and was immediately struck by the scale, shape and the direction of the pathway, which suggests gravitational ebbs and flows when walking through the sculpture.

My own personal observation is corroborated by reviews of the work around this time: in his article for the British newspaper *The Independent* in 2008, Michael Glover provides a detailed account of his experiences within the sculptures, noting the "velvety, terracotta-ish" texture and colour of the steel material, the altered nature of time and the "claustrophobic" effect of certain parts of the journey, before finally emerging "into the bright, relaxed space of the gallery" (Glover, 2008, unpag.). One can argue that an existential semiotic process takes place here, wherein we are literally "seeing the signs from the inside" (Tarasti, 2000, p. 6). Following Eero Tarasti's path of existential semiotics, we can observe a transcendence from everyday life to a domain that involves unknown experiences through these maze-like installations (disorientation, loneliness, "anxiety", etc.) before re-emerging from within the installation with new knowledge, or as *The Independent* expresses, as "a changed man" (Glover, 2008, unpag.).① Building on Jacob von Uexhüll's model, Tarasti's discussion on the interactivity between the *Umwelt* (the subjectivity of "the self") and the objectivity of the "actual physical surroundings" of the *Umgebung* seems relevant here (Tarasti, 2000, p. 38). A walk through Serra's installation arguably involves direct involvement in endosemiosis, which entails an understanding of "the processes of sign transmission inside the organism" (von Uexhüll, Geigges and Herrmann, 1993, p. 5).

Such ruminations on the relevance of existentialism in Serra's work should be supported with the note that Serra had indeed studied existentialism as part of his undergraduate studies, and was influenced in particular by

---

① See Eero Tarasti's chapter "On the Paths of Existential Semiotics" in Tarasti, 2000, pp. 3—16.

Alberto Giacometti and Albert Camus[①], although Serra once proclaimed that he did not consider himself "part of the existential tradition" (Ottmann, 1989, p. 4). Moreover, Buchloh discusses the influence of phenomenology on the sculptor—a branch of philosophy that clearly relates to the existential tradition due to its predilection with the subjectivity of experiences (Buchloh, 2007, p. 57), particularly in relation to space and time.[②] Rocío von Jungenfeld's following statement provides a succinct explanation of such aesthetic involvements: Serra's "work is not about representation, but about process, movement, measure, *Dasein*, and the phenomenology of place" (von Jungenfeld, 2011, p. 7).

The site-specificity and subjective involvement in the perception of Serra's installations results inherently in a strong psychological and emotional impact upon the perceiver. In musical terms, Glass' works for string quartet or the piano holds resonances with the interiority of Serra's sculptures: his String Quartet No. 2, originally commissioned for Mabou Mines's production of Samuel Beckett's existential monologue, *Company* (1979), centres on the pervading inner thoughts of an individual lying in darkness.[③] Indeed, String Quartet No. 2 is a prime example of a work that sees a shift in Glass' compositional style. Keith Potter writes: "From 1970, Glass began his move away from a hard-line structuralist approach to one involving a more malleable attitude to sound and an increased concern with the sensuous effect of his music on the listener." (Potter, 2000, p. 269) This notion of the "sense" forms an obvious association with Sartrean existentialism, as opposed to the objectivity and impersonal state of structuralism in Glass' earlier works up to *Einstein on the Beach* (1976) (see Tarasti, 2000, p. 105). We can argue

---

① Buchloh refers to the fact that Glass and Serra frequented the La Coupoule brasserie in Montparnasse during their period in Paris, where Giacometti was a regular customer, although they never met (Buchloh, 2007, p. 44). The brasserie was also popular with other existentialists including Jean-Paul Sartre, Simone de Beauvoir and Samuel Beckett to name but a few.

② Serra refers to artists' awareness of existentialism and phenomenology in Serra, 2003, p. 36.

③ Glass chose to write a string quartet for Beckett's play as he considered that the genre matched the contemplative nature of the work: "the musical equivalent of that kind of reflective piece is normally a string quartet. The works which are considered the most introspective and private works of composers are often string quartets" (Zurbrugg 1999, p. 144).

that the malleability of Serra's materials, and the natural curves of his sculptures are equally comparable to examples of Glass' approach to musical time and harmonic voice leading.

Glass' "Façades" is a work that can be drawn out as an example of a similarity between undulating musical and visual lines.① By adopting and adapting Schenkerian techniques for the study of the piece, as apparent in the graphical reduction of Example 1, we can notice how the upper and lower voices are clearly interweaving in contrary motion—the oscillating motion of Glass' harmonic progressions, often based on semitonal steps—creates curving musical lines comparable to Serra's "Open Ended" installation, for instance.② The use of such harmonic progressions create a sense of gravitational ebbs and flows (also evident in "Opening" from *Glassworks*, as McClary noted), and the minor tonality creates a sense of bleakness within a repetitive framework altogether in contrast to the optimism of the "Heroes" Symphony as discussed earlier. Finally, the tension and release effect of Glass' harmonies form a direct connection with the terminology used by Serra to describe the resulting effect of his most recent works. "7 Plates 6 Angles" (2013) employs more defined angles than "Open Ended" for instance, creating a sense of "compression and release" according to Serra (Crow, 2013, unpag.).

Example 1 Harmonic Reduction of "Façades" from *Glassworks* (1981)

① The title of the piece reveals a predilection with the surface or outward appearance (which is compatible with the minimalist aesthetic as mentioned at the outset of the essay). The music was originally intended for Godfrey Reggio's film *Koyaanisqatsi* (1982), accompanying shots of New York's Wall Street, but was not used in the final soundtrack.

② Buchloh notes that Giacometti also influenced another American sculptor, Barnett Newman, whose work addressed "the sculptural dialectics of liquidity and rigidity, of flow and arrest, of uprightness and gravitational pull" (Buchloh, 2007, p. 44).

Glass and Close

In addition (or indeed in contrast) to the fluidity of the harmonic progressions apparent in "Façades", Glass' modular repetitive structures (often based on the addition or reduction of material) can be compared to those apparent in Chuck Close's artistic techniques. Since the mid-1960s, Close has drawn numerous portraits of Glass, the first of which was entitled "Phil" (1969), based on photographs subsequently transferred by hand into repetitive modular blocks on an enlarged canvas. In return, Glass wrote a two movement work entitled *A Musical Portrait of Chuck Close* (2005) —the first comprises alternating major/minor chords, sequences extensive scallic passages and unexpected shifts in tempo, while the second movement opens with a more subdued and dark ambience. In response to the question of whether the pieces were an accurate portrait of the artist, Close once commented: "Unless you have music that attempts to sound like rain or something like that, it's not likely that visual images come to mind. But the first movement is more like my earliest work, much more minimal and reductive, almost black and white. And the second is the musical equivalent of a riot of color." (Kazanjian, date unknown) Close's observation highlights the subjectivity of the music, a comment that resounds with Glass' views on the distance between audience and artist—an open ended-ness that allows for a subjective interpretation of music and visual art.

The ability of Glass' music to coincide with the visual domain is also strongly apparent within a filmic or televisual context, as seen earlier in the case of the Eurostar commercial. In fact, Glass' entrance to the world of film music began with a documentary film on the abstract expressionist sculptor Mark di Suvero, entitled *North Star* (1978), which paved the way for his subsequent career in film music production—a career that has brought minimalist music to mainstream Hollywood blockbusters, art films and documentaries alike. Most recently however, Glass' work has even entered into the new digital media domain.

Glass Apps—Interactive Minimalism

The release of Glass and Beck's *Rework* album in 2012 brought together

Glass' pre-existing works and the contribution of twelve artists with backgrounds in a vast array of genres such as indie rock, folk, chillwave, acousmatic, electro pop, jazz and post-classical styles. Artists including Beck, Peter Broderick, Amon Tobin, My Great Ghost and JóhannJóhannsson—to name but a few—remixed an extensive amount of minimalist works, including *Einstein on the Beach*, *Glassworks* and *North Star*. Both Glass and his music have ventured into techno and post-rock environments on several previous occasions, however what sets the REWORK-compilation even further apart from earlier efforts is its co-release with a downloadable multimedia application for iPhone and iPad. ① The app offers graphical visualisations of eleven tracks whereby the graphical material interacts with such musical parameters as rhythm, tempo and structure, and offers scope for user's interaction due to the capability of adapting the patterns slightly by using the touchscreen. Jóhann Jóhannsson's reworking of "Protest" from the opera *Satyagraha* (1979), for example, features weaving lines and descending rectangles that correlate with the falling 4th intervals on violin, followed by shapes that loosely represents faces and mouths when lyrics are sung. Peter Broderick's ethereral interpretation of "Islands" from *Glassworks* is accompanied by images resembling constellation maps that are continuously changing.

Additional to the visual representation of the music tracks, the REWORK app offers a "Glass Machine" —a function that allows the user to create basic musical patterns in the style of Glass' early works. Glass' collaboration on the project consequently demonstrates a venture into a more accessible form of association between the perceiver and the perceived, and an increased involvement in the production of minimalist based sounds—whereby, as Glass notes, "the listener becomes the artist"②.

The desire to create such a system was evident during the mid-1990s, as

① The app was developed by Snibbe Studios, who have released numerous music apps, including Metric's Synthetica, Björk's Biophilia and Bubble Harp.

② See <http://www. snibbestudio. com/rework/>.

another composer influenced by minimalist music, Brian Eno[①], presented his manifesto for the development of user generated music, or "generative music"[②], in order "to be able to sell systems for making [his] music as well as selling pieces of music. In the future, you won't buy artists' work-you'll buy software that makes original pieces of 'their' works, or that recreates their way of looking at things. You could buy [...] a Brian Eno box (Kelly, 1995, unpag. in Dietz, 2013, p. 301).

Over fifteen years later, Brian Eno's ideas were indeed realised, and the release of his "Bloom, Trope and Scape" offered different ways of interacting with visualised ambient music on a smartphone or tablet computer. While Eno's apps are more exclusively involved in user generated music and graphics, Glass's REWORK app offers an array of reworked versions of Glass' music in addition to the pattern making capabilities of the "Glass Machine". The REWORK project is consequently situated at the crossroads of minimalist music, art and new media—a scenario in which the perceiver is empowered to develop the product even further.

Conclusions

This investigation has brought to light many interconnections between various media influenced by the minimalist style. Discussions have often hinged on binary relationships—musical/artistic material, individual/society, old/new, structure/content, inside/outside, subject/object, or similarity/difference. Yet despite these formal underpinnings, the relationships are mediated in different forms, particularly as a result of their involvement with new media. Such paradigms as colour, shape, space, time, form, emotion, signification, accessibility, repetition are seemingly occupying similar grounds within different minimalist contexts. As implied by the reference to title of Serra's sculpture, the potential for perceptual interpretation and development

① British composer Brian Eno initially studied art at the Colchester Institute, thus his formative interests in music and art were intermingled.

② Steve Dietz explains that in Eno's form of "generative music" "some part of the 'decision making' process is out of Eno's hands and mind" (Dietz, 2013, p. 301), thereby the involvement of users in the creation of the music is evident to a certain extent.

of minimalist music, art and new media is consequently "open ended".

References:

Battcock, G. ed., (1995). *Minimal Art: A Critical Anthology*, Berkeley: University of California Press.

Bernard, J. W., (1993). "The Minimalist Aesthetic in the Plastic Arts and in Music", *Perspectives of New Music* (31/1): 86—132

Bernard, J. W., (2003). "Minimalism, Postminimalism and the Resurgence of Tonality in Recent American Music", *American Music* (21/1): 112—33.

Blake, C. N., (1993). "An Atmosphere of Effrontery", in Richard Wightman Fox & T. J. Jackson Lears, eds., *The Power of Culture: Critical Essays in American History*. Chicago: University of Chicago Press.

Buchloh, B. D. H., (1978). "Process Sculpture and Film in the Works of Richard Serra", in Hal Foster, ed., (2000). *Richard Serra* (October Files). Cambridge. MA: MIT.

——, (2007). "Richard Serra's Early Work: Sculpture between Labor and Spectacle", in Kynaston McShine and Lynne Cooke, eds., *Richard Serra Sculpture: Forty Years*. New York: MOMA, pp. 43—60.

Chave, A. C., (1990). "Minimalism and the Rhetoric of Power", *Arts Magazine* (64/5): 44—63.

Crow, K., (2013). "Richard Serra's Stonehenge Period", *Wall Street Journal*.

Dietz, S., (2013). "Learning from Eno", in Christopher Scoates. ed., *Brian Eno: Visual Music*. San Francisco: Chronicle.

Glover, M., (2008). "Steel Yourself: Richard Serra's Monumental Sculptures", *The Independent*.

Grimshaw, J., (2002). " 'High', 'Low', and Plastic Arts: Philip Glass and the Symphony in the Age of Postproduction", *The Musical Quarterly* (86/3): 472—507.

von Jungenfeld, R. (2011). "Intersubjectivity and Intermediality in the Work of Serra", *CLCWeb: Comparative Literature and Culture*, 13.3 <http://www.dx.doi.org/10.7771/1481—4374.1810>.

Kazanjian, D., <http://www.metoperafamily.org/metopera/news/interviews/detail.aspx? customid=3459>.

Kelly, K., (1995). "Gossip is Philosophy", *Wired*. <http://www.wired.com/wired/archive/3.05/eno.html>.

McClary, S., (2001). *Conventional Wisdom: The Content of Musical Form*. Berkeley: University of California Press.

Ottmann, K., (1989). "Richard Serra", *Journal of Contemporary Art*. <http://www.

jca-online. com/serra. html>.

Potter, K., (2000). *Four Musical Minimalists*. Cambridge: Cambridge University Press.

Serra, R., (2003). "Serra at Yale, The Original Work of Art: What It Has to Teach", *Yale University Art Gallery Bulletin*, pp. 26—39.

Strickland, E., (2000). *Minimalism: Origins*. Bloomington: Indiana University Press.

Suzuki, D., (2013). "Minimalism in the Time-Based Arts: Dance, Film and Video", in Keith Potter, Kyle Gann & Pwyllap Siôn, eds., *The Ashgate Research Companion to Minimalist and Postminimalist Music*.

Tarasti, E., (2000). *Existential Semiotics*. Bloomington: Indiana University Press.

Tusa, T., (2002). "The John Tusa Interviews: Transcript of the interview with Richard Serra". <http://www. bbc. co. uk/radio3/johntusainterview/serra_transcript. shtml>.

Von Uexhüll, Th., Geigges, W., & Herrmann, J., (2009). "Endosemiosis", *Semiotica*, pp. 5—52.

Zurbrugg. N., (1999). "Interview with Philip Glass", in Lois Oppenheim, ed., *Samuel Beckett and the Arts*. New York: Garland, pp. 143—9.

Discography:

Richard Serra—Sehen ist Denken [*Richard Serra—Thinking on your Feet*]. DVD. Dir. Maria Anna Tappeiner. 2005—2007. WDR Mediagroup.

Author:

Tristian Evans, lecturer in School of Music at Bangor University, research coordinator for the "Companion to Welsh Music" project, founded by the Welsh Federal College.

作者简介：

崔斯坦·埃文斯，英国威尔士班戈大学院音乐学讲师，威尔士联合大学“威尔士音乐指南”项目研究协调员。

E-mail: tristian. evans@bangor. ac. uk

网络公共事件中的叙事原型*

李　红

摘要：叙事原型作为一种深层的文化范型，是一种集体解释世界和处理问题的模式。网络公共事件中，对相关原型的征用常常能增强舆论的召唤力。各个主体总是试图通过叙事建构和发掘有利于自己的原型，并在此过程中经历原型冲突、原型转移和框架重建。

关键词：网络公共事件，叙事原型，框架

Narrative Archetype in Network Public Events

Li Hong

Abstract: As a deep cultural paradigm, narrative archetype is a collective model to explain the world and to deal with problems. In network public events, some archetypes are often expropriated to enhance the force to appeal the public opinion. Each subject always tries to construct and discover some archetypes to help himself, in the process of which, archetype conflict, archetype transformation and framework reconstruction happen.

Key words: network public events, narrative archetype, framework

在网络公共事件叙事中，千差万别的表层叙事之所以具有几乎类似的舆论召唤力，在于其叙事中具有深层的结构，这种结构不断表现为结构模型，而且体现为一定的原型意象和原型母题，这种原型往往成为网络公共事件叙事的深层框架。网络公共事件中的叙事原型不仅仅来自文本自身，而且来自

* 本文系笔者主持的教育部人文社科基金青年项目“符号、语境、传播及意义的生成——网络舆论的符号学分析”（项目编号：11YJC860022）的成果。

原始记忆和集体记忆，是一种集体无意识，这就导致众多事件体现出几乎同样的舆论取向。这种叙事原型往往指向现实的社会矛盾和问题，具有深刻的历史根源和现实困境，并由此沉淀到集体的叙事、记忆和认知当中。

一、叙事原型：根源与功能

网络公共事件是一种公共性的体验和书写，而不是个体的，因此，应该将其放入社会历史的语境中去进行认知和解读。它是一种集体无意识的结果，其中的原型就成为社会交际的基础，没有这一基础，就无法进行有效的沟通。

“原型”的英文为“archetype”，源自希腊文“architypos”；archi 为“初始”“首例”之意，typos 则意为“形式”“痕迹”。柏拉图用这个概念指事物的理念，认为现实事物不过是理念的影子。荣格（Carl G. Jung）则在其心理学的背景中将原型与集体无意识相结合，认为“个体无意识的绝大部分由‘情结’所组成，而集体无意识主要是由‘原型’所组成的”，并且认为原型作为一种“预先存在的形式”总是“到处寻求表现”[①]。弗莱（N. Frye）则将作品视为“社会性的事实和交际模式的文学”，研究需要“将单篇诗作放回到作为一个整体的诗歌系统中去”[②]，认为原型存在于作品的“置换变形”（displacement）之中。

基于上述哲学、心理学和文学批评的传统，我们认为所谓原型是叙事中的一种原初模式，这种模式建立在社会历史的沉淀和叙事文本的关联之中，是一种文化的产物，体现出人类解决问题的集体模式。比如，世界各文明的创世神话都有关于天地分离的叙事，从心理学的意义来看，荣格的弟子纽曼（N. Neumann）就认为“创世神话表现了人类意识发展进化的重要阶段，天父地母的分离表明意识已脱离浑然不分的无差别状态，开启了二元对立的认知编码模式”[③]。

网络公共事件作为社会叙事的一种，即使其符号具有深刻的现实指涉性，但是其叙事的深层却具有某些自古延续而来的原型，由此成为能够在各个舆论主体之间进行交际的深刻根源。弗莱就认为，“运用众所周知的联想的诗人

① ［瑞士］荣格：《集体无意识的概念》，叶舒宪编选，《神话—原型批评》，陕西师范大学出版社，2011 年，第 99～100 页。

② ［加］弗莱：《作为原型的象征》，叶舒宪编选，《神话—原型批评》，陕西师范大学出版社，2011 年，第 155 页。

③ 转引自叶舒宪：《苏美尔神话的原型意义》，叶舒宪编选，《神话—原型批评》，陕西师范大学出版社，2011 年，第 374 页。

将更为迅速地同读者建立交往关系”[①]，荣格也认为，“当原型的情境发生之时，我们将会突然体验到一种异常的释放感也就不足为奇了，就像被一种不可抗拒的强力所操纵”[②]。而这种原型的情境，在网络公共事件中是通过不同叙述者的叙事博弈所建构的，那些展现出特定原型的网络公共事件总是具有强大的舆论召唤力。

原型是潜藏在众多的叙事文本当中的深层文化范型，荣格认为它是一种集体无意识，是文化的遗传机制在起作用，这种认识具有巨大的争议性。弗莱就认为原型并非遗传所导致，而是一个象征、一个意象，是“在文学作品里反复出现”的文学经验的总体，是“指文学作品里的因素；它或是一个人物、一个意象、一种叙事定式，或是一种思想，这些因素均可从范畴较大的同类描述中抽取出来”[③]，是“一些联想群（associative clusters）”，而“特定文化中的大多数人都很熟悉它们”[④]。原型在网络公共事件叙事中的存在和显现不同于文学作品，因为网络公共事件具有更多的现实经验性，除了符号叙事以外，还有更多的身心体验，在对此进行探讨时，必须有更多现象学的考量。因此，在探讨网络公共事件中的原型时，除了追溯社会历史和文本的根源以外，还必须追溯其现实经验的传递和现实根据。如果说在神话叙事和文学叙事中远古的原始经验已经变成“集体无意识”，不能被明确意识到，需要通过原型批评（archetypal criticism）加以还原和认知的话，那么网络公共事件中的“原型”则具有现实性，通过相关事件的抽象分析就可以把握。当然，其社会历史的记忆和原初的经验也是应该考虑的，比如网络公共事件中关于“无官不贪”的原型，就是在中国文化对于官场腐败的描述中延续下来的文化范型，这在众多的文学作品和历史叙事中皆有呈现。现实的众多新闻事件中，官员的贪污腐败、大众的现实体验以及网络公共事件中贪污腐败现象的层出不穷，都通过不断的重复在叙事中和大众意识中建构出了这种原型。反过来，这种原型又成为大众叙事和认知的框架，使得相关的政府官员被置于一种经常被“污名化”的叙事逻辑中。

---

① ［加］弗莱：《作为原型的象征》，叶舒宪编选，《神话－原型批评》，陕西师范大学出版社，2011年，第158页。

② ［瑞士］荣格：《论分析心理学与诗的关系》，叶舒宪编选，《神话－原型批评》，陕西师范大学出版社，2011年，第96页。

③ 周发祥：《西方文论与中国文学》，江苏教育出版社，1997年，第232～233页。

④ ［加］弗莱：《作为原型的象征》，叶舒宪编选，《神话－原型批评》，陕西师范大学出版社，2011年，第157～158页。

“人类对客观世界的认识是通过原型实现的”[①]，荣格就认为“原始意象寻求自身表现的斗争之所以如此艰巨，是由于我们总得不断地对付个体的、非典型的情境”[②]，而原型作为一种应对现实问题的文化范式，其实就是在纷繁复杂的现实生活中建构意义，将个别的事物和行为归入秩序之中。弗莱也认为，“仪式和梦”就成为原型的“叙述和意义内容”；而仪式是“重复出现的象征交际活动”，梦所体现的意义是“愿望与经验之间的关系”，在愿望的满足和阻碍之间“存在着一种道德辩证法”，即是对愿望满足的欣喜和愿望受到阻碍的嫌恶，因此，原型体现一种“循环的模式”和一种“辩证的模式”。[③]

在面对网络公共事件的时候，众多的叙述者和受述者总是基于相关的原型建构事件的叙事框架和阅读框架，并将此原型与原始集体无意识、历史记忆和现实体验等结合起来，意义由此在历史的纵聚合和现实的横组合中得以显现。有关“官二代”“富二代”的网络事件叙事，体现的正是中国社会两极分化的集体无意识，因为集体无意识既不是推测性的也不是哲学性的，而是经验性的。[④] 这种原型认知体现在基尼系数的日益增高上。国家统计局称“2010 年基尼系数略高于 2000 年的 0.412”[⑤]，这种模糊的表达正说明了问题的严重；国家统计局公布 2012 年的基尼系数为 0.474，而民间的调查却显示基尼系数达到了 0.61[⑥]。所谓的“仇官”“仇富”，体现的是一种对权力和财富的嫌恶，这种嫌恶与现实的社会结构密切相关，也来自那些遥远的历史记忆，这些记忆充满了对权力的恐惧和对财富的鄙夷。原型的辩证模式在网络公共事件中体现为对彭宇案、小悦悦事件等道德沦丧的痛心，也体现在对 2012 年“仁义哥”王冬事件的颂扬中[⑦]，对于道德的渴求成为中国文化的集体

---

① 延俊荣、戴建东：《论隐喻建构的基础》，《山西师大学报》（社科版），2005 年第 2 期。

② ［瑞士］荣格：《论分析心理学与诗的关系》，叶舒宪编选，《神话—原型批评》，陕西师范大学出版社，2011 年，第 96 页。

③ ［加］弗莱：《作为原型的象征》，叶舒宪编选，《神话—原型批评》，陕西师范大学出版社，2011 年，第 161 页。

④ ［瑞士］荣格：《集体无意识的概念》，叶舒宪编选，《神话—原型批评》，陕西师范大学出版社，2011 年，第 101 页。

⑤ 国家统计局：《中国全面建设小康社会进程统计监测报告》（2011），< http://news.ifeng.com/mainland/detail_2011_12/21/11474801_0.shtml>。

⑥ 孙春祥：《中国首度公布基尼系数》，《北京晨报》，2013 年 1 月 19 日，<http://www.morningpost.com.cn/szb/html/2013-01/19/content_205914.htm>。

⑦ 新华网：《撞倒老人坚持送医，“仁义哥”赖着不走主动担责》，2010 年，<http://news.xinhuanet.com/yzyd/society/20121119/c-113718303.htm>。

无意识。上述这些事件中的原型体现着中国社会转型期的深刻矛盾，也体现着中国自古以来的文化矛盾，而如何解决这些矛盾，自然就成为所有叙事的原型，也成为网络公共事件叙事试图解决的“愿望与经验之间的关系”问题。

如上所述，原型的产生并不是凭空而来的，而是面对经验的一种解释世界和处理问题的模式，体现了人类的共同思维，是一种集体无意识，因为“每个意象中都凝聚着一些人类心理和人类命运的因素，渗透着我们祖先历史中大致按照同样的方式无数次重复产生的欢乐与悲伤的残余物”①。正是因为如此，就其影响力来说，“谁讲到了原始意象，谁就道出了一千个人的声音，可以使人心醉神迷，为之倾倒。与此同时，他把他正在寻求表达的思想从偶然和短暂提升到永恒的王国之中。”② 可以说，原型并不是一种信息的传递，而是一种信息和仪式的共享，它作为一种社会性的中介能够将个体和社群整合起来。在网络公共事件中，原型能够将某些事件作类型化处理，将既有的叙事框架和认知框架套到新事件中。比如，以“彭宇案”作为原型，就有“郑州‘彭宇案’”③“温州‘彭宇案’④”等。这种类型化处理使得认知上忽略了事件之间的差别，往往会遮蔽事件本身的其他问题；使得人的认知过程得以简化，从而避免了复杂认知的负担。某些当事人当然会抱怨这种对事件类型化叙事的方式，但是某些弱势的当事人正是需要利用这一原型化的处理吸引舆论的关注，获得个别性事件无法获得的舆论支持。

原型也不是一成不变的，原始时代的原型往往变成一种集体无意识，需要通过原型批评才能将之复原；原型也并不是非得要回溯到原始时代不可，每一种反复出现的记忆都有可能成为原型，网络公共事件中的众多原型就属于这一类。原型之所以变化，原因有四点：社会问题得到了解决；集体经验发生了变化；社会叙事发生了转移；大众记忆被抹杀。因此，要消除不利的原型，就需要在对话的基础之上着手解决实际的社会问题，以此重构集体经验，由此，原型所体现的矛盾和问题将会自然消解。社会叙事的转移也是一种有效的策略，但是，对这种叙事的接受必须建立在认同基础之上，否则其

① ［瑞士］荣格：《论分析心理学与诗的关系》，叶舒宪编选，《神话－原型批评》，陕西师范大学出版社，2011年，第96页。

② ［瑞士］荣格：《论分析心理学与诗的关系》，叶舒宪编选，《神话－原型批评》，陕西师范大学出版社，2011年，第96页。

③ 新华网：《郑州版“彭宇案”判决引起争议》，2010年，<http://news.xinhuanet.com/mrdx/2010－01/10/content_12784451.htm>。

④ 新华网：《温州版“彭宇案”：老人摔倒司机送医汽车被扣》，2008年，<http://news.xinhuanet.com/legal/2008－03－/03/content_7709137.htm>。

叙事就是无效的，官方叙事和民间叙事出现裂隙的原因就在这里。对大众记忆的抹杀在极权主义之下更容易办到，通过重新叙述历史和遮蔽现实就能做到。极权主义下的记忆抹杀常常跟暴力和话语高压联系在一起，但是在这个媒介高度发达的社会，这并不容易。

二、网络公共事件中的主要原型类型

荣格认为集体无意识的主要内容是原型，但是原型不一定限于无意识或集体无意识，而可能是意识、观念、习俗、文化等，生活中有多少典型情境就有多少原型，可以是一个故事、一个形象，也可以是一个过程等。[①] 正如上节中弗莱所言，原型的类型包括：人物、意象、叙事定式和思想，这已经超出了集体无意识的范围，是那些反复出现的、约定的联想物，而不再局限于意象或原始意象。网络公共事件作为中国转型社会、媒介化社会中的特定叙事形态，其中蕴含了中国传统的文化原型和现实矛盾原型。其中的原型就有："无官不贪"原型（周久耕事件、广州房叔事件等[②]）、高衙内原型（"我爸是李刚"事件、哈尔滨警察打死人事件等[③]）、欺压百姓原型（宜黄拆迁事件、罗彩霞事件等[④]）、文字狱原型（跨省追捕王帅事件、任建宇事件、彭水诗案等[⑤]）、反抗外辱原型（抵制家乐福事件、抵制 CNN 事件等[⑥]）、黑幕与

---

① 程金城：《原型的内涵与外延》，叶舒宪编选，《神话—原型批评》，陕西师范大学出版社，2011 年，第 125 页。

② 人民网：《从一包烟说到网络反腐：盘点周文耕案前前后后》，2009 年 10 月 23 日，<http://npc. people. com. cn/BIG5/28320/80577/10241045/. html>。新华网：《广东"房叔"涉嫌受贿275万元，获刑11年6个月》，2013年9月12日，<http://news/xinhuanet. com/politics/2013－09/12/c－125374260. htm>。

③ 人民网：《"我爸是李刚"案专题》，2010 年 12 月 1 日，<http://legal. people. com. cn/GB/43027/213230/index. html>。人民网《哈尔滨 6 警察打死一男子》，2008 年 10 月 21 日。<http://pic. people. com. cn/GB/1098/8206644. html>。

④ 新华网：《宜黄折迁自焚事件：责任人受到处理　1 名伤者不治身亡》，2010 年 9 月 18 日，<http://news. xinhuanet. com/2010－09/18/c－12583597. htm>。人民网：《"罗彩霞案"专题》，2010 年 8 月 16 日，<http://edu. people. com. cn/GB/8216/20025/index. html>。

⑤ 新华网：《发贴举报遭遇跨省追捕》，2009 年 4 月 14 日，<http://news. xinhuanet. com/local/2009－04/14/content _ 11183875. htm>。人民网《任建宁：被劳教的材官》，2012 年 11 月 26 日，<http:/sc. people. com/cn/n/2012/1126/c346334/17771134. html>。人民网：《公务员短信针砭时弊被拘续：彭水县委书记被免职》，2007 年 11 月 9 日，<http://society. people. com. cn/GB/1062/5305268. html>。

⑥ 人民网：《抵制家乐福：让理性和热情走向同一条路》，2008 年，<http://www. people. com. cn/GB/32306/33232/7145516. html>。人民网：《中国网民反击 CNN 辱华言论行动升级》，2008 年，<http://opinion. people. com. cn/GB/1036/7125177. html>。

冤案原型（华南虎事件、躲猫猫、赵作海案、钱云会案等[①]）、道德沦丧的原型（小悦悦事件、彭宇案[②]）等。

在中国人的文化意识里面，几乎是无官不贪，而清官是少数，在《儒林外史》里就有“三年清知府，十万雪花银”的俗谚。中国历史中的贪官污吏最为著名的有《世说新语》里记载的石崇与王恺、唐朝的杨国忠、北宋的蔡京、明朝的严嵩父子、清朝的和珅等，他们不但位高权重，而且穷奢极欲。新中国成立后，有著名的刘青山、张子善、成克杰、王怀忠等高官贪污腐败。腐败问题已经成了目前中国社会的重大挑战，普通老百姓对此具有切身的体验，中央也意识到了这个问题的严重性。2012 年 11 月 15 日，习近平在其当选中国共产党总书记的记者见面会上说，“一些党员干部中发生的贪污腐败、脱离群众、形式主义、官僚主义等问题，必须下大气力解决”，将腐败问题列为众多问题之首。基于这样的历史原型、现实情况和经验感知，贪官原型已经成为中国政治话语中的核心原型，这在网络公共事件中总是被不断地重复和唤起。在南京“周久耕事件”、陕西“表叔杨达才事件”、广州“房叔蔡彬事件”等事件中，网民从最初对其别的行为的不满，发展到搜索其腐败的证据，目的在于报复其不当言行。从怀疑，到最终的坐实，这进一步验证了网民和媒体的原型想象。正是因为贪污腐败在中国历史和现实中的严重性，它已成为每一个中国人内心中最敏感的一部分，任何对贪污腐败的只言片语都会引起极大的舆论反响，贪污腐败已经成为中国网民揭发权力者的一种叙述原型。在中国政治历史上，要想揭发一个当权者，最好的策略就是将对方置于贪污腐败的叙事原型中，因为在中国以人格作为核心政治素养的传统中，贪污腐败是人格的致命伤。

至于社会的等级化和权力的污名化，也是中国文化中最具悖论色彩的问题：一方面充满了对等级秩序和权力的向往——读书人的终身理想就是进入等级和权力体系之中；另一方面又体现出对等级和权力的对抗和恐惧——侠

---

① 人民网：《新闻背景：陕西“华南虎照”事件大事记》，2008 年，<http://society.people.com.cn/GB/42733/8116288.html>。人民网：《“躲猫猫”引起网络关注，云南省公开征集网民参与调查》，2009 年，<http://cpc.people.com.cn/GB/64387/8838943.html>。人民网：《办案机关承认“赵作海冤案”存在刑讯逼供》，2010 年，<http://society.people.com.cn/GB/42733/11560395.html>。人民网：《乐清村长被碾死案》，2010 年，<http://legal.people.com.cn/Gb/43027/211348/index.html>。

② 新华网：《反思“小悦悦”事件：“见危不救”是否应入罪》，2011 年，<http://www.xinhuanet.com/chinanews/2011-10/22/content_23951856.htm>。《“彭宇案一场没有赢者的游戏”》，《中国青年报》，2012 年 1 月 17 日，<http://opinion.people.com.cn/GB/16894019.html>。

文化、隐逸文化和臣民文化体现的正是这点。中国文化中关于“纨绔子弟”“高衙内”“仗势欺人”等的记忆成为大众认知的原型，在网络公共事件中就体现为“官二代”“富二代”“强拆”等。比如，在“哈尔滨警察打死人事件”中，由于打人者的警察身份，舆论起初一边倒指责警察；而当被打死的大学生林松岭嚣张的录像被公布和其有“背景”的传言散布开来后，舆论发生转向。在此过程中，舆论转向体现出的，正是对于权力的对抗和恐惧。在“杭州飙车案”中，胡斌的一帮朋友在车祸现场勾肩搭背、抽烟嬉笑的照片激起了大众关于“纨绔子弟”的原型想象，再加上“飙车”、其母亲现场“不断打电话”等细节，进一步坐实了对于权力的固有原型想象，这也为后来的“胡斌是替身”的怀疑埋下了伏笔。如果说在传统的舆论格局和制度格局之下，对权力的怀疑和对抗不能也敢公开进行的话，那么在这个宣扬法治和民主的社会中，通过网络舆论对抗等级和权力则是名正言顺，而且可以通过舆论的道义力量得以实现。因此，在中国文化的社会历史和现实语境中，“富二代”“官二代”“有背景”“有权力”等，常常被视为标出项，是异于正项和中项的异项，具有贬义性，其本人也往往对此加以否定。那些与权力有关的人和机构，总是在网络公共事件中得不到大众的信任，原因在于大众固有的对于“官官相卫”“托关系”等原型的想象。

网络公共事件是一种符号化的建构物，言语是其中的核心，没有言语的空间，网络公共事件将无法形成。因此，网络公共事件的兴起，可以反映出中国言论空间和言论平台的开放，但是，这种开放更多是传播的技术平台所带来的，是一种开放的可能性，并在实然层面实现了某种程度的突破；不过，在正式的规定和规范层面，言论空间的开放尚需时日，这就形成了“倒逼”的态势。言论空间本身的开放意味着文化和制度的变革，但是，这种变革是一种渐变的过程，中国文化中对于言语本身的原型想象总是会横亘在集体文化心理之中。其中就充满着悖论：既注重文章的教化作用，又对言语不信任；既崇拜文化人又提防文化人，比如焚书坑儒、文字狱等体现的就是对言语和文化人的不信任与恐惧，历史上其他“因言取祸”的案例不在少数。对言语的恐惧其实体现的是一种符号想象与符号巫术，是对言语力量的一种夸大，认为“一言可以兴邦，一言可以丧邦”（《论语·子路》），并将其上升到“经国之大业，不朽之盛事”（曹丕：《典论·论文》）的地位。当然这也与将国家和政府神圣化的观念密切相关，皇帝及其皇族被神圣化，政府成为不容置疑的主体，任何通过言语对政府的质疑都被视为大逆不道。

就网络公共事件来说，互联网不断的技术革新使得信息与言论的表达和传递实现了全民参与，言论平台的开放使得言语对事件的建构能力增强。但是与此相对的，是某些政府官员或群体在观念层面的固有原型没有跟上时代的进步，那种对言语的恐惧和不信任深藏在其集体无意识中，他们对相关言论者随意使用暴力，往往使一个普通事件成为网络公共事件，反而将事态进一步扩大。技术平台提供的言论可能性与对待言论的固有观念之间的张力，成为很多网络公共事件得以发酵的催化剂。比如 2009 年，在上海工作的王帅，因为在网上发帖披露了家乡河南灵宝市政府违法“租”地的事实，被“跨省追捕”。政府在最初给媒体的回复中称，王帅“严重损害了灵宝的形象。特别是伤害了市抗旱工作指挥部和市水利局负责同志”，“严重侵犯了其人格和身心健康”①。正这种对言论的惩罚，将事件推向了舆论的风口浪尖，最后官方不得不承认对王帅的拘留是违法，征地也是违规的，并且强调要“牢固树立依法行政理念”②。没有网络和媒体的介入，也许事件不会发生：王帅不会参与其中，也不会有网民大规模参与，事件也只不过是个征地案件。但是，当地政府因为言论而处罚王帅，就触动了“因言获罪”的原型，进而激起了舆论的极大反响。类似的事件还有 2006 年“彭水诗案”、2011 年“任建宇案”等。重庆彭水县公务员秦中飞因为写了一条针砭时弊的短信《沁园春·彭水》并在 QQ 里传播，而被以“诽谤罪”刑事拘留，后此事因李星辰在博客上披露而引起舆论的反弹，最后秦中飞无罪释放，得到公安局道歉并获国家赔偿。同样是在彭水县，2011 年，大学生村官任建宇，因为在微博和 QQ 空间里复制、转发和点评“一百多条负面信息”，被以涉嫌“煽动颠覆国家政权罪”拘留并劳教了 15 个月，其订购的印有“不自由，毋宁死”字样的文化衫也被作为犯罪证据。这些“因言获罪”的网络公共事件，体现出了某种官方言语巫术的原型记观念与民间“文字狱”原型记忆之间的冲突，官方言语巫术原型最终不得不在舆论和法制的审判之下向民众和法律妥协。

在中国式的冤案原型中，总是会有清官的原型与之相随，从而让叙事获得一种“圆满”，但是，在作为真实叙事的网络公共事件中，这种清官原型很难塑造，而且，制度的合法性更需要摒弃清官原型，变“魅力型权威”为“法理型权威”，这种权威类型则需要通过整个制度的设计和持续规范运行来树立。网络公共事件作为一种真实的、即时性的叙事，对于真相的展现总是

---

① 灵宝市信息中心：《关于〈一篇帖子换来被囚八日〉一稿有关情况的回复》，灵宝党政公众网，2009 年 4 月 10 日，<http://tieba.baidu.com/f?kz=563016230>。

② 灵宝市委、市政府：《关于对“王帅发帖事件”处理情况的答复》，《中国青年报》，2009 年 4 月 16 日。

逐步进行的，里面充满了各种叙事权力的博弈，官方的叙事总是面临网络叙事的挑战。在此过程中，网民常常征用的原型是“冤案”，这在“华南虎事件”“躲猫猫事件”“钱云会案”等事件中皆有体现。比如，在2010年的“钱云会案”中，浙江乐清县村支书钱云会被工程车碾压致死，警方将事件界定为“交通肇事”，而网络舆论则更多相信是“谋杀”，是“冤案”，是“被五个人按在地上压死”，这与死者钱云会多次因征地上访、现场录像失灵、村民的“目击”、村民被捕、105万的巨额赔偿等语境联系起来，更增强了网络舆论和媒体的怀疑。虽然，事件最终被判决为“交通肇事”，但是由于网民认为警方叙事有众多不合理，真相仍然处于扑朔迷离之中。没有真相，“冤案”的原型也就无法消解，这在众多的网络公共事件叙事中反而得以强化。比如，在“华南虎事件”中，周正龙也被认为是“替罪羊”；而“躲猫猫”“俯卧撑”等不合逻辑的事件解释，则将网民和媒体集体无意识中的冤案原型召唤出来。在面对网民和媒体的原型想象的过程中，网络领域的争辩最为核心的两点共识就是：真相和制度，即要求信息公开和制度合法性的建构。正是现实中这两点没有办到，才导致舆论的反弹；而连作为权威的信息宣布者的警方都不再令人信服，可见的确是信息透明度和制度合法性出现了问题。

当然，网络公共事件中的原型远不止上述这些，上述对典型事件的原型分析，只是为了展示网络公共事件中的深层文化影响和制度影响，而假如只是就事论事，就无法达到应有的深度。

三、原型冲突、原型转移与框架重建

网络公共事件叙事具有深刻的对话性，事件各个主体的声音都得到了呈现，并且处于相对平等的地位，声音彼此之间存在着互动和回应，这区别于许多文艺叙事的独白，也区别于传统新闻报道中只有政府立场的独白。在对话中，各个主体所征用的原型不可避免地存在冲突，但是，具体哪种原型在受众那里能引起共鸣和认同，则又与受众集体无意识中的原型想象密切相关。在此过程中，传播者所征用的原型和框架常常面临着转移和重建，整个社会的文化原型也会在此过程中经历转移和重建，因为“原型有强劲的继承性、传播性和无限生成转换性”[①]。

网络公共事件中的原型冲突，体现在事件中作为传播者的当事人之间，也体现在传播者与受众之间，还体现在整个文化的传统与现代之间。网络公

① 张中载：《原型批评》，《外国文学》，2003年第1期。

共事件中，作为当事人的地方政府常常征用的原型是“刁民”、符号巫术、政治斗争等原型，而与其对应的则是事件相对方采用的“权力暴力”“文字狱”“冤案”等原型。权力暴力是自古至今社会集体无意识中的原始创伤，因而，暴力总是会激起整个舆论的反感，这与上述“文字狱”“冤案”等原型共同构成了与官方所征用的原型之间的冲突。但是，这种冲突并不是不分高下的，而是会经历法理和道德的追问，以及经历舆论的审判，在网络公共事件中，就体现为网民和媒体是否认同，体现为上级政府对事件的处置。在“王帅发帖被跨省追捕事件”中，将当地政府所说的言论造成的“诽谤”“伤害”“干扰”等放入法制的视野中进行审视，就会发现罪名是“莫须有”的。其结果自然是，上级政府在舆论压力之下介入事件，道歉、赔偿、处分责任人等，错误得以纠正，原型冲突表面上得以消解，至于深层的集体无意识的改变，则远非一日之功。

原型并不是一成不变的，其内涵总是会随着时代的变化而发生转化，因为每个时代的内在矛盾和心理创伤不一样，因而，集体无意识就会存在巨大差异。比如，“红颜祸水”原型在新的时代已经不再常常显现；而“为富不仁”原型在中国社会历史中频繁出现，在现实语境中也屡见不鲜。这在关于慈善的新闻报道和网络公共事件中具有鲜明的体现。中华慈善总会的统计显示，他们所获捐赠的70％都是来自国外和港台地区，国内富豪的捐赠仅占不到15％[①]，与此相对的是他们的偷税漏税、挥土如金等。原型的转移在网络公共事件中其实表现得很明显，那就是固有的原型在其他原型的压力和竞争之下，在新的文化语境之下常常无法胜出，从显性转化为潜隐状态。比如，关于“符号巫术”的原型总是对言语充满着恐惧和仇视，认为任何的“负面”言语都会造成极大的社会伤害和个人伤害，从而想当然地夸大其“损害”。但是，这一原型在新的法制环境和民主观念之下，在新媒体的语境之下，就面临着前所未有的理论压力和舆论压力。虽然在某些事件中它还有所显现，但是随着越来越多的类似原型想象被宣布为“非法”，这一原型的空间将被大大压缩，从而转化成潜隐的集体无意识状态。

原型并不是如荣格所言是遗传的，而是通过文化进行传承的，只不过那些遥远的记忆因为现代人的经验缺失而变成了一种无法明确意识到的集体无意识。如果说个体无意识能解释私人性的心理，那么原型则是解决“普遍矛

---

① 凤凰网：《中国富豪为何“远离慈善”》，2009 年 8 月 24 日，<http://gongyi.ifeng.com/shehui/200908/0824_6688_1316384.shtml>。

盾的问题”以及非私人的“‘社会的’现象”，而“原型支配下的精神病人没有一个不成为其牺牲品的”，比如纳粹的狂热就跟反犹等原型的唤起密切相关。[①] 在解决普遍矛盾和社会现象的过程中，原型得以形成，网络公共事件叙事中的原型不但与历史记忆有关，而且也是现实矛盾和想象的产物，是试图通过叙事来解决问题的一种尝试，其中就体现了官民冲突、阶层冲突、民族主义、秩序混乱等中国转型期的典型问题。在相互冲突的原型之中，某些原型总是会受到理想的文化范型、现实的力量对比、舆论的指向、潜在的文化规则（潜规则）、原始的文化意象等的推动或者制衡，从而出现博弈。那些在各种力量对比中胜出的原型就成为显现的原型，那些被压抑的原型就会变成集体无意识，在适当的时候才会被召唤出来。

在网络公共事件的原型研究中，原型与框架（framing）存在着某种关联，框架能起着唤起原型的作用。框架是一个认知心理学的概念，后被戈夫曼引入社会学研究中，“指人们用来认识和解释社会生活经验的一种认知结构，它‘能够使它的使用者定位、感知、确定和命名那些看似无穷多的具体事实’”[②]，框架具有选择和凸显作用，能够“促成一个独特问题的界定、因果解释、道德评价以及如何处理的忠告”[③]，也是一种建构意义、探寻原因和后果的观察事物的世界观。如果说框架是在某种叙事文本中选择的显性而可见的结构，那么原型则是在文本之间、历史传承和记忆中的深层结构。深层原型可以表征为一定的叙事框架，通过合适的框架召唤起舆论，而那些不合适的框架在框架冲突中往往受到受众的抵制，最终就需要框架调整和重建。“瓮安事件”最初的叙事框架是“黑恶势力对政府的挑衅”[④]，当地政府和当地媒体最初就采用这一框架，省委书记石宗源起初也采用这一叙事框架[⑤]，对涉事人员的抓捕和定性也是在这个框架内展开的。但是，这种框架中所采用的陈词滥调使得广大公众和网民习惯性地不信任和对抗，于是令人匪夷所

① 荣格：《集体无意识的概念》，叶舒宪编选，《神话—原型批评》，陕西师范大学出版社，2011年，第103页。

② 甘莅豪，樊小玲：《“精品”与“合作”：两岸“××制造”形象广告的框架分析》，《当代修辞学》，2011年第2期。

③ Entman, R. M., “Framing: Toward Clarification of a Fractured Paradigm”, *Journal of Communication*, 1993, vol. 43, no. 4.

④ 《贵州黔南州召开常委会议通报瓮安事件》，《黔南日报》，2008年07月02日，<http://news.ifeng.com/mainland/special/wengan628/news/200807/0702_3932_629648.shtml>。

⑤ 《贵州省委书记赴瓮安指挥6·28突发事件善后工作》，《贵州日报》，2008年07月01日，<http://news.ifeng.com/mainland/200807/0701_17_626485.shtml>。

思的“俯卧撑”这个细节就成为广大网民戏谑的由头。媒体对这种陈词滥调的框架也不认同，这从凤凰网所收录的媒体评论可以看出：

- 《法制日报》：反思瓮安事件，民生的背后是民权
- 时评：瓮安尸检，展示技术细节的价值
- 时评：瓮安公安局长为什么等到免职才讲真话？
- 贵州反思瓮安事件：真相是消弭谣言的“良药”
- 评论：从瓮安事件看地方政府公共权力的行使方式
- 《法制日报》“瓮安事件”三细节决定处置之失①

如上可见，媒体并未将事件置于“黑恶势力挑衅”的框架进行解读，而是希望通过政府的努力解决深层次的社会问题。这与后来贵州省委书记石宗源所重建的框架相吻合，他认为事件“背后深层次原因却是瓮安县在矿产资源开发、移民安置、建筑拆迁等工作中，侵犯群众利益的事情屡屡发生，而在处置这些矛盾纠纷和群体事件过程中，一些干部作风粗暴、工作方法简单，甚至随意动用警力”。不再将事件归咎于黑恶势力，而是承认了“官民矛盾”这一框架，从而将问题凸显出来以引起思考、讨论和解决。后续的对有关责任人的处罚，也是基于这一框架，网民和媒体的框架与官方的框架在此相吻合，这也成为舆论转折的关键点。事实上，“黑恶势力”“不明真相”“煽动”等是一种政治的框架，这种具有特定时代特色的框架在这个利益多元、情况复杂、日益法制化的时代下不再是一种有效的深层原型，相反，“官民冲突”“贫富差距”等矛盾成为受众心里的主要原型。那种将社会事件随意政治化的叙事框架，往往会受到抵抗，在此框架下对事件的处理也会更固化那些主要原型想象，从而诱发更大的社会危机。

作者简介：

李红，新闻学博士，西北师范大学传播学院副教授。

Author:

Li Hong, Ph. D. in Journalism, associate professor in College of Communication and Media, Northwest Normal University, Lanzhou.

E-mail: yoyohei@163. com

① <http://news. ifeng. com/mainland/special/wengan628/>。

The Invention of Tradition: The Case of *Pasta*, a Symbol of Italian Identity

Simona Stano

Abstract: Local food is generally regarded by Italians as one of the most representative aspects of their national identity, a feeling that can sometimes lead to real forms of patriotic fervour, if not even open chauvinism. But if, on one hand, the Italian gastronomic universe includes many regional and local components which are not reducible to a single tradition and to a few stereotyped dishes; on the other hand, Italians' collective passion for their "own" cuisine makes reference to a well-defined and limited *imaginarium* which finds in *pasta* its most representative element. Why? How does pasta emerge as a Value-Object that can seduce the Subject ("Italians"), making them—as Roland Barthes (1977) would say—"fall in love" with their country? And what are the values with which this Object is invested? Focusing on advertising, which is both the mirror and generator of sociocultural values, and building on the semiotic analysis of some relevant case studies, this paper aims at pointing out how collective passions and representations are produced and enhanced by mass media and their discourses.

Key words: pasta, identity, *imaginarium*, advertising, semiotics

传统的生成：意大利面何以成为意大利人民族认同的象征？

西蒙娜·斯坦诺

摘要： 意大利人多把本土食物视为民族认同最具有代表性的方面，这种感受有时会导向真实的爱国热情。然而，如果说意大利的美食图谱包含了诸多地区性的、地方性的成分，这些成分不能被简单地视为某种单一的传统或为数不多的传统菜系，那么另一方面，意大利人对他们“自己”的美食的集体热情暗示了一种明确而有限的想象，而意大利面则是这种想象最典型的体现。意大利面何以成为，又是如何成为一个价值对象，使得主体（意大利人）如罗兰·巴尔特所说的那样，“爱上”他们国家？这一对象被赋予了什么价值？本文探讨了广告这一社会文化价值的镜像和催生器，对一些相关案例进行了符号学分析，旨在揭示出大众媒体及其话语是如何生产并加强了集体的热情和表现。

关键词：意大利面，认同，想象，广告，符号学

Ⅰ. Introduction

"*Macaroni*, you provoked me, and I'll destroy you now, *macaroni*. I'm gonna eat you, ahmmm" (Vanzina 1954). With these words, Nando Moriconi, the *American in Rome* of Steno's movie①, temporarily abandons his infatuation with the American way of life to fully *re*-discover his Italian identity in his relationship with food. Local food, in fact, is generally regarded by Italians as one of the most representative aspects of their national identity, a feeling that can sometimes lead to real forms of patriotic fervour, if not even open chauvinism. But if, on one hand, the Italian gastronomic universe includes many regional and local components which are not reducible to a single tradition and to a few stereotyped dishes; on the other hand, Italians' collective passion for their "own" cuisine makes reference to a well-defined and limited *imaginarium*② which finds in *pasta* its most representative element.

---

① *An American in Rome*/*Un americano a Roma*, Steno, 1954, Italy.

② The term *imaginarium* is here used to refer to the socially shared depository of images—or, more generally, of *figures*—which comprises part of a cultural *encyclopaedia* (cf. Eco 1975; 1979; 1984) directing and regulating its imaginative paths according to the dual dimension of an "internal imaginarium" (intended as a "cultural pattern for the production of images and figures," Volli 2011: 35 [translation of mine]) and an "external imaginarium" (conceived as a "material system of production and storage of [these] images," Volli 2011: 35 [translation of mine]). Several works have investigated the term and its meanings, which are not easy to define; in particular, cf. Leone 2011: *passim*).

Why? How does pasta emerge as a Value-Object that can seduce the Subject ("Italians"), making them—as Roland Barthes (1977) would say—fall in love with their country? And what are the values with which this Object is invested?

Ⅱ. Italians and Pasta: a Brief Historic Outline

Pellegrino Artusi's *Science in the Kitchen and the Art of Eating Well* (1891) represents the first formal attempt to unify the various culinary traditions of the Italian peninsula and to create "a national identification code" (Camporesi, 1970: XVI) which, while not erasing the specific regional features, translates the different local food dialects into a common language. In such national language, pasta does not seem to play a key role: Artusi hints at the Italian passion for *macaroni*, but he explicitly refers to pasta in only two recipes ("with béchamel sauce" and "with breadcrumbs").

Similarly, if we refer to the history of Italian cuisine—or, rather, cuisines—we see that pasta "was for a long time a food among many others" (Capatti and Montanari, 1999: 66, [translation of mine]): only between the 17th and 18th centuries did its consumption begin to spread widely, and we have to wait until the post-unification period (1880 – 1920) and the mass emigration to the United States of America for its election as symbol of Italian identity. Before 1700, pasta could be found in some Italian regions—such as Liguria and Sicily—but it was a food for small, privileged groups of people. The change came with the so-called "Neapolitan Food Revolution": "the application on a mass scale of a previously existing technology until then exclusively limited to the handcrafted universe probably allowed the development of the first 'modern' food in our country," as Peppino Ortoleva (1992: 11 [translation of mine]) states. As a consequence of the food crisis of those years, in fact, it was decided to avoid the high costs of transportation of leafy vegetables (the so-called "foglia") —a poor, aqueous and highly perishable foodstuff which previously formed the basis of popular Neapolitan diet—replacing it with a dry and easily storable food product: *wheat*, which is an ingredient that, mixed with water, could be easily transformed into a nutritious low-cost food dough.

The Neapolitan food revolution then slowly spread to other regions and, gradually, from metropolitan areas to rural ones. But it was only with the Italian emigration in the early 20th century that pasta started to be considered the "Italian" food *par excellence*. By virtue of its *adaptability* and *modularity*, that is, its "tendency to be combined with a high number of dressings, sauces and ingredients, and so to match fields even quite different from the original one" (Galli della Loggia, 1998: I [translation of mine]), pasta became the main symbol of identity of Italian communities in the United States. "Unlike other immigrated groups, such as Irish, who were very cohesive thanks to Catholicism, or the Jews, who were unified by their religious endogamy, the religion of the migrated Italians consisted in 'domesticity'." (La Cecla, 1998: 55—56 [translation of mine]) This value then came to be represented by *pasta*, "the most accurate artefact of a home cooking" (La Cecla, 1998: 56 [translation of mine]), which requires a certain degree of knowledge on cooking times and methods of preparation. As La Cecla states, pasta became the "flag" under which a whole nation found a shelter where to protect its fragile identity (1998: 58).

If "identity is defined even (or perhaps especially) as a *difference*, that means in relation to others" (Capatti and Montanari, 1999: VIII [translation of mine]), then pasta, the essential feature of an identity that must be claimed and somehow protected from external interferences, is no exception. It has become one of the most common symbols of Italian identity, which comes to be firmly associated with a universe of values centred on the basic ideas of *domesticity*, *authenticity*, *tradition*, and *conviviality*.

Ⅲ. From History to Collective Imaginary

Beyond the historical and material variables that have led to the creation of a certain Italian culinary imaginary, it is interesting to investigate what happens in terms of *signification*, analysing how pasta comes to embody the values of "Italian identity", thus creating the conditions for that "conformity of essence" between Subject and Object of the passion that Roland Barthes described as central for the *Lover's Discourse* (1977): "I want to be the other, I want the other to be me, as if we were united, enclosed within the same sack of skin." (ET, 1979: 127–28)

In such a perspective, it is very important to consider the language of advertising, which is both the mirror and generator of similar values. The objective of this article is precisely to analyse how, in the context of advertising discourses, different forms of representation and promotion of pasta are associated with particular *mises-en-scène* of "Italian identity." Specifically, in what follows we will consider some audiovisual campaigns promoting *Barilla*, the world leader in the pasta market.

1. Barilla, the "Traditional" Italian Pasta

The Barilla brand was created in 1877, when Pietro Barilla opened a bakery in the city of Parma. After initial difficulties, the small enterprise started to grow, becoming, in 1910, under the direction of Pietro's sons Gualtiero and Riccardo, the first factory equipped with a continuous furnace, employing eighty workers. Immediately realising the importance of advertising, the two brothers gave rise to a trend that, over the years, had led the Parmesan company to collaborate with leading Italian and international artists to create calendars, posters, packaging and eye-catching audiovisual commercials. With Pietro (the founder's grandson), the advertising and marketing strategy of the brand came to a turning point: pasta, originally a "humble" product, became a real *object of worship*, as it represented "a simple and genuine Italy, made of refined and genuine things" (Rai Educational, 2011 [translation of mine]).

Leaving aside the printed advertising production, this article will focus on some audiovisual commercials commissioned by Barilla, which represent a decisive stage of this process of establishing pasta as the symbol of Italian identity.

2. The First Carosello (1958): Giorgio Albertazzi and Dante

A few months after the first *Carosello*① in 1958, Barilla decided to

① Carosello (Italian for "carousel") was an Italian television advertising show, broadcast on RAI-Italy's national public TV from 1957 to 1977. It generally included short sketch comedy films or other entertainment shows followed by commercials.

commit the advertising of its products to television. This gave birth to the first Barilla *Carosello*, hosted by Giorgio Albertazzi, who, after reciting the famous sonnet from Dante Alighieri's *Vita NovaTanto gentile e tanto onesta pare* ("So gentle and so honest she appears", 1292 — 1293), presented Barilla's new gluten pasta, introduced by a cheerful group of children of different ages dancing around a huge box of pasta. The decision to have a sonnet by Dante Alighieri, the "father of the Italian language", thereby suggests that Barilla pasta is also to be understood as representing quite essential Italian spirit.

Another relevant factor is the logo that introducing the *Carosello*. Its roundish font, combined with the choice to put the Barilla logo inside of an ellipse, which is in turn surrounded by a "bright" spiral, simultaneously both evokes the image of an egg (the basic ingredient of the product) and announces the *Ring a Ring o' Rosest* hat will take place in the final scene.

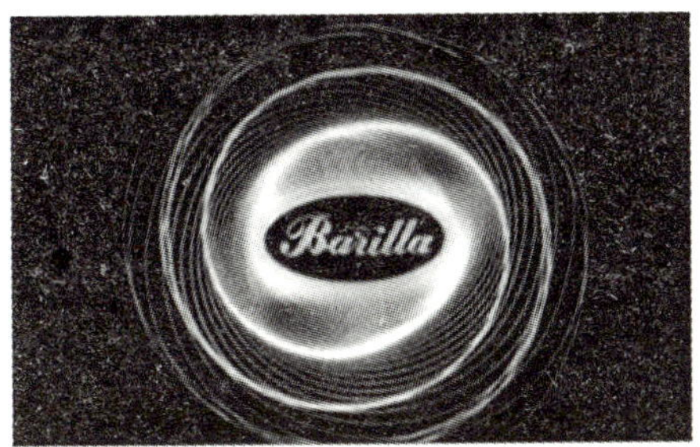

Figure 1 **Barilla Logo and Children Dancing**, ***Carosello***, 1958 (© **Barilla**)

An interesting parallelism on the topological level is thereby established, with the creation of a relationship, describable in terms of the oppositions between circumscribing/circumscribed and peripheral/central, between the spiral-circle of children and the logo-product. This stresses the importance of Barilla, whose logo is in this way inextricably linked to the two terms used in the second image to describe the contents of the box ("gluten pasta"), as well as to the figure of the child. Childhood, an element that is at the same time circumscribing-peripheral and central-circumscribed, plays a central role in the commercial, as clarified by the voiceover ("A safe food product for children and all stages of life") and the children's choir ("We are healthy babies, do you know why? / Our mom found it! / She gives us the new

Barilla pasta / that is gluten pasta." Barilla, 1958 [translation of mine]). This leads one to remark on the strong *practical* valorisation (cf. Floch, 1986 and 1990) of the product: Barilla is praised for its nutritive capacity (as it can provide the body with the energy it needs to grow in a healthy way) — that is, it is presented in accordance with those *use values* (Floch, 1986 and 1990) that make it a "safe food product for all stages of life" (Barilla, 1958 [translation of mine]). This idea is further enhanced by the hyperbolic exaggeration of the size of the box of pasta, which assumes gigantic proportions, reaffirming the importance of the product for proper nutrition and children's growth and investing then Barilla pasta with that "miraculous" nature described just before in the verses of Dante recited by Albertazzi: "and it seems a thing that has come from heaven to earth to show forth a miracle." (Alighieri 1292—1293, [1863]: 81)

3. The Commercial *High Society* (*Alta società*) —*Rigatoni Barilla* by Fellini

In the commercial *High Society* (*Alta società*) —*Rigatoni Barilla* by Federico Fellini (1986), a refined and seductive lady, after examining a rich menu of dishes with resounding French names, orders, winking at the maître, a portion of *Rigatoni*. The waiter then responds "Ha... So we echo: 'Barilla.'" Afterwards, while a series of concentric circles (the reference is again to the egg, as well as to the idea of perfection expressed by the circular shape) that light up in succession invades the shot, the other guests of the restaurant repeat "Barilla" in unison, strengthening the echo effect announced by the waiter. This is the denial of those use values exalted in the previously analysed *Carosello*: pasta Barilla is no longer presented as a nutrient food product necessary to grow healthy and strong, but as an object of luxury and refinement. And for this reason it is preferred to the common dishes of a cuisine generally recognized as one of the most prestigious in the world (the French one). The intention, therefore, is to dignify pasta, which emerges no more as a plebeian (as its origins are) product, but a "chic", high-class food, subjected to a *ludic* or *aesthetic* (cf. Floch, 1990) valorisation. *Perspective*① (cf. Ferraro, 1998) heroine of the commercial, the woman refuses any external and pre-established definition, going against the tide and bringing the entire group of guests to a kind of orgiastic ecstasy which, in turn, makes them repeat in unison, as if they had been struck by a kind of "enlightenment", the name of the brand-deity, *Barilla*.

Figure 2 The Commercial *Alta Società* by Fellini, 1986 (© **Barilla**)

4. "Where There is Barilla There is a Home"

In the late 80s and early 90s, Barilla commissioned a series of commercials called *Dove c'è Barilla c'è casa* ("Where there is Barilla there is a home"), characterized by the presence of the jingle *Hymn* by Vangelis.

(1) *The Little Girl with the Yellow Raincoat* (1987)

In the first commercial of the series, a little girl just got out of school, having missed her bus, starts to walk towards her house protected from the rain by a yellow raincoat. Meanwhile, a woman (presumably her mother),

① Building on the opposition between the *subjective* level, which is related to the Subject, and the *objective* level, which stresses the socially and inter-subjectively recognised values, as well as on the contrast between the *relative* and *absolute* axis, Guido Ferraro (1998) identifies four *discursive regimes*. In the *causal* regime the emphasis is put on objective facts, and what one does defines what one is. The *positional* regime is based on the subject, whose actions are defined by his same essence; this is the realm of tradition and socially recognised roles. The third discursive regime is the *perspective* regime: the "perspective hero" is someone who does not accept any external definition, going against socially established roles and values and acting according to his own feelings and nature. The *multiperspective* regime, finally, identifies the "seducer", the one who is able to be for others what they want him to be. In Ferraro's view, in fact, seduction is essentially an interpretative process, which consists in grasping other people's desires and breaking into their narrative programs as a value-object.

while waiting for her husband (who will appear shortly afterwards) and her daughter, is cooking pasta. The camera then moves to the clock and the worried expression of the two parents: it is almost one o'clock in the afternoon (Italian lunch time!) and their daughter has not returned home from school. Along the way, in fact, the child finds a lost kitten and she stops to put it under her raincoat and take it home with her. Suddenly, the man sees the daughter from the kitchen window and he goes with his wife to the door. Here their worried and almost reproachful expression immediately makes room for a moment of hilarity: the little girl extracts the kitten from the raincoat and smiles looking at the mother, who, returning the smile and inviting them to enter. The commercial then closes with the scene of the woman placing on the ground a bowl of milk to feed the little cat and then hugging her daughter, while in the background the father brings to the table a dish full of pasta. Finally the tagline "Where there is Barilla there is a home", reiterated by the voice-over, appears on the screen, followed by the logo Barilla (updated, but always shaped to make reference to the egg).

Figure 3 **Commercial** ***The Little Girl with the Yellow Raincoat***, 1987 (© **Barilla**)

An interesting element which clearly emerges in the commercial is the chromatic rhyme between the yellow colour of the child's boots and raincoat, of the bus, and of pasta (both the one shown on the packaging and the actual one, cooked by the woman), which gives a sense of continuity to the represented scenes and helps to put the emphasis on the product, linking it to the message expressed by the slogan. As a result, we have a *utopian* (cf. Floch, 1990) valorisation of pasta, whose exalted *basic* values are conviviality, family, and hospitality. The mini-story that is presented, whose beginning is characterised by scenes of solitude (the little girl who loses her bus and walks alone on the street, in the rain, and the abandoned kitten meowing for help), has a happy ending, due to those basic values that make Barilla, and more generally, pasta, the incarnation of the house, as it is generally conceived in Italian culture: home, protection, love, and joy of staying together.

(2) *Travels and Fusilli* (1988)

A man, surrounded by his children, is packing his case (so that we can understand that in a short he will leave). Then the product appears, as the voice-over says: "Fusilli Barilla. Made to tie together the finest flavours of your kitchen" (Barilla, 1988 [translation of mine]). So the camera moves back to the man and his family, shot while eating together and then on their way to the airport. When they are in the car, his daughter furtively enters *fusilli* (which is a particular type of pasta) in his jacket pocket, then giving a smile of complicity to her brother. After saying goodbye to his family, the man appears alone in a hotel room, while sadly looking out of the window. This is the moment when, finding *fusilli* in his pocket, he smiles, smelling the piece of pasta. Then the voice-over—as always, with the logo in superimposed—comes in to say: "Where there is Barilla there is a home."

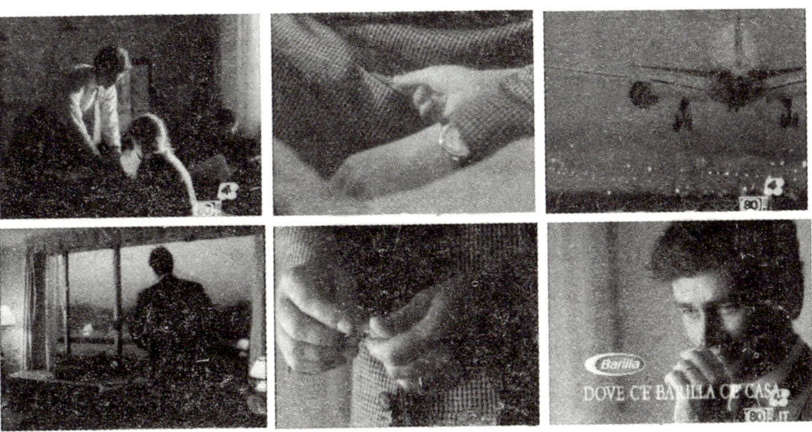

Figure 4 **Commercial** ***Travels and Fusilli***, 1988 (© **Barilla**)

It is very interesting, first of all, to consider the contrast between the warm colours of the early scenes, in which the man is happily surrounded by his family, and the cold colours of the final ones, in which the man is alone and sad. Cold colours, however, also refer to the usual packaging of Barilla: a packaging on which, such as in the commercial, suddenly breaks in the warm colour of pasta, which, unexpectedly found in the jacket pocket, makes the man feel at home and close to his family (to which also the wedding ring at the man's ring finger refers), despite the miles of distance. Finally, the slogan comes to argue that, regardless of one's physical location, Barilla makes it possible to feel at home.

(3) *Pasta and Conviviality* (1992)

The commercial opens at an airport, with the arrival of a Cambodian girl, accompanied by a flight attendant, and a man and a woman (probably her adoptive parents) who are waiting for her and cheerfully receiving her. The joy of the two adults, however, does not match that of the child, who appears rather lost and sad. Then we see the scene of a phone call to home, where an old lady surrounded by some children responds with joy to the phone. Suddenly the voice-over breaks in, saying "Spaghetti Barilla adds flavour to a new romance" (Barilla, 1992 [translation of mine]). Finally, the characters are sitting at the table, where the grandmother has just placed a pan full of *spaghetti* with tomato sauce and basil. The child enigmatically looks at the fork, a tool probably totally unknown to her, so the other child shows her how to use it, sucking with joy the last *spaghetti* from the just taken forkful. Then she imitates him, fully integrating the hilarity of the scene with a big smile. Finally the slogan and the logo can appear, reminding, thanks to the usual voice-over, that "Where there is Barilla there is a home" (ibid.).

Again, the contrast between warm and cool colours, now presented in alternating scenes, refers to the opposition between conviviality, community, and harmony, on the one hand, and loneliness and melancholy, on the other one. The first one is the case of the family gathered around the table or in other places (e. g. the airport). The second one is that of the little child, just introduced to a new and unknown world. Here again pasta breaks in to unify colours and moods, melting the initial coldness and marking the triumph of those basic values identified in the previous case: conviviality, sharing and joy of staying together. Such values are strong enough to erase not only the physical distance, as we saw in the case of *fusilli*, but also cultural differences.

Figure 5 **Commercial *Pasta and Conviviality***, 1992 (© **Barilla**)

Finally, it is also very interesting to note the tricoloured flag identifiable in the baking dish brought by the grandmother, which refers to the Italian tradition, stressing the *utopian* valorisation of the product, and making manifest the *positional* regime of the commercial. We assist to a situation where *one does what one is*, and what one is is "Italians", that is cheerful and friendly people, whose table and hearts are always open to the "Other".

5. The Commercials with Mina: *Family, Friendship, and Joy of Staying Together*

In 2009, Barilla entrusted the voice of its advertising campaigns to Mina, one of the icons of Italian music and culture.

It is very interesting to analyse the commercial dedicated to family: the commercial opens with a shot of some clothes and a teddy bear hanging out to dry. Meanwhile the singer's voice-over says: "It is our starting line; it is the family. Sometimes it protects you; sometimes it supports you. Sometimes you cannot wait to have one; sometimes you try to escape from it. You think that alone you will go further, but when you're there in the middle of your family, you realize that, to be truly free, you must have roots. *Lasagne Emiliane Barilla*, the joy of staying together." (Barilla, 2009 [translation of mine]) In the mean time, a series of scenes of familiar hilarity among more or less young people appear on the screen, leading to the last image, which depicts these characters all gathered around a table and the dish of pasta still steaming that the head of the family is putting on it. Then a red line surrounds them, stressing the importance of the friendly, relaxed atmosphere that has been created and announcing at the same time the logo Barilla, which will appear shortly afterwards.

Figure 6 ***Family, friendship, and joy of staying together***, 2009 (**© Barilla**).

Again, therefore, the emphasis is put on the values of conviviality and the "joy of staying together", as well as on tradition (the "roots"). Such tradition, however, is able to link the past, the present, and the future, as evidenced by the inclusion in the commercial of characters from different generations and the red ellipse that comes to surround them all, in addition to what is stated by the voice-over: it is precisely from the roots and family that can come individual freedom.

Here, then, Barilla emerges as the true Subject of the advertisement, marking the transition from the *positional* to the *multiperspective* regime, as Guido Ferraro (1998) would say: able to be for others what they want it to be, pasta meets different ages and desires, solving quite insuperable value oppositions and collecting at the same table both those who cannot wait to have a family and those who do not want anyone. Hence the equation presented in the final part: Barilla, seducer subject able to conciliate all, is reason and essence of that typically Italian "joy of staying together" celebrated by the hilarity of the final scene and by the tagline.

Ⅳ. Conclusions

Which forms of Italian spirit or identity, then, emerge from the so far described representations and valorisations of pasta? And how do similar combinations take place?

We have seen that, with the exception of the first two cases, the valorisation chosen for the advertised product is the *utopian* one: rather than on the basis of use values, pasta Barilla is celebrated according to the basic values of conviviality, sharing, and joy of staying together. It is crucial, in this sense, the figure of the house and the family, often recurring in the commercials analysed not only in their concrete manifestations (the space of the house, the wedding rings, the table, the family gathered around it), but also with reference to the ideas of domesticity, simplicity, and tradition.

But if, on the one hand, it is stressed the importance of roots, using a *positional* discourse (cf. Ferraro, 1998) that links the Italian traditional values of hospitality, family and domesticity; on the other hand, the intention is rather to highlight the relevance of spheres of values such as individual freedom, exclusivity, and sophistication.

After all, not necessarily must these two sides be in mutual opposition. As Franco la Cecla reminds, in fact,

> the Italian case is [...] unique. His "modest", home-made nature makes [...] the Italian cuisine [...] a cuisine that becomes at one point "Haute Cuisine" by exaggerating its "simplicity", "soberness", its *simple living* (1998: 73 [translation of mine]).

At this point, therefore, it should not surprise too much the combination established between pasta and class restaurants in the commercial by Fellini (cf. § 2. 3).

And with regard to the conflict between the individual and the family, tradition and innovation, old and new generations, however, it seems to be functional, as we have seen, to express the seductive extent of the product:

capable of grasping the desires of other people and breaking into their narrative programs (cf. Greimas, 1966) as a value-object (Ferraro, 1998), pasta emerges as a seducer subject that is in constant fluctuation between use and basic values, objective and subjective dimension, absolute and relative positions. This leads to a situation that could be described making reference to what Roland Barthes describes as the moment of love encounter: "a gradual discovery (and a kind of verification) of affinities, complicities, and intimacies" in which "at every moment, [one] discover[s] in the other another [oneself]" (1977: 198—99).

A moment when the same previously mentioned Nando Moriconi, having fallen in love with the American way of life, recognising American food as a "rubbish" for cats, mice, and bugs, *re*-discovers himself as fully Italian while eating the *macaroni* cooked by his mom. A moment when the entire Italian community emigrated abroad, having to redefine itself as well as to define itself to the eyes of the Other, *re*-discovers its identity in pasta and in the universe of values in which its preparation as well as its consumption are inscribed: the tradition, the joy of staying together, domesticity, simplicity, sharing, and the ability to adapt to changeable situations. Because we should not forget that, "such as language, food defines man in his appropriation of himself and of the world surrounding him" (Marin, 1986: 30 [translation of mine]).

References:

Alighieri, D., (1292—1293). *Vita Nova*, in G. B. Giuliani, ed. (1863): 1—215.

Artusi, P., (1891). *La scienza in cucina e l'arte di mangiare bene*. Florence: Landi.

Barthes, R., (1977). *Fragments d'un discours amoureux*. Paris: Editions du Seuil. English Translation (1978) *A Lover's Discourse: Fragments*. New York: Hill and Wang.

Camporesi, P., (1970). Introduction to P. Artusi (1891), XV—LXXVIII.

Capatti, A., Montanari, M., (1999). *La cucina italiana: storia di una cultura*. Rome: GLF Editori Laterza.

Cook, I., Crang, P., (1996). "The World on a Plate: Culinary, Culture, Displacement and Geographical Knowledge", *Journal of Material Culture*. 1 (2): 131—153.

Ferraro, G., ed., (1998). *L'emporio dei segni*. Rome: Meltemi.

Floch, J.-M., (1983). "Le carré sémiotique. Pour une topographie du sens", *Sémiotique*

& *Publicité II*. Paris: Institut d'Etudes et de Recherches sur la Publicité , pp. 57—79.

——, (1990). *Sémiotique, marketing et communication*. Paris: PUF.

Galli della Loggia, E. (1998). Introduction to F. La Cecla (1998) , I—II.

Greimas, A. J. , (1966). *Sémantique structurale: Recherche de méthode*. Paris: Larousse.

Giuliani, G. B. , ed. , (1983). *La Vita Nuova e il Canzoniere*. Florence: Barbera.

La Cecla, F. , (1998). *La pasta e la pizza*. Bologna: Il mulino.

Leone, M. , ed. , (2011). *Immaginario / Imaginary—Lexia*, 7—8. Turin: Aracne.

Marin, L. , (1986). *La parole mangée et autres essais théologico — politiques*. Paris: Méridiens Klincksieck.

Montanari, M. , (2010). *L'identità italiana in cucina*. Rome—Bari: Laterza.

Ortoleva, P. , (1992). *La tradizione e l'abbondanza. Riflessioni sulla cucina degli italiani d'America*. Turin: Edizioni della Fondazione Giovanni Agnelli.

Rai Educational, (2011). "La storia siamo noi". Retrieved from<www. lastoriasiamonoi. rai. it/puntata. aspx?id=416. x. >.

Sereni, E. , (1958). "I napoletani da 'mangiafoglia' a 'mangiamaccheroni'. Note di storia di alimentazionenel Mezzogiorno", *Cronache Meridionali* (4): 272—295; (5): 351—377; (6): 398—422.

Serventi, S. , Sabban, F. , (2000). *La pasta. Storia e cultura di un cibo universale*. Rome: Laterza.

Sorcinelli, P. , (1999) *Gli italiani e il cibo: dalla polenta ai cracker*. Milan: Mondadori.

Teti, V. , (1999) *Il colore del cibo. Geografia, mito e realtà dell'alimentazione mediterranea*. Rome: Meltemi.

Volli, U. , (2011). "L'immaginario delle origini", *Immaginario / Imaginary—Lexia*, 7—8, 31—61.

Filmography and Analysed Commercials:

Barilla, (1958). *Carosello*. Retrieved from <http://www. youtube. com/watch? v = 974r1GTWrB8>.

Barilla, (1998). *Fusilli Barilla*. Retrieved from <http://www. youtube. com/watch?v= XZkpr09Rnrc>.

Barilla, (2009). *Lasagne Emiliane Barilla*. Retrieved from <http://www. youtube. com/watch?v=9GcEQd7sNGo>.

Barilla, (1987). *La bambina con il keeway giallo*. Retrieved from <http://www. youtube. com/watch?v=giwQmBfKNEg>.

Barilla, (1992). *Spaghetti Barilla*. Retrieved from <http://www. youtube. com/watch?v =kvAht2F8nzs>.

Fellini, F. , (1986). *Alta società—Rigatoni Barilla* [Video]. Retrieved from<http://

www. youtube. com/watch?v=we3ozyRfsJE>.
Steno, (1954). *Un americano a Roma* [Movie].

Author:

Simona Stano, Ph. D. candidate in Sciences of Language and Communication at the University of Turin and in Science of Communication at the "Università della Svizzera Italiana". He currently focuses on semiotics of food and cultural identity, visual and urban studies, semiotics of culture, food studies, and media.

作者简介:

西蒙娜·斯坦诺，都灵大学语言与传播学及提契诺大学传播学博士，研究方向为食品与文化身份、城市视觉、文化符号学、食品研究、媒介研究。

E-mail: simona. stano@gmail. com

中国现代幻想文学叙述研究之构想

方　芳

摘要：从20世纪90年代末至今，幻想文学在全球范围内呈现出繁荣的态势，在中国尤甚。本文对这种文学现象进行了概括，分析了叙述学在幻想文学研究领域的优势，在总结前人理论的基础上尝试对中国现代幻想文学的叙述研究提出几点构想。

关键词：幻想文学，叙述学，述真，世界建构，跨媒介叙述

A Narratological Study of Modern Chinese Fantastic Literature

Fang Fang

Abstract: Since the late 1990s, there has been an astonishing boom of fantastic literature around the word, paricularly in china. Giving a description of this phenomenon, this paper pvovides a narratological analysis of the genre, making a critical survey of the field. Summing up the theoretical contributions by other narratologists, this paper makes some suggestions to the future studies on modern Chinese fantastic literature.

Key words: fantastic literature, narratology, veridiction, world-building, narrative across media

一、幻想文学潮及其国际影响力

20世纪90年代末，幻想文学在全球范围内掀起一股热潮，至今仍未减势。

在欧美文学领域，英美的奇幻文学创作继续强势推进。美国奇幻作家乔治·马丁（Geoger Raymond Richard Martin）有“史诗奇幻”之称的《冰与火之歌》（*A Song of Ice and Fire*）从1996年最初问世起就一直引领着出版界的狂潮，马丁被美国《时代》杂志评选为2011年影响世界的一百人。英国作家罗琳于90年代末期创作的《哈利·波特》（*Harry Potter*）系列陆续被翻译成74种语言，在全世界两百多个国家累计销量达5亿多册，位列史上非宗教、市场销售类图书首位。英国奇幻作家柴纳·米耶维（China Miéville）以融推理、奇幻和科幻为一炉的“新怪谭”（New Weird）风格奠定国际声誉，从《鼠王》（*King Rat*，1998）到《伪伦敦》（*Un Lun Dun*，2011），其作品屡获雨果奖、世界奇幻奖、阿瑟·克拉克奖等重要国际幻想文学奖项。在电影领域，幻想文学更是大放异彩。《黑客帝国》（1999—2003）、《魔戒》（2001—2003）、《哈利·波特》（2002—2010）、《纳尼亚传奇》（2005—2011）、《变形金刚》（2007—2011）、《第九区》（2009）、《阿凡达》（2009）、《盗梦空间》（2010）、《源代码》（2011）、《云图》（2012）、《地心引力》（2013）……各种类型的幻想电影风起云涌，不断刷新受众的想象极限。

在亚洲文学领域，中国作家莫言凭借带有神话及寓言色彩的《生死疲劳》等作品荣获2012年度的诺贝尔文学奖，其获奖理由为莫言“用魔幻现实主义的写作手法，将民间故事、历史事件与当代背景融为一体”，评委会在授奖词中称“莫言的想象力翔越了人类存在的全部”。而同时受到评委会青睐的还有日本作家村上春树，一位同样以卓越的想象力著称的作家。其《世界尽头与冷酷仙境》《寻羊历险记》《奇鸟行状录》《海边的卡夫卡》等作品创造出一个个现实与幻想融合的世界。作为严肃文学评判的风向标，诺奖似乎传达出一个信息：幻想文学，或者带有幻想因素的文学作品也开始进入了阳春白雪的视野。在科幻领域，中国科幻领军人物刘慈欣在2006—2010年间创作的《三体》三部曲，被业界人士认为比肩于阿西莫夫的《基地》三部曲，将中国的科幻创作推向世界的高度。此外，作为中国独有的幻想文学类型，武侠小说自诞生起一直处于文坛的边缘位置，直至90年代才开始迅速升温，精英知识分子开始研究武侠，金庸等作家的作品得以进入经典的殿堂，这说明，武侠小说得到了新的评估，不再仅仅是消遣之作。而带有神话和武侠色彩的电影也层出不穷，如《青蛇》（1993）、《风云之雄霸天下》（1998）、《卧虎藏龙》（2000）、《蜀山传》（2001）、《英雄》（2002）、《神话》（2005）、《无极》（2005）、《画皮》（2008）、《狄仁杰之通天帝国》（2010）、《少年派的奇幻漂流》（2012）等均取得了不凡的票房成绩。

此外，随着动漫与游戏这两大文化产业的不断升级和成熟，这两个备受幻想文学影响的领域也不再仅仅被青少年青睐，而是赢得了更多成年人的市场。

这些领域及行业的动向都说明了，从20世纪末迄今，在全球范围内，人们对幻想文学及与之相关的文化产业出现了旺盛的需求，且有增无减，促成了创作与市场的双赢。并且，幻想文学及其带动的相关文化产业已经成为文化市场的强心剂，也成为促进各国文学、文化交流的新名片。我国目前对国产动漫产业的强力扶持就并非偶然之举。那么，幻想文学在这个阶段异军突起的原因是什么呢？它又给文学创作和研究提出了哪些新问题呢？

二、幻想文学在当代的认识论意义

意义不在场的时候才需要符号，我们必须探究，是什么催生了幻想文学的虚拟世界？这涉及幻想文学的认识论意义，时代不同，认识论的意义也不同。如果说远古的幻想文学如《山海经》主要缘于人类对于自然的不可知的敬畏，其后在佛家与道家思想的影响下出现了对现实世界的投射与反思，形成《西游记》《镜花缘》等寓言性的写作，那么，当代幻想文学如武侠及“新神话主义”创作的态度就体现了现代人对世界认识的根本性偏差。启蒙理性的一个显著的后果就是经验世界与超验世界的断裂，现代人的认识论框架局限于经验世界，从而排除一切非经验性真理。当代幻想文学正是在这一层面上反思理性主义的，它试图超越经验“现实”，恢复人们对超验世界的意识，以帮助现代人摆脱物质世界的限制，获得一定意义上的超脱。

除了超越现实之外，幻想文学还可以以其独特的方式关涉现实。关于“幻想文学”最宽泛的定义莫过于弗莱提出的“在幻想世界中的人物可以做任何事”，那么，我们并不难理解为什么每个时代都需要幻想。在现实世界，正义并不总能战胜邪恶，好人并不一定有好报，梦想常常破灭，爱情难以圆满，人不能超越自然法则，也无法和其他生命形态交流。而在幻想世界里，人神共处，万物有灵，正义必然得到伸张，有情人终成眷属。即便是关于成长的题材中，主人公受尽磨难，却是“天将降大任于斯人”的磨难，并不灭绝希望，通常有个好的结局，也就是托尔金所谓的“善灾”（eucatastrophe）。并且，幻想文学常常以寓言的形式，以讽喻或戏谑的态度批评现实世界的阴暗面，虽不是秉笔直书，但却可以使人对号入座；而现实主义文学在处理此类题材时若写得过于隐晦，也许会被批评为不够“现实”。因此，幻想文学也被称为“成年人的童话”。

此外，幻想文学不仅是对现实的“补充”，还在更深层的意义上与现实对抗。社会批判学家阿多诺（Adorno）认为，艺术的本质就在于幻想，而幻想的本质在于想象力，是对现实世界的否定性认识。艺术是对尚未存在的东西的把握，现代艺术追求的是那种尚不存在的东西，从而，艺术是对现实世界的疏离和否定，现代艺术是对完满的感性外观的扬弃。基于此，文艺理论家赛普斯（Jack Zipes）认为如今的幻想文学是“令人绝望的”，因为我们曾经在幻想文学中求得对世界的认识，“正是通过建立在个人经验之上的虚构的想象，我们得以掌握、解释、改变以及评判现实”。而今，“它们每时每刻都在被现实利用，即便是在梦中”。幻想文学及其副产品所带来的巨大的经济效益使其在某种程度上成为意识形态与消费主义的工具，而人们看奇幻，在很大程度上不过是为了消遣。在这些力量的共同作用下，幻想文学沦为垃圾速食。但是，从幻想（fantasy）的词源义出发，他同时也指出，幻想的本义就是“显现”和“使……被看见”，是“一种使人产生错觉的想象或幻觉，表现并不存在的事物的一种能力或结果，对并不实存之物的想象”，是一种可以“无中生有并使其艺术化”的能力。① 所以，它的本质就是对“实存之物”，也就是对现实的反抗，是化陈词滥调之腐朽为神奇的力量，并因此获取无尽的生命力。或许，这才是幻想文学为何在当代如此重要的原因。

三、西方对幻想文学的叙述学研究

或许，我们早已远离了文学的“外部研究”和“内部研究”之争。如今，从作者传记、心理学、思想潮流、社会环境因素、与其他艺术的关系等角度研究文学作品的外部研究，与从文体、修辞、叙述特征、类型等角度研究文学的内部研究，并没有轻重与高下之别。我们需要做的，是针对不同的研究对象寻找合适的研究方式。而对于幻想文学而言，大概没有比叙述学和符号学更为适合的研究方式，因为对于这种将虚构推向极致的文学，形式方面的要素已成为其重中之重。或者，更确切地说，幻想文学充分证明了索绪尔提出的比喻，他说符号的能指与所指如同一枚硬币的两面，须臾不可分离。在研究所谓现实主义文学作品的时候，我们通常会忽略这一点，似乎研究叙述就可以搁置内容，研究意义就可以暂时不考虑形式。这是因为，我们自认为对于现实世界是如此熟悉，以至于常常脱离字词去思考意义，哪怕这意义在

---

① Jack Zipes, *Why Fantasy Matters Too Much*, CLCWeb, *Comparative Literature and Culture*, Purdue University Press, vol. 10, issue 4 (December 2008), article 3.

很大程度上是哲学、心理学或者伦理学的意义，而这种做法在研究幻想作品时就显然行不通了。面对一个完全由作者的想象构筑的世界，如果我们脱离了文学表现形式，便无从认识这个世界。

20世纪中后期，对于幻想文学进行叙述学研究的著作逐渐呈现出来，在对幻想文学的早期研究中，比较有代表性的是托多罗夫、曼勒等人的著述。托多罗夫第一次自觉地将幻想文学作为一种类型（genre）进行考察，他的《对于幻想文学的结构主义分析》[①] 呈现出鲜明而严肃的结构主义的态度。在这本小说诗学中，托多罗夫试图同时考察文学的一般理论及一种特殊的类型，试图为他所关注的各类幻想文学文本的结构性特征找到语言学的基础。通过对《驴皮记》（*The Magic Skin*）、《一千零一夜》（*The Arabian Nights*）、《魔鬼恋人》（*Le Diable Amoureux*）等具体作品的分析以及对于现存理论，如弗莱（Frye）神话原型理论等的纠偏，托多罗夫往返于幻想文学自身的理论以及元理论的建构之间，提出了关于类型研究的两个重要的概念，即历史类型（historical genres）和理论类型（theoretical genres），他认为一个批评家应该在理论与历史、理念与事实之间往返，是文学类型研究的重要方法。

在曼勒的《现代幻想》中，类型读者的概念被进一步引入。为什么幻想作品的读者“应该”对虚拟世界中的超自然成分“至少在一定程度上感到熟悉”[②] 呢？这里的“熟悉”（familiar）莫如说是“亲切”，因为只有对这些在现实世界中的“不可能存在”感到“亲切”的读者才乐于享受这种“惊奇感”（wonder），而另外一些读者也许会感到荒谬和不知所云。进一步，“惊奇感”缘何而生？曼勒谈到了距离，即“真实与幻想世界、自然与超自然之间的距离”[③]，并认为这是幻想意义呈现的基本问题。这里的真实是现实世界的真实，而惊奇感正源于与此真实相背离的幻想世界的“真实”。

此后，大量学者对幻想文学进行了叙述学及符号学方面的研究。罗斯玛丽·杰克逊的《幻想：颠覆性的文学》[④] 试图将幻想文学定义为一种特殊的叙述。她通过引入精神分析的理论对托多罗夫的思想体系作了进一步的延伸，

---

① Tzvetan Todorov, *The Fantastic: A Structural Approach to A Literary Genre*, trans., Richard Howard. Ithaca: Cornell University Press, 1975.

② C. N. Manlove, *Modern Fantasy—Five Studies*. Cambridge: Cambridge University Press, 1975, p. 1.

③ C. N. Manlove, *Modern Fantasy—Five Studies* Cambridge: Cambridge University Press, 1975, p. 258.

④ Rosemary Jackson, *Fantasy: The Literature of Subversion*. Massachusetts: Methuen Company, 1981.

将幻想视为一种无意识冲动的表达，强调了弗洛伊德以降的精神分析学家关于双重/多重自我、镜像、变形、身体瓦解等方面的学说。布鲁克－罗丝在《虚构的修辞：对幻想的叙述以及结构研究》① 中引入了俄国形式主义及结构主义的理论，考察幻想小说在叙述与结构方面与现实主义小说的本质区别。法拉·孟德尔颂的《幻想修辞学》② 通过分析创作者与幻想世界的关系区分出幻想的四种类型：探索式（portal-quest）、沉浸式（immersive）、侵入式（intrusion）以及阈限式（luminal）。借由这套体系，孟德尔颂认为，正是作者对创作类型的选择决定了他最终的写作体裁。

随着幻想文学主题的不断演变以及表现形式的丰富，一些跨学科的前沿问题陆续进入幻想叙述的研究视野，比如虚构述真的问题、可能世界的问题，以及跨媒介叙述的问题，对目前国内的幻想文学研究都具有极大的启发意义。

四、当代中国幻想文学叙述学研究现状及构想

中国拥有丰富的奇幻文学资源，上古神话有《山海经》，至六朝出现志怪奇谭，之后有唐传奇、明清神魔小说，进入现代后则出现武侠小说，当代则有科幻以及融神话、武侠、怪谈为一体的奇幻小说。可以说，中国的幻想文学创作从未中断过。而孕育于老庄道教、佛教禅宗等思想中的中国式幻想思维也在本土与外来文化的碰撞与激荡中不断生长，成为儒教正统文化的有力补充。儒道释三教合流，方使中华文化焕发出独特辉光。关于中国传统文化及思想源流的研究著述甚多，然而在文学领域，幻想文学相较于主流文学受到的关注却远远不够，现有的著述也大多采用文献考古、宗教溯源等方法，在形式论研究方面明显滞后于西方。

可喜的是，国内已经有学者开始了这方面的认真探求。在宏观理论的建构方面，当推王阳的《虚拟世界的空间与意义》③ 和张新军的《可能世界叙事学》④。前者是对作者之前在《小说艺术形式分析——叙事学研究》中所提出的叙事学理论的发展，该书在与国内外叙事理论的对话中提出了自己的文学符号学思想，探讨了文本意义结构的形式规则，从多个侧面对文学文本的符号结构和文本内外诸种可能世界的主体、意义及关系进行了描述。后者借

---

① Christine Brooke-Rose, *A Rhetoric of the Unreal: Studies in Narrative and Structure, Especially of the Fantastic*. Cambridge: Cambridge University Press, 1983.

② Farah Mendlesohn, *Rhetorics of Fantasy*. Connecticut: Wesleyan University Press, 2008.

③ 王阳：《虚拟世界的空间与意义》，宁夏人民出版社，2006 年。

④ 张新军：《可能世界叙事学》，苏州大学出版社，2011 年。

用可能世界与量子理论的相关思想，建构“可能世界叙事学”的理论模型，从虚构性、叙事性、经验性三个方面描述叙事虚构世界与现实世界的心理表征之间的互动关系。两本著作的共同点在于其目的都是要建构一个新的模态逻辑系统，以超越和补充传统文学审美偏重直觉、感悟的局限。应该说，这两本著作在探讨虚构叙述方面具有重要的开拓性的意义。

以前人的理论贡献为基础，在此我仅提出几点对于目前国内幻想文学叙述研究的构想。

（一）虚构的述真：“假戏真看”与“假戏假看”

在幻想文学的研究领域，托多罗夫较早对幻想文学进行较为系统的叙述学研究，并取得突破性进展。今天我们再回过头去看托氏的观点，虽然明显表现出时代与结构主义的局限性，但他的确敏锐地抓住了幻想文学的一些核心特质，为我们今天的研究奠定了方向性的基础，也留下了空间。

托多罗夫认为幻想文学的特质就是“一个只了解自然法则的人在面对明显的超自然事件时所经历的犹疑”[①]。这里的“犹疑”（hesitation）指人物和读者在“真”与“假”之间的摇摆和徘徊，实际上已经触及虚构如何述真这个实质问题。赵毅衡在论述符号“述真”时曾指出，符号可以用来“说谎”，并由此提出“说谎者”（符号发送者）与接受者之间的八种类型。其中，由成功营造艺术文本的“逼真性”（verisimilitude）而使符号接收者“信以为真”的类型称为“假戏真看”型；而作者与读者达成某种默契，分别分裂出一个人格进入文本游戏，“将计就计”“以伪为伪”的类型称为“假戏假看”型，其中镶嵌了“真戏真看”的诚意正解的格局。[②] 这两种类型便是艺术符号表意过程的主要类型。实际上，虚构世界与现实世界之间的“疏离”与“对应”正是营造艺术作品“逼真性”和构建作者与读者默契的两面，幻想文学的审美张力即由这两面的相互拉扯而实现。

有论者在探讨梦意识时曾引入“格位”的概念，认为做梦的我与梦中之我虽然是两个不同的我，但却分享着同一个格位。作者并未对“格位”这个概念多加解释，或许可以按字面意义和上下文理解为“安放人格的位置”：“某些情况下，现实之我完全占据着格位；在另一些情况下，它则完全让位于

---

① Tzvetan Todorov: *The Fantastic: A Structural Approach to A Literary Genre*, trans., Richard Howard. Ithaca. Cornell University Press, 1975, p. 25.

② 赵毅衡：《符号学：原理与推演》，南京大学出版社，2011 年，第 273 页。

虚构之我；还存在着两个我以不同的方式同时占据格位的情况。”① 当现实之我完全占据格位时，人处于清醒状态；当虚构之我完全占据格位时，人完全进入梦境；当两者同时占据格位时，产生“清明之梦”（lucid dream）的现象，即“我知道我在做梦”。假若我们同意在符号表意接受过程中产生了人格分裂的说法，那么“述真”与梦意识在结构上便呈现出类似的特征。当读者没有（或没能）分裂出一个人格进入文本中的某个视角，即读者自我完全占据格位时，便呈现出“拒绝接受”表意的类型；当读者分裂出的人格（相当于虚构之我）进入文本中的某个视角并完全占据格位时，便呈现出“假戏真看”的类型；当分裂出的人格与自我同时占据格位时，便呈现出“假戏假看”的类型。

（二）世界建构

在讨论幻想文学这一类型时，托多罗夫反复强调的一个问题是形式与内容的不可分割，必须要打破形式与内容之间的差异性。他提出：“在文学中，我们表达了什么和用什么方式表达是同样重要的，‘说了什么’和‘怎样说’同样重要，反之亦然……但是，我们不能想当然地认为，在这两种倾向的混合状态中找到平衡点就是正确的态度，我们并不是要在形式与内容的研究之间找到一个合理的比例。……结构这个概念的‘存在理由’之一即在于此：超越旧有的形式与内容之间的分裂，以便将作品视为一个整体，并且是一个动态的统一体。”② 托多罗夫非常敏感地意识到了在奇幻这一领域中，形式与内容之间的微妙的关系，奇幻这一类型也充分证明了，托氏反对文学“释义学”是言之有理的。在阅读奇幻的过程中，我们更关注的是作者“创造”了什么，而不是“揭示”了什么。而“创造了什么”（说了什么）与“如何创造”（怎样说）的确是息息相关的。

遗憾的是，受研究对象与方法论的限制，托氏虽然提出了这个问题，却没有将它解决好。在幻想文学作品中，引发读者犹疑或者惊奇的情绪的，已经超越了托氏提出的“自我主题”（变形，物我两忘）和“他者主题”（欲望与暴力奇观），而是超自然的世界本身。也就是说，对于当代的幻想文学创作来说，如何去界定以及建构一个幻想世界是首要的任务。在讨论可能世界理

---

① 高松：《梦意识现象学初探——关于想象、梦与超越论现象学》，《现代哲学》，2007 年第 6 期。

② Tzvetan Todorov, *The Fantastic: A Structural Approach to A Literary Genre*, trans., Richard Howard. Ithaca: Cornell University Press, 1975, pp. 93–94.

论时，赵毅衡提出，“虚构世界是心智构成的，是想象力的产物，因此虚构文本再现的世界是一个‘三界通达’的混杂世界”[①]，即一个由可能世界、不可能世界和实在世界共同构筑的世界。讨论世界建构，必须厘清三界之间的关系。世界建构（world building）即指用一套哲学理念，创造出一个既明显区别于现实世界但又有现实世界投射的可能世界/不可能世界的过程。这是一个大问题，此处单以对细节量的处理论之。

根据幻想世界时间轴向的不同，中国现代幻想文学的世界大概呈现出三分的局面：指向古代，以武侠为代表，如金庸的江湖世界；指向当代，以憍妄现实主义为代表，如莫言的高密乡；指向未来，以科幻为代表，如刘慈欣的“三体”。这三种世界的形态与特征虽各有不同，但有一点是相同的，即要无中生有造出一个世界，并让它有真实感，那么文本势必要拥有足够的细节量。细节饱和度是实在世界区别于异世界的特征之一。异世界的细节量无论怎样增加，永远无法与现实世界的细节饱和程度相匹敌，但异世界却能够通过局部细节量的渲染与饱和而显得“真实”，幻想文学的魅力正在于通过强有力的局部细节饱和让读者去相信不可能之物。麒麟、凤凰、夔牛、赑屃等神兽原本只是以无发送符号的形式存在，却在各类幻想故事中由于强有力的细节表现而让人觉得实有其物。武侠小说中的一招一式在现实中也不可能发生，却因为作者的刻意设计而让人觉得过瘾、好看。此外，幻想往往着力以细节渲染人物超越常人的感官能力，如武侠中的“听风辨形”、“聚音成线”等，使现实中的不可能成为想象中的可能。

细节饱和度与细节量有一定的关系，但并不一定成正比。也就是说，并不是细节量越大，细节饱和度就一定更高。如一张清明上河图和一张只有一丝白云的天空的照片，后一张图片的细节饱和度可能更高，因为它更“真实”。让人感觉“真实”的原因在于信息量达到了一定程度，而且意义的传达没有受阻。这说明，信息量与细节量也不一定成正比，某些信息量也许通过“空缺”产生，比如国画的“留白”，大量的信息通过“象外之象”与联想生成。由此，我们便可以解释，为什么一部设计繁复、细节密度大的巨著可以构筑世界（如《西游记》），而“一沙一世界”也可以传达出“世界”的意味。

（三）跨媒介叙述

随着科技的不断发展进步，纸质图书在文学承载与传播上占有绝对优势

---

① 赵毅衡，《三界通达：用可能世界理论来解释虚构与现实的关系》，《兰州大学学报》（社会科学版），2013 年第 41 卷第 2 期。

的时代已经过去。如今网络写手风起云涌，经由小说改编而成的电影、电视、游戏、动漫等也成为意义播散更为广泛、迅速的新兴媒介。如今，人们的文学阅读与欣赏习惯已从昔日的以纸质图书阅读为主变为今天的以数码阅读与观赏为主，在幻想文学领域尤为明显，光怪陆离的幻想世界在电影与游戏的特效中带给了观众和玩家远远超越纸质图书的体验。在研究幻想文学，尤其是现当代的幻想文学时，必须要重视新媒介的独特意义。新媒介突破了传统纸质图书以文字作为主要载体的形式，融图像、声音、电脑特效等为一体，文学的叙述方式与意义的生成方式得到了极大的拓展。在“语言学转向”以及“叙述学转向”之后，“数码的转向”（digital turn）成为学界研究的新领域。“数码的转向”不仅使人们认识到什么是“新媒介”，对传统媒介对于思维的“构形”功能也进行了重估。跨媒介叙述要解决的几个基本问题是：叙述的意义如何通过语言外的媒介建构？在一个“多媒介”的作品中，不同类型的符号是如何协调起作用的？新媒介的诞生创造了哪些新的叙述形式？

跨媒介叙述的确为当代的叙述学研究开拓了更为广阔的视野。同样是《西游记》中的“大闹天宫”的故事，可以纸质图书、电影、电视剧、动漫、游戏等多种形式表现出来，我们能否归纳出它们各自的叙述语法，并且，每种媒介表意的独特性何在？或者，李安导演的《卧虎藏龙》，其运镜、配乐、灯光、布景、服装造型等，如何完成了“合谋”，讲述出一个“中国的武侠故事”？再比如，张系国的科幻小说《城》里的地图是否体现出叙述的功能？尚有大量课题可以讨论，此处不再赘述。

作者简介：

方芳，四川大学文学与新闻学院在读博士，符号学—传媒学研究所成员，昆明理工大学讲师。研究方向为现代华语奇幻文学的符号学研究。

Author:

Fang Fang, Ph. D. Candidate of Collage of Literature and Journalism, Sichuan University Lecture in Kunming University of Science and Technology, mainber of the ISMS Research Team. Her research mainly focuses on semiotic studies of modern Chinese fantastic literature.

E-mail: soleil99@163. com

2013年中国符号学年度发展报告

刘一鸣　齐千里

摘要：本文从专著、论文、会议三方面来呈现2013年中国符号学发展状况，并从理论和应用两个维度入手，对上述三方面进行分析，总结出2013年度中国符号学发展的基本特征：符号学学科化趋势进一步加强，符号学学科门类进一步增加，符号学理论探索则相对较少。

关键词：符号学，发展状况，年度报告

2013 Annual Report of Chinese Semiotics Studies

Liu Yiming　Qi Qianli

Abstract: This paper endeavors to sketch the development of the Chinese semiotic studies in 2013. After reviewing selected papers, monographs and academic conferences, and studying the activities in semiotic application and theory, this study generalized a trend of Chinese semiotics: semiotic disciplines has been rapidly developed; meanwhile, the theoretical study of semiotics is still not adequate.

Key word: semiotics, development, mannual report

就目前来说，中国符号学仍处于并将长期处于发展的过程中。发展，即意味着进步的可能。在这样的局势下，总结学科现有得失，看清学科大致发展趋势，将有力地保证其在未来向前、向上地发展。这样看来，将编写中国符号学学科总结的年度发展报告作为例行事宜，是亟待我们中国符号学人重视的必行之事。

一、2013年中国符号学发展情况扫描

（一）专著

专著，是学术创造力的集中体现，是学科发展的关键所在。整个2013年，中国符号学界出版了20余本符号学相关专著或译著。[①] 这些著作或是直接涉及符号学的研究，如保罗·科布利的《劳特利奇符号学指南》[②]；或是用符号学方法讨论某一具体问题的著作，如徐瑞的《〈周易〉符号学概论》[③]，舒惠芳的《人造天书——民俗文化中的神秘符号》[④]。同去年相比，今年的专著对符号学的研究更细致，层面更广，层次更深，符号学正在对更多门类的学科产生着影响，而对于符号学早已涉及的学科，又在过去的基础上有了新的、更深入的讨论。

值得注意的是，四川大学符号学-传媒学研究所与四川大学出版社在2013年底开始了两套大型丛书——《中国符号学丛书》（唐小林主编）、《当代符号学译丛》（赵毅衡主编）的出版合作。这两套丛书有几十本的规模，将在2016年之前陆续面世。其中赵毅衡多年的研究成果《广义叙述学：叙述的符号学研究》已在2013年12月出版，作为这两套丛书的第一本，奉献给读书界和学界。这是将叙述学、符号学两个学科结合起来的第一本书，值得关注。

（二）论文

论文是反映符号学研究发展最为直接和迅速的信息。而在数据库的选择方面，由于“中国知网”（CNKI）是国内较完善、较权威，并具有极大影响力的数据库，所以本文延续了去年的方法[⑤]，依旧是以“知网”作为本次数据搜索、采集、整理的平台。而在检索关键词的选择方面，本文与去年不同，只选取了“符号学”作为检索关键词，而未选用“符号”。这是由于以“符号”为主题的文章大多数与符号学并无关联。“符号”一词几乎可以作为任何

---

① 本报告所统计的专著、论文指的是2013年1月至11月中旬中国大陆的符号学研究成果，因时间和资料的限制，未能覆盖到台湾和香港地区，特此说明。

② ［英］保罗·科布利：《劳特利奇符号学指南》，周劲松、赵毅衡译，南京大学出版社，2013年。

③ 徐瑞：《〈周易〉符号学概论》，上海科学技术文献出版社，2013年。

④ 舒惠芳：《人造天书——民俗文化中的神秘符号》，中国财富出版社，2013年。

⑤ 饶广祥：《2012年中国符号学发展报告》，《符号与传媒》（总第6辑），四川大学出版社，2013年。

学科的关键词，如电信技术学科中的“符号定时”“符号率”，计算机学科中的“地图符号”“符号执行”等。但上述这些看似与符号学无关的学科，又的确有关于符号学的讨论，且人文社科论文分类下以“符号”为关键词检索出的论文，也并不都涉及符号学，所以无法贸然用学科来进行筛选。不分学科，以人工统计，由于论文量过大（超过 1 万），也并非现实的选择。而以“符号学”作为检索关键词，虽有可能漏掉少数有关符号学的讨论，但由于基数较大，故整体上不会过多影响对符号学学科分布情况、总体发展趋势的分析。

在“中国知网”中，以“符号学”为主题搜索全年文献（2013 年 1 月 1 日至 2013 年 11 月 12 日），一共搜到 708 篇文章，高于去年同期（648 篇），根据“中国知网”的学科分类，在这 708 篇以“符号学”为主题的文章中，中国语言文字学类别的文章最多，有 136 篇；其次是美术、书法、雕塑与摄影学科，一共有 98 篇；新闻与传媒类以 67 篇位居第三。排名第 4 至第 10 位的学科分别为：戏剧电影与电视艺术（52 篇）、世界文学（52 篇）、外国语言文字（52 篇）、建筑科学与工程（39 篇）、文艺理论（31 篇）、中国文学（27 篇）、文化（26 篇）。这些也的确是与符号学关联较紧密的学科。此外，还有轻工业手工业类 21 篇，哲学类 18 篇，工业通用技术及设备类 17 篇，旅游类 17 篇，社会及统计学类 13 篇，音乐舞蹈类 12 篇，贸易经济类 11 篇，教育理论与教育管理类 8 篇，计算机软件及计算机应用类 7 篇，中等教育类 6 篇，体育类 6 篇，企业经济类 5 篇，电信技术类 5 篇，行政学及国家行政管理类 5 篇，高等教育类 4 篇，心理学类 4 篇，民族学类 4 篇，人物传记类 4 篇，宗教类 3 篇，伦理学类 3 篇，工业经济类 3 篇，美学类 3 篇，出版类 2 篇，政治学类 2 篇，经济理论及经济思想史类 2 篇，一般服务业类 2 篇，民商法类 2 篇，医学教育与医学边缘学科类 2 篇，物理学类 2 篇。

（三）学术会议、学科建设方面

从整体情况看，今年符号学研讨活动较为活跃，全年举办了多场以“符号学”为主题的会议、研讨会，这些会议为分布在各地的符号学学者提供了一个面对面交流的机会。通过这些会议，学者们交流学术心得，探讨学术成果，交换学术意见，这种积极的学术沟通对符号学的发展很有益处。复旦大学在 2013 年一共召开了两次以“符号学”为主题的会议、研讨会，分别为 4 月的“符号学研讨会：符号/逻辑方阵与文学意义”和 11 月的“符号与记忆”研讨会。两次会议都邀请了来自海峡两岸的学者对符号学学术活动进行深刻探讨，不同思想的交流和碰撞，为符号学研究注入了新的生命力。另外，

2013年5月19日和6月30日分别于阿坝和兰州召开的“符号学-叙述学”圆桌会议和“西北青年符号学-传媒学”座谈会上，与会者们就各种与符号学相关的话题进行了热烈的讨论，彼此之间虽有争论，但也正是这样的思想碰撞，体现出学者们对符号学的热情，而这样的思想交流，也为符号学研究提供了新的观点、新的方向。

在2013年的6月和7月，第四届“全国语言与符号学高层论坛”和第二届“中国符号学论坛”分别在贵州和兰州召开。两次会议都吸引了众多学者出席。来自不同学科却对符号学都有所涉猎的学者们围绕不同的学科与符号学的结合展开讨论，探讨了符号学在不同学科中的发展情况，对符号学今后的发展方向有一定的指导作用。

在讲座方面，2013年5月6日至23日，芬兰符号学家阿赫蒂·皮耶塔里宁（Ahti Pietarinen）教授在中国开展了一系列的巡回讲座，所到之处包括西南大学、湖南大学、浙江大学和复旦大学。讲座共举行了8场，涉及的领域包括皮尔斯研究、认知符号学、语言学、视觉符号学等。皮耶塔里宁是赫尔辛基大学哲学历史系教授和爱沙尼亚塔林技术大学哲学系的首席教授，研究范围相当宽泛，尤其对皮尔斯的理论有相当程度的深耕。

值得注意的是，读书会作为一种较为轻松的交流形式，也开始为全国各地的符号学活动所采用。比如，兰州大学国际文化交流学院举办“语言与符号学读书月”活动，活动由该院文学与比较文化教研室主任祝东博士主持，分专题展开座谈研讨，主要议题有“发展中的符号学”“语言与元语言”“组合与聚合——从语言到文化”“符号修辞”“视角修辞与文化传播”等。四川大学文艺学教研室也举行了每月一次的读书会，讨论卡西尔、巴尔特、热奈特等人的符号学、叙述学理论。

学科建设方面，2013年10月29日，四川大学研究生院网站公布了2014年博士研究生的招生专业，将符号学设立为二级交叉学科，该学科将于明年开始招收博士。这是川大继2009年开设“符号学与传播学”博士方向之后，进一步提升符号学的学科独立性的又一举措。

二、2013年中国符号学研究的内容

上文数据已经表明，符号学在各个学科都有广泛的应用。下面将从符号学应用的主要学科领域分析其具体应用，以呈现符号学的具体研究动向。

在专著方面，2013年共有24本有关符号学的专著面世。如前文所言，这些著作中有直接涉及符号学的研究，如纳尔逊·古德曼所著的《艺术的语

言：通往符号理论的道路》[①]；也有用符号学方法讨论某一学科领域具体问题的著作，如黛比·米曼的《品牌这样思考：一场以设计、人类学、符号意义颠覆创意、品牌行销思维的大师对谈》[②]、陈峻俊的《符号的魅惑：网络消费文化研究》[③] 和金华的《俄语句义层次的语言符号学阐释》[④]。还有著作介绍了著名符号学家的一生及其科研成果，如法国作家罗歇所著，张祖建翻译的《罗兰·巴尔特传：一个传奇》[⑤]。这些专著所涉及的领域各不相同，但都与符号学紧密相连，通过和符号学研究的结合，使原领域的研究成功更加丰富。

在理论译著方面，保罗·科布利的《劳特利奇符号学指南》是一本符号学理论专著，作者不仅对符号学领域的重要学者和核心概念进行了翔实的介绍，也为进一步拓展该领域的学习提供了详尽的阅读指南。

论文方面，2013 年关于符号学的 708 篇论文，在各个学科都产生了不少的研究成果。中国语言文字学学科下的 136 篇论文和去年的情况大致相似的是这些论文仍是致力于反映国内符号学理论研究的发展情况，其中既有对符号学发展的回顾与展望，也有对符号学相关议题的讨论。谭晓庆的《从符号学角度看影像表意的多义性》[⑥] 从符号学角度，并依据影像符号语义、语法的不同呈现，来解读影像表意的多义性。

在美术、书法、雕塑与摄影学科下的 98 篇文章里，符号学被用作分析的工具，用于分析文本意义，指导艺术实践。在这个领域中，符号学的研究对象囊括了服饰、雕刻、平面设计、室内设计、家具设计、陶瓷器物。经分析，这 98 篇论文的特征和去年大致相同，覆盖对象全面，运用符号学分析解读的方式将符号学和艺术结合。由此，符号学跨学科研究的可行性得到进一步证明，表现出该理论强大的生命力。陈丽萍和郭伟所著的《从陶艺作品〈岁月荷莲〉中探究其符号学的内涵》[⑦] 试图通过符号学的研究，以陶艺作品《岁月荷莲》为例，从理性认知的角度，将作品的构成元素以数学式的研究模式进行解构，并通过对解构后的陶艺符号进行逐一分析，来研究作品各个角度

---

① ［美］纳尔逊·古德曼：《艺术的语言：通往符号理论的道路》，北京大学出版社，2013 年。

② ［美］黛比·米曼：《品牌这样思考：一场以设计、人类学、符号意义颠覆创意、品牌营销思维的大师对谈》，商周出版社，2013 年。

③ 陈峻俊：《符号的魅惑：网络消费文化研究》，中国社会科学出版社，2013 年。

④ 金华：《俄语句义层次的语言符号学阐释》，世界图书出版公司，2013 年。

⑤ ［法］罗歇：《罗兰·巴尔特传：一个传奇》，张祖建译，中国人民大学出版社，2013 年。

⑥ 谭晓庆：《从符号学角度看影像表意的多义性》，《中国报业》，2013 年第 10 期，第 81～82 页

⑦ 陈丽萍 郭伟：《从陶艺作品〈岁月荷莲〉中探究其符号学的内涵》，《佛山陶瓷》，2013 年第 7 期，第 42～44 页。

的艺术内涵。

新闻与传媒是符号学应用的另一大领域，该领域下的符号学相关论文数量较去年的49篇有一定增长。新闻与传媒学科主要是运用符号学方法分析媒介事件、媒介理论。如刘小波的《符号学视阈下〈中国好声音〉之文化现象解读》[①]在符号学视域研究这一文化现象，用符号学伴随文本理论，分析《中国好声音》携带的大量伴随文本。再如蒋晓丽的《从"客体之真"到"符号之真"：论新闻求真的符号学转向》[②]，以符号学为理论视野，讨论了新闻真实性这一新闻传媒界内永恒的话题。

戏剧电影与电视艺术学科下共有52篇符号学相关文章，逐渐发展为符号学研究领域的新宠。该学科主要从以下几个方面展开符号学研究：第一，对西方电影符号学理论的解读，如李丹所著的《从大众审美角度解读电影符号学的语言体系》[③]和梁国杰的《电影话语多模态连贯叙事的社会符号学视角》[④]；第二，从符号学角度分析电影文本，如杜哲的《没野心有梦想——对美剧〈破产姐妹〉的符号学分析》[⑤]和袁嘉的《电影〈人再囧途之泰囧〉的符号学解读》[⑥]。从这些文章中可以发现，此学科的符号学研究紧跟潮流，对最新、最火热的话题进行分析讨论。同时，也不乏一些俗称"接地气"的话题讨论，如卢晓侠的《东北喜剧小品中的乡土符号及其意义》[⑦]将东北喜剧小品这样贴近大众的话题同高度抽象的符号学理论文本结合，降低了大众接触符号学的门槛，对符号学的发展有着正面意义。

世界文学这一学科有关符号学的文章数量较去年的39篇也有了较为明显的增多。除了对西方经典符号学家理论的解读，不少学者采用符号学的理论去解读文学作品。李小华的《符号学视角下〈到灯塔去〉的女性主义解读》[⑧]

---

① 刘小波：《符号学视阈下〈中国好声音〉之文化现象解读》，《四川戏剧》，2013年第6期，第16～20页。

② 蒋晓丽：《从"客体之真"到"符号之真"：论新闻求真的符号学转向》，《国际新闻界》，2013年第6期，第15～23页。

③ 李丹：《从大众审美角度解读电影符号学的语言体系》，《大众文艺》，2013年第7期，第220页。

④ 梁国杰：《电影话语多模态连贯叙事的社会符号学视角》，《电影文学》，2013年第15期，第16～17页。

⑤ 杜哲：《没野心有梦想——对美剧〈破产姐妹〉的符号学分析》，《电影评介》，2013年第7期，第14～15页。

⑥ 袁嘉：《电影〈人再囧途之泰囧〉的符号学解读》，《电影文学》，2013年第13期，第79～80页。

⑦ 卢晓侠：《东北喜剧小品中的乡土符号及其意义》，《新世纪剧坛》，2013年第2期，第26～30页。

⑧ 李小华：《符号学视角下〈到灯塔去〉的女性主义解读》，《大众文艺》，2013年第4期，第25～27页。

从符号学的角度对弗吉尼亚·伍尔夫著名小说《到灯塔去》进行重新解读，认为小说中的灯塔是一个巨大的符号，具有独特的所指，小说最后的灯塔之行是对男女二元对立系统的颠覆，最终实现了二者的和谐统一。崔晓娟的《〈一个陌生女人的来信〉中的象征——重要意象的符号学分析》[①] 将符号的概念作为工具，利用相关的符号学思维方式、分析方法对小说中的意象进行探究，以深刻把握其与主题之间的关系，使《一个陌生女人的来信》中的重要意象从科学的角度得到阐释。

外国语言文字学科下，张荞荟、胡璇所著的《BBS 论坛中字母使用的功能分析》[②] 从 BBS 论坛中的字母使用情况出发，探讨了在符号学功能指导下论坛中的字母使用情况。这种新颖的研究在来年会有怎样的发展，令人不禁心生期待。

如上文所说，文艺理论学科中有关符号学的论文一共有 31 篇，其中大多是通过对文艺理论和符号学的探讨，来探索文艺理论的发展，如左茜茜的《澳洲土著艺术与其符号阐释》[③]。其他学科的符号学研究的方向和趋势与上述学科接近，本文就不再详细阐述。

三、2013 年中国符号学发展特征

（一）符号学学科化趋势进一步加强

学科化是衡量符号学发展水平的重要指标之一。一个研究领域要成为教育体系内的一个学科，一般需具备两方面的条件：该领域获得多数人的认可和接受，并具备系统理论。符号学发展百年，在中国传播了半个多世纪，已经为各高校接受。目前全国高校已经开设了总计 100 门左右的符号学课程，每年也产生 700 篇左右论文，其中有不少是硕、博士论文。

但若将符号学作为专业或者学科，则是近几年的事情。四川大学从 2009 年开始在新闻学博士点下设置“符号学与传播学”方向，正式开始招收了符号学方面的博士和硕士；南京师范大学外语学院也在俄语语言文学专业下面设置了“诗学与文化符号学”方向；天津外国语大学也在外国语言学及应用

① 崔晓娟：《〈一个陌生女人的来信〉中的象征——重要意象的符号学分析》，《青年文学家》，2013 年第 9 期，第 42～43 页。

② 张荞荟、胡璇：《BBS 论坛中字母使用的功能分析》，《传奇. 传记文学》，2013 年第 4 期，第 45～46 页。

③ 左茜茜：《澳洲土著艺术与其符号阐释》，《美术学刊》，2013 年第 2 期，第 33～34 页。

语言学科下设置了语言符号学。

多数情况下，符号学往往需要挂靠在其他学科下面，才能获得自己的位置。上文所提到过的四川大学将符号学设置为独立的二级学科，应该算是今年符号学界的一大进展。这意味着符号学在高校体系里获得了独立学科的位置，并形成独立的培养体系。四川大学符号学二级学科属于交叉学科，这也体现了符号学的人文学科基本方法论的属性，该学科在研究符号学理论的同时，可以为传媒、艺术、广告、品牌等方面的研究者提供学习的平台。

（二）门类符号学发展迅速

由于早期研习符号学的学者不少是外语学界的，所以符号学在外语学界有更大的影响力，也正因为如此，不少学者强调符号学要走跨学科的道路。检视今年的符号学文献，就会发现：符号学的跨学科发展迅猛，已成为符号学研究的主流。今年的708篇论文中，有500多篇是符号学在非语言领域里的应用与探索。这些领域极广：广告、品牌、艺术、建筑、法律、计算机等都有涉及。符号学方法推进了各个学科的发展，提出不少论点。王峰、明庆忠、熊剑峰将符号学方法应用到旅游中去，尝试构建一个系统的理论体系[①]；彭佳梳理、概括了民族符号学作为一门学科在多学科的理论研究铺垫之下产生和展开的过程，展示了它从符号研究向文本研究的转变，尤其是“空间”这一概念的引入对它的影响[②]。

不过我们应该注意到，虽然中国符号学跨学科的趋势越来越明显，也的确有一些可喜成果，但很多跨学科的文章对符号学理论理解不够，运用不到位，更无法与全球符号学理论进展保持同步，导致其论文空有其表。这在另一方面也提示我们，符号学界的任务不应仅是号召跨学科，更关键的应是学习、推进符号学理论研究，从而为整个符号学的发展提供原动力。

（三）理论符号学的探索与应用可以进一步系统化

符号学原理探索是符号学研究最重要的方面，今年也有学者在这方面展开了研究。专著方面，《劳特利奇符号学指南》较全面地介绍了符号学研究作为交叉学科的相关研究。论文方面，赵毅衡在《重新定义符号与符号学》中，将符号定义为“被认为携带意义的感知”；把符号学定义为“研究意义的学

① 王峰、明庆忠、熊剑峰：《旅游符号学研究框架体系的建构》，《旅游论坛》，2013年第3期，第11～15页。

② 彭佳：《民族符号学研究综述》，《三峡论坛》，2013年第2期，第97～101页。

说”，定位为“不仅讨论表意批判而且讨论解释”。① 唐小林的《索绪尔局限与朗格难题——论符号诗学推进的几个关键问题》，从朗格艺术符号的讨论切入，回应了索绪尔语言符号学模式的困境与缺陷，指出中国符号学不应再局限于索绪尔符号学的窠臼之中，并对符号诗学的发展方向作了系统地探讨。② 皮特·特洛普的《符号域：作为文化符号学的研究对象》讨论了符号域在文化符号学中的地位和作用。③ 卢德平通过对符号学发展史的反思，特别是对自索绪尔之后的符号学研究的透视，揭示符号学思想在戈夫曼那里所获得的巨大变革。④

从总体上来看，与跨学科趋势不相协调的是符号学理论探索的研究较少，对理论进行系统研究的佳作更是屈指可数。我们可以看到，近两年来，国内符号学理论专著极少，前两年的有赵毅衡的《符号学》、丁尔苏的《符号与意义》，去年还有一系列的译著，而今年符号学理论方面，除了南京大学出版社出版的译著《劳特利奇符号学指南》之外，几乎没有任何此方面的专著。在七百多篇论文中，探讨符号学原理的论文不超过10篇。这也体现了符号学研究发展存在的问题：大多数研究停留在结构主义符号学的阶段，缺乏对新理论的关注、研究和探讨。这也正是中国符号学发展亟待解决的问题。

作者简介：

刘一鸣，四川大学符号学-传媒学研究所驻所研究员，研究方向为传播学与符号学。

齐千里，四川大学符号学-传媒学研究所驻所研究员，研究方向为理想主义、马克思主义。

Authors:

Liu Yiming, member of the ISMS Research Team. His research covers communication and semiotic studies.

E-mail:231617291@qq. com

Qi Qianli, member of the ISMS Research Team. His research mainly focuses on idealism and Marxism.

E-mail:qiqianli1121@163. com

---

① 赵毅衡：《重新定义符号与符号学》，《国际新闻界》，2013年第6期，第6～14页。

② 唐小林：《索绪尔局限与朗格难题——论符号诗学推进的几个关键问题》，《文艺争鸣》，2013年第3期，132～135页。

③ ［爱沙尼亚］皮特·特洛普著，赵星植译：《符号域：作为文化符号学的研究对象》，《符号与传媒》（总第6辑），四川大学出版社，2013年，第157～166页。

④ 卢德平：《从索绪尔到戈夫曼：符号学的转折》，《当代外语研究》，2013年第9期，第10～13页。

西安批判符号学派专辑

编者按

主持人：李军学

毋庸讳言，符号学作为一种现代理论研究形态发端于西方学界，怒放于各学科之中。作为一种现代理论形态，“符号学转向”对于克服笛卡尔式二分，走出西方传统哲学困境功莫大焉。然而西方符号的形式化、系统化特征终又使得以心控身的二分传统走向了以符控身这一死地。立足于象形文字的悠久滋润，基于东方身道传统的绵绵不绝，一种中国式的符号学研究既为必要又为重要。本次所编选的三篇文章，其着力点即在于展开一种符号的中国式分析。张再林通过对早期典籍，如《周易》中的有别于西方基于主客二元对立的中国式符号学思想的深入挖掘，为我们昭示了一条步出西方符号学危机的可能途径。李军学的文章着重分析当代符码社会的运作机制，使我们警觉于日用而不知的符号所可能带来的对自身和社会的影响。张兵的文章透过西方符号在身体史上的载沉载浮，分析了西方意识式符号自身所蕴含的内在矛盾及在此冲突下符号话语系统的崩溃，提示了一种非西方文化视野的符号学研究的必要。

从《周易》的“交道”到《周礼》的“象征性交换”*

张再林

摘要：正如《说文》“爻，交也”这一释义所指，以“爻”为元符的《周易》实质上指向了阴阳之交，并且《周易》的“近取诸身”的致思方式又决定了，这种阴阳之交最终体现为人类的“男女之交”。这种“男女之交”隐含着一切人际交往的历史和逻辑上的真正隐秘，也使一种亦社会亦自然的“生命交往”方式得以确立，并最终易、礼相通地使《周礼》中礼物“象征性交换”之旨大白于世。因此，《周礼》的“礼尚往来”与其说是一种抽象的物的属性的交往，不如说是一种具体的人的生命的交往。

关键词：爻，阴阳之交，男女之交，象征性交换

From “Jiaodao” in *Zhou Yi* to “Symbolic Exchange” in *Zhou Li*

Zhang Zailin

Abstract: Just as the definition in *Shuo Wen*, “Yao”, regarded as the original sign in *Zhou Yi*, actually refers to the exchange of *Yin* and *Yang*. The thinking mode of “taking from the body” in *Zhou Yi* determines that the exchange of *Yin* and *Yang* is ultimately expressed as human copulation which is the genuine secret behind all interpersonal relationships historically and logically, and also establishes the pattern of “life interaction” both socially and naturally. In addition, it

* 本文为教育部人文社会科学研究规划基金项目“中国古代家的哲学及其意义”（项目编号：08JA720022）的阶段性成果。

reveals the decree of "symbolic exchange", characterized by exchanging gifts in *Zhou Li* through intercourse of *Yi* and *Li* . Therefore, "reciprocity" of *Zhou Li* is not so much an abstract and physical attribute as a specific intercourse of human's life.

Key words: *Yao*, exchange of *Yin* and *Yang*, exchange of man and woman, symbolic exchange

对符号的崇拜似乎是人类这一符号的动物与生俱来、挥之不去的宿命。从迷信"魔咒"的原始神巫时代，到热衷于数字编码的信息时代，人类都一无例外。故为了破译古老而又神秘的中国《周易》之谜，还是要先从《周易》的基本符号谈起。

一、"爻，交也"

"造化合元符，交媾腾精魄。"无疑，一旦我们染指以穷神知化为所指的《周易》的符号世界，我们就会发现，由 64 卦、384 爻构成的符号世界，是以"– –""—"这一阴阳两爻为其基本符号的，借用李白诗里的表述，即为所谓的"元符"。

那么，什么是阴阳两爻之"爻"?《说文》谓："爻，交也。象《易》卦六爻相交。"又，徐灏《段注笺》谓："交者交错之义。六爻为重体，故作重乂象之。"因此，爻这一符号看似极其神秘，实则明白平易，它实际上以"乂"这一象形的形式表示事物（更确切地说，阴阳二者）之两两相交。而这种两两相交之旨对《周易》来说是如此的至关重要，以致不仅"物相杂，故曰文"（《周易·系辞下》)，且一部《周易》，就是与《说文》所谓"错画也，象交文"这一"交错为文"的"文"的释义一致，以事物（阴阳）相交为内容的"互文主义"的符号系统，"文不当，故吉凶生焉"（《周易·系辞下》)。阴阳相交与否实际上决定了其或吉或凶的价值形态判定。或换言之，若阴阳相交者则为吉，若阴阳不交者则为凶。

以《周易》的"泰"卦为例。"泰"卦之所以被占断为吉祥、亨通，乃至引申出的汉语"泰"字所具有的诸如通达、安宁、宽裕、美好、极其等义涵，恰恰在于在"泰"卦（䷊）中，下卦（乾☰）与上卦（坤☷）不仅适成所谓"天地交泰"之趣，而且各自的第一爻、第二爻、第三爻（即"初"与"四"、"二"与"五"、"三"与"上"）也完全相交。在这方面，"泰"卦毋宁说与它适成其反的"否"卦这一至为不吉利之卦形成鲜明的对比。后者下卦（坤☷）

与上卦（乾☰）“天地不交”，且各自每爻之间的乖背睽离亦与“爻”的两两相交之旨完全相悖。

因此，《周易》所谓的“简易”，乃是将一切事物表象形式还原为阴阳相交形式的“简易”；所谓的“变易”，乃是将阴阳相交形式“因而重之”“参伍错综”而生发出的“变易”；所谓的“不易”，乃是指虽繁且富，但却万变不离其宗地以阴阳相交为基础的“不易”。这一切不啻意味着，无论是“简易”之“易”、“变易”之“易”，还是“不易”之“易”，最终都可一言以蔽之为“交易”之“易”。故“定其交而后求”（《系辞下》），一如《周易》所指出的那样，真正的易道实际上是“交道”之道。唯有从这种“交道”出发，我们才能无入而不得地进入易学的领域，并最终纲举目张，领悟到大易之道的穷神知化的至胜之谛。

“阴阳和合”，这种至胜之谛也即中国哲学无比心仪的所谓宇宙中的“和”的真理。正如“乂”这一象形符号为我们所表示的那样，“和（hé）”即“和（huò）”也，这种“和”既非指向事物间了无干系的绝对差异，也非指向事物间完全重叠、重合的绝对同一，而是以其两两交汇、交合，为我们指向了事物间的异中之同。故“和而不同”，“和”的真理与其说是体现了一种所谓“同”的真理，不如说体现了一种彼此之间因交而通的“通”的真理。孙子曰：“我可以往，彼可以来，曰通。”（《孙子·地形》），章学诚说：“《说文》训通为达，自此之彼之谓也。通者，所以通天下之不通也。”（《文史通义·释通》）如此种种对“通”的论述，无一不可视为同样也是对“和”之旨的解读。无怪乎《周易》在极其推崇阴阳和合之“和”的同时，又为我们如此前所未有地彰显了物物相通之“通”义，其谓“天地交而万物通也”，谓“感而遂通”，谓“通则久”。以至于可以说，《周易》一书既以其“太和所谓道”的主张而堪称中国古老的“和谐”之说的鼻祖，又以其之于“以‘通’训‘道’”“道通为一”的阐释[①]，而实发人类今天“沟通”理性的端倪。

一旦我们把《周易》定位为道出了“和”的真理，那么，我们就不仅领悟了《周易》何以是一种“关系论”的真理，而且还进一步使这种“关系论”真理中关系算子“三”之谜、关系界定“际”之谜得到破解。也就是说，《周易》之所以一如老子坚持“三生万物”那样，对“三”推崇有加，提出“三极之道”，提出“兼三才而两之”恰恰在于，其所谓的“三”，与其说是数学

① 关于“道”与“通”的关系，可参看唐君毅所著《中国哲学原论·原道篇二》（中国社会科学出版社，2006年）一书31页。

意义上的“三”，不如说是阳爻（—）的奇数与阴爻（– –）的偶数之和意义上的“三”，是“叁”，即“参”（参与、参加）这一“关系算子”意义上的“三”，它实际上不过是异中之同的“和”的真理的体现。同理，《周易》之所以一如船山强调的那样，以究“天地之际”之“际”为归趣，正是因为其所谓的“际”，与其说是“分际”“边际”意义上的“际”，不如说是“交际”意义上的“际”，是船山所谓“天地万物消长通塞之机，在往来之际”[①]，所谓“大辨体其至密，而至密成其大辨”[②] 这一“关系界定”意义上的际，它同样与《周易》“和”的真理深深相契。明白了这一点，我们就不难理解为什么《周易》会提出“闔闢成变”的命题，热衷于“门”的哲学隐喻。《说文》谓：“际，壁会也。”段注：“两墙相会之缝也。引申之凡两合皆曰际。际取壁之两合，犹‘閒’取门之两合也。”[③]《说文》又谓：“閒，隙也。”段注：“隙者，壁际也。引申之凡有两边有中者皆谓之隙。隙谓之閒。閒者，门开则中为际。凡罅缝皆曰閒，其为有两有中一也。”[④] 在这里，古人在解读出“门”“有两有中一也”这一深邃的“际”的含义的同时，不也使《周易》“和”的隐秘一起地大白于世了吗？

“同则不继，和实生物。”如果说“同”意味着生命的终结的话，那么，“和”则意味着生命的诞生。故庄子谓“交通成和而物生焉”（《庄子·田子方》），《淮南子》谓“阴阳和合而万物生”（《天文训》）。因此，“生生之谓易”（《系辞上》），以“交”为旨的大易之道在使我们去向一个异中有同的“和”的世界的同时，也为我们催生了一个生生不息的“生”的世界。这决定了“往来不穷谓之道”（《系辞上》），“（易之）为道也，屡迁”（《系辞下》），《周易》的交道并非是一成不变的，而是无限进行的；并且也决定了，这种交道的能指并非是一种完成时态的“静止的互文”的形式，“爻”的符号形式所示，以其“乂”的“感应交织，重重无尽”，是一种行进的“动态的互文”的形式。以《周易》的“既济”卦为例。在“既济”（䷾）卦中，不独上卦坎（☵）与下卦离（☲）对应相交，不独上卦与下卦各自每爻对应相交，且其六爻无不各就其位而得正。故始于“屯”卦的阴阳交构形式至此臻至完善，并且在这方面比“泰”卦有过之而无不及，因为后者六爻中尚有两爻并未各就其位而得正。然而，也正是由于其完善至极，它也走向生命的尽头，没有进

① 王夫之：《〈周易〉内传》，《船山全书》第一册，岳麓书社，2011年，第142页。

② 王夫之：《〈周易〉外传》，《船山全书》第一册，岳麓书社，2011年，第852页。

③ 许慎撰，段玉裁注：《说文解字注》，上海古籍出版社，1997年，第736页。

④ 许慎撰，段玉裁注：《说文解字注》，上海古籍出版社，1997年，第589页。

一步发展的余地和空间。故“既济”卦虽被占为“亨”，却是“小者亨也”，仅有小的作为而难有大的作为；其虽被占断为“初吉”，却有“终乱”与之相伴相随，而这种所谓的“终乱”也即“终止则乱，其道穷也”（《系辞下》）。

分析至此，作为《周易》“元符”的“爻”的符号形式的所有内涵可谓一览无余。如上所述，它以“立象以尽意”的方式，为我们表达出其所指世界两两相交的“交”的真理，以及从“交”中所生发出的“和”的真理、“生”的真理，同时，也标志着中国式的符号形式的真正确立，并使自身与西方式的符号形式形成鲜明对比。众所周知，从索绪尔语言学开始的西方式的符号系统，与其说是一种基于“阴×阳”的符号系统，不如说是一种基于“A/非A”的符号系统。在这种符号系统中，不是代表相交的“×”而是代表分隔的“/”是其符号系统中的元符。正因如此，如果说中国式的符号形式集中体现了一种两两相交的“交”的真理的话，那么，西方式的符号系统则集中体现了一种各自分隔的“分”的真理，由此，英国语言学家约翰·莱昂斯（John Lyons）认为，“二元对立是掌握语言结构的最重要的原则之一”[①]，俄国语言学家雅各布森宣称，“二元主义是基本的；没有它，语言的结构将不存在”[②]；进而，如果说中国式的符号形式以其“交”道之异中有同为我们指明了“和而不同”的“和”的真理的话，那么，西方式的符号形式则根据雅各布森的“标记理论”（Theory of Markedness），以其对看似“严格的差异”的坚持，实质上却为对“绝对的同一”的强调，使自己从属于“同而不和”的“同”的真理。“和实生物，同则不继。”如果说，中国的符号形式从“和”的真理出发，最终走向了对生生不息的“生”的真理的肯定的话，那么，西方的符号形式则从“同”的真理出发，使“死”的真理成为其最后归宿。

我们无意否认西方符号形式之于人类文明的功绩。我们深知，若无这一符号形式的确立，便没有现代科学文明。然而，人们又不能不看到，这种符号形式在为我们构建了辉煌的现代科学文明的同时，又为我们筑起一道不可逾越的高高的栅栏，使我们与那个我们深深根植于其中的、复杂而和谐的、充满无限生机的原生态的世界一刀两断。因此，以《周易》“×”符为元符的中国符号形式虽去今已远，却具有不可磨灭的胜义。它不仅以一种清醒的符号形式取代了巫魅的魔咒，使我们民族一跃跻身文化人“符号动物”之列，并且更重要的是，也在现代二元对立文明所向披靡之际，以一种独特的符号

---

① John Lyons: *Semantics*, vol. 1. Cambridge: Cambridge University Press, 1977, p. 271.

② Roman Jakobson: *Some Questions of Meaning*, *On Language*, Linda R. Waugh, Monique Monville Burston, ed.. Cambridge: Harvard University Press, 1990, p. 321.

形式，为我们另辟一条通向原生态世界的通道，使我们得以重返天地万物相交、相和、相生之境。

二、阴阳之交与男女之交

“一阴一阳之谓道。”（《系辞上》）然而，一旦追问“何谓阴阳”，我们就会由于“其称名也小，其取类也大”（《系辞下》）、“触类而长，物貌难尽”（《文心雕龙·物色》），而陷入中国式符号形式所特有的“无穷所指”的窘境之中。阴阳或被指称为天地，或被指称为日月，或被指称为寒暑，或被指称为水火，或被指称为刚柔、动静，如此种种以至无穷。但是，“阴阳者，数之可十，推之可百，数之可千，推之可万，万之大不可胜数，然其要一也”（《黄帝内经·素问·阴阳离合论》）。当我们穷追不舍，再对这种阴阳之“要”进一步追问之时，我们就会发现，《说文》以“腰”训“要”，“要”乃涉身性概念，“阴阳”之“要”也不例外，它同样为涉身性所指。而这种涉身性所指，与其说是以一种“远取诸物”的方式，指向自然界的某两种事物及其属性，不如说是以一种“近取诸身”的方式，指向人类男女两性。

这一结论不仅与“依形躯起念”“用身体知道”这一中国式的身体思维方式相吻合；与“象，犹类也”[①]，也即与抽象的、无穷的“类”恰恰就体现在具体的、有限的“象”这一中国式的“类取”原则同旨；也和《周易》所谓“乾道成男，坤道成女”（《系辞上》）这一表述完全一致。同时，既然阴阳被还原为男女，那么，所谓“阴阳之交”也就理所当然地被还原为“男女之交”。故尽管随着《周易》作为“大叙事”的“经”的地位的确立，使后来的道学家们对该书中的“男女之交”讳莫如深，但这些描述是如此的坦率直白，以致无论人们如何遮掩，都难以将其一笔勾销。“男女构精，万物化生”（《系辞下》）谈论的是“男女之交”；“夫乾其静也专，其动也直，是以大生焉；夫坤其静也翕，其动也辟，是以广生焉”（《系辞上》）谈论的亦是“男女之交”。“阖户谓之坤，辟户谓之乾，一阖一辟谓之变，往来不穷谓之通”（《系辞上》）——“阖辟”当为上文的“翕辟”，“门”当为老子所谓的“玄牝之门”，谈论的同样的是“男女之交”。除此之外，对“男女之交”的暗示还体现在《周易》中“屈信相感而利生焉”（《系辞下》）这一极富“性暗示”的说法，以及《周易》中可视为古人生殖崇拜的孑遗的“龙蛇隐喻”。凡此种种，郭沫若、周予同和钱玄同等人视阴阳两爻为男根女阴象征这一观点，虽至少有猜

① 焦循：《易学三书》卷七，九州出版社，2004年，第322页。

测成分，却也不乏合理性。

《周易》中的“咸”卦可以印证“男女之交”一说。“咸之为道，固神化之极致也”[①]，“卦以利用，则皆亲乎人之事，而唯咸则近取诸身”[②]。“咸”卦占有“取女吉”，被荀子称作为“易之咸，见夫妇”（《荀子·大略》），被孔颖达解读为“婚媾之善”，其卦象下卦“少男”与上卦“少女”相会，“咸其拇”“咸其腓”“咸其股”，“欲思运动以求相应”，是对“憧憧往来，朋从尔思”这一男女交媾过程细致入微的描绘。[③] 故整个“咸”卦，与其说是理学家们所解读的“心所感通者，只是理也”[④]，是一种高高在上，的“天理”的哲学脚注，不如说是对“男女之交”的直白书写，并以其对《周易》所谓“一阴一阳之谓道”明白体现，而为我们指明了“房中者”这一古人所谓的“至道之际”。

而在《周易》中，男女之交之所以可以被视为“至道之际”，恰恰在于，它在使我们切身体验到大易“交道”的同时，也从发生学、逻辑学出发把这种“交道”演绎到了极致。正是这种男女之交，以一种历史与逻辑相统一的方式，为我们揭示出了大易“交道”的真正隐秘。

从发生学出发，男女之交在一切人际交往中具其发生学意义上的优先性。“有男女，然后有夫妇；有夫妇，然后有父子；有父子，然后有君臣；有君臣，然后有上下；有上下，然后礼仪有所错。”（《序卦传》）。这一论述正是对此优先性的明示，它为我们明确宣布，就其生命发生谱系而言，人类的一切社会交往皆源于男女之交。《周易》如是说，对于以易为宗的儒家学说来说也理应如此。否则，那些儒家信徒无论如何高抬“父子之际”，都会不得不在面对《中庸》“君子之道造端乎夫妇”这一圣训时，保持难堪的沉默，陷入尴尬的境地。

从逻辑学出发，它告诉我们男女之交与一切人际交往具有逻辑上的同构性。也就是说，“不同而一，夫是之谓人伦”（《荀子·荣辱》），而这种“不同而一”的人伦逻辑，恰恰与男女之交“惟异相感”的逻辑完全契合。这意味着，与异性的关系是如此集中地体现了一个人的道德品质，以至于可以说，一个人如何对待身边的女人，那么，他也就会如何对待社会中一切他人。无

---

① 王夫之：《〈周易〉内传》，《船山全书》第一册，岳麓书社，2011 年，第 277 页。

② 王夫之：《〈周易〉外传》，《船山全书》第一册，岳麓书社，2011 年，第 903 页。

③ 参看拙文《咸卦考》，《学海》，2010 年第 5 期。

④ 程颢，程颐：《二程集》上册，中华书局，1981 年，第 56 页。

怪乎唐甄宣称："五伦百姓，非恕不行；行自妻始。不恕妻而能恕人，吾不信也"。[①] 在这里，这位"夫妇伦理"的力挺者，不仅继《周易》之后再次肯定了夫妇之交的优先性，并且还更进一步，把一切人际交往之道与夫妇之道视为别无二致的东西。

这样，发生学上的优先性和逻辑学上的同构性使男女之交道成为一切人际交往的真正依据。故归根结底，《周易》所谓的"交"实际上不过是男女之交的"交"，《周易》所谓的"和"实际上不过是"男女亲和"的"和"，《周易》所谓的"生"实际上亦不过是"男女生殖"的"生"。因此，"圣人通神明之德，类万物之情，亦近取诸身而已矣"[②]。诚如易学大师焦循所说，与那种"道在迩而求诸远，事在易而求诸难"的好高骛远的学说相反，中国哲学是卑之无甚高论的。《周易》同样也是卑之无甚高论的。为《周易》所无比推崇的"交道"之道看似远在天边，实际上却近在眼前，看似神秘莫测，实际上却寻常平易，它就亲切地体现在我们个体之身与异性之身的两情缱绻之中，体现在二者不言而喻的"身体话语"里。同时，也正是在这里，我们不仅无比真切地体会到了什么是"大辨体甚至密，而至密成其大辨"，亲历"男女相感于一旦，初不必有固结之情，而可合以终身"[③]，进而领悟到"易"即"不易"的道理。

值得注意的是，无独有偶，《周易》也现之时，恰是中国历史上"夫妇文明"发蒙时期。这一惊人的巧合又一次暗示《周易》的"交道"与男女之交的内在默契。

王国维在其《殷周制度论》中称，中国政治与文化之变革，莫剧于殷周之际，而这种变革实自其制度始矣。在他看来，周人制度之大异于商者有三：一曰立子立嫡之制，二曰庙数之制，三曰同姓不婚之制。其中第三项的"同姓不婚之制"是指，与周时男子称氏、女子称姓相应的严格的同姓不婚之制。《礼记·大传》所谓的"系之以姓而弗别，缀之以食而弗殊，虽百世而婚姻不通者，周道然也"之说，适可为此明证。

关于周人的同姓不婚之于整个宗周文明变革的意义，王国维先生已有中肯的阐述。然而，遗憾的是，他仅将其简单地归纳为"异姓之国，非宗法之

---

① 唐甄：《潜书》，中华书局，1955 年，第 79 页。

② 焦循：《孟子正义》下册，中华书局，1957 年，第 521 页。

③ 王夫之：《〈周易〉内传》，《船山全书》第一册，岳麓书社，2011 年，第 278 页。

所能统者，以婚媾甥舅之谊通之”[①]，未能点明其深义。其深义在于，正是由于同姓不婚，女性才从同姓的“自家人”变为异姓的、陌生的“他者”，从而才有“取妻不取同姓，以厚别也”（《礼记·坊记》），“取于异姓，所以附远厚别也”（《礼记·郊特牲》）的说法，两性关系中真正的“男女之别”也才成为可能。进而，“男女有别而后夫妇有义”（《礼记·昏义》），以其男女之“大辨”适成其“大密”，最终“合两姓之好”，使亲密无间的专偶式夫妇关系得以真正确立。再进而，“夫妇有义而后父子有亲”（《礼记·昏义》），随着这种专偶式夫妇关系的确立，人类告别了知其母而不知其父的群婚制形式，父子相续的代际关系也应运而生。

因此，周代文明的变革与其说是王国维先生论述的那样，始于父子之间的“立子立嫡”之制，不如说是始于“同姓不婚”之制：由“同姓不婚”之制而生“立子立嫡”之制，再由“立子立嫡”之制而生“庙数”之制，如此而已，岂有他哉！周人以阴阳两爻为我们演绎出重重无尽的易象，与此相应，周人也从夫妇之际出发，使“郁郁乎文哉”的周文明勃兴于中华大地。

按古人“礼义以为文”（《荀子·臣道》）的说法，这种周文明也即“礼”的文明。既然周文明深深地植根于夫妇之际，那么，“礼”与夫妇之际应当存在着内在的、固有的联系，或者毋宁说，“异姓主名治际会”（《礼记·大传》），夫妇之际也恰恰就是备受孟子推崇的所谓“礼际”[②]。这样，我们的讨论就从《周易》过渡到《周礼》，并且接下来的考证将使我们发现，正是《周易》推崇的男女之交为我们开辟了一条通向《周礼》的道路，使作为“象征性交换”而非抽象的“物的交换”的“礼”的真正实质得以破译。

三、从《周易》的“男女之交”到《周礼》的“象征性交换”

如前所述，《周易》之所以一如我们分析的那样，把男女之交视为所谓“至道之际”，不仅在于男女之交以其切身性成为一切人际交往的集中体现，同时还在于，它如《周易·系辞》中“乾（天）道成男，坤（地）道成女”所喻，如“咸”卦中的男女之“感”乃为无“心”之“咸”那样，为我们指向自然界交往的至极真理。因此，它是人际交往与自然交往的高度统一，是伦理之理与生理之理的高度统一。这种高度统一，意味着一个善待女人的男人，必将在善待一切他人的同时，也善待自然万物；并且意味着，当他在做

① 王国维：《殷周制度论》，陈其泰编，《二十世纪中国礼学研究论集》，学苑出版社，1998年，第299页。

② 见《孟子·万章下》：“苟善其礼际矣，斯君子受之。”

到这一切之时，也就理所当然地达到古人所谓的“天人之际”。或一言以蔽之，一种真正的“男女之交”恰恰无外乎为古人所高标的真正的“天人之际”，那种看似难以穷极的“天人之际”，恰恰就体现在我们用自己的身体书写的“男女之交”里。无怪乎《中庸》宣称：“君子之道，造端乎夫妇；及其至也，察乎天地。”这与其说是“夫妇”与“天地”并举，不如说是二者根本一致。

如同存在主义认为此在乃完整的“生命化的存在”（existence）那样，男女交往亦为完整的生命的交往。在这种交往中，个体为自己选择了最为孤注一掷、最具风险的投资，“以身相许”，交给对方自己的整个生命，而对方亦应也必以自己的整个生命做筹码来回报。在这种交往中，双方是如此地慷慨无私，以至于在这里，无论是金钱和地位，还是疾病和生死都可以被当事人置之度外，都无碍当事人义无反顾；以至于在这里，生命的一次感动，却可以赢来双方生死相依，双方一生一世的不弃不离。也正是在这里，爱情在浮世俗尘中脱颖而出，以其人性的象征而成为与生死并举的人类千古不灭的永恒语题，不仅使古人以男女之爱比“天地之际”，为我们写下“天地合，乃敢与君绝”这样的爱的盟誓，写下“死生契阔，与子成说；执子之手，与子偕老”，使我们在见证到什么是男女之爱的矢志不渝的同时，洞观何为以“志”为旨的诗的至真至胜之谛；也正是在这里，我们才能为“情为何物”这一千古之谜找到真正的谜底，并且才能理解为什么现代哲学家阿多诺指出，“在人情浇薄的大众社会里，婚姻是维护人性细胞的最后机会”①。

“究天人之际”必然也意味着“通古今之辨”。一旦我们像古人那样，把男女之交定位为一种亦人亦天的“生命交往”，我们就可以古注今，通向今人所谓礼物交换的“象征性交换”，看清两种交往方式的内在联系。

熟悉当代法国思想的人应知道，所谓礼物交换的“象征性交换”（symbolic exchange），是在人类学家莫斯的理论基础上，由后现代主义的“大祭师”鲍德里亚大力发明的一种极其重要的文化概念。这一概念肇始于西方人文知识分子之于愈演愈烈的现代文明的一种深深的“忧患意识”。这种忧患意识所面对的，是源于“/”这一西方文化之元符的二元对立原则，以及从这种二元对立原则中产生的绝对同一性原则的统治。这种统治虽使一种真理性的识辨系统成为真正可能，却也不可避免地以其高度抽象、垄断且无比僵

---

① Theodor W. Adorno, *Minima Moralia: Reflexion aus dem beschädigten Leben*. Frankurt am Main: Suhrkamp, 1969, p. 3.

化的“权力话语”将人与人之间的现实的、生动的和丰富的交往属性彻底葬送。为巴塔耶、鲍德里亚等所刻画的当代社会中无所不在的“物的秩序”“物体系”的统治，恰恰是对此的现实写照。这种统治带给我们的，不仅是人们对物质利益的无比的贪婪，对经济利益最大化的不可遏止的渴求；更为触目惊心，还是随着交往媒介的“物”的作用和地位的日益凸显，随着交往目的最终让位于手段，人际关系被商品交易关系所偷换，“一切人都成为商人”的“商业社会”降临，社会中“买方”与“卖方”人格彻底丧失，人与人之间的脉脉温情荡然无存。

我们看到，也正是值此完全物化的人际交往方式大行其道之际，西方人文主义思想家在对这种非人性的交往方式大加鞭挞的同时，通过把目光转向作为西方文明的“他者”的异域文明，一种迥异于西方现代交往方式的古老而又富有活力的，也即“礼物交换”的方式开始进入他们的视域。在他们看来，这一交往方式以其物际与人际的真正统一，避免了物化的偏执，为深陷入人际交往困境的当代人类文明带来了一线生机。

礼物交换之所以迥异于商品交换，首先在于礼物与商品虽同为“物”，但商品的“物”实质上是商业价值，是一种“抽象的物”，而礼物的“物”其“本身却是有活力的”，其“本身原本也具有人格和品性”①，是人自身的具体的“生命的象征”。按“衣服是人身体的第二层皮肤”这一说法，礼物之“物”就是人的活脱脱的生命本身。其次还在于，虽同以物为媒介，但商品交换是以物易物的物的交往方式，而礼物交换则是生命之于生命的交往方式。用莫斯的话来说，“在给予别人礼物的同时，也就是把自己给了别人；之所以把自己也给出去，是因为所欠于别人的正是他自己——他本身与他的财物”，礼物交换“归根结底便是混融。人们将灵魂融于事物，亦将事物融于灵魂。人们的生活彼此相融”。② 这样，礼物交换在使人们同样以物为媒介进行交际的同时，也使“一种主动、充分而又直接在场的人际关系建立起来了”③。而这种人际关系的建立，一方面表明了正如礼物交换乃礼物馈赠－回赠的循环往复那样，存在礼物交换的社会中的人际关系自始至终都是“相互”的；另

---

① ［法］马塞尔·莫斯：《礼物：古代社会中交换的形式与理由》，汲喆译，上海人民出版社，2002年，第139、140页。

② ［法］马塞尔·莫斯：《礼物：古代社会中交换的形式与理由》，汲喆译，上海人民出版社，2002年，第79、45页。

③ William Merrin, “Television is Killing the Art of Symbolic Exchange: Baudrillard's Theory of Communication”, *Theory*, *Culture & Society* 16 (3), 127.

一方面，还表明了“既然它们并不依赖于经济交换，它们也就不屈从于商品及其交换价值的体系化”[①]，在这里，随着这种人际关系的确立，礼物交换实际上最终为当代文明的“物体系”之权力话语统治敲响了丧钟。

笔者无意像发现了远离尘嚣的一首田园诗那样，将这种礼物的“象征性交换”完全地理想化。实际上，鲍德里亚由于受尼采“权力意志”思想的影响，对这种“象征性交换”的描述和解读也不乏自相矛盾之处。[②] 我们感兴趣的，仅仅是他对这种“象征性交换”中特有的“生命交往”的性质的揭示，因为正是这一特质为我们敞开了一个不同于现代交往世界的“他者”世界中礼的交往，使长期以来扑朔迷离的中国古老的交往形式，即《周礼》之谜得以真相大白。众所周知，这种《周礼》曾为素有“礼仪之邦”之称的中国古代社会的交往标准，随着时代的推移，世人对其内在的奥义却日益陌生。

《周礼》之谜之一：礼为何物？也就是说，《周礼》的礼物无疑是物，那么，这种物到底是“商品”之物，还是人自身的“生命象征”之物？显然，正如莫斯、鲍德里亚的“象征性交换”理论所揭示的那样，答案只能是后者而非前者。在周人那里，商品之物与其说是礼物，不如说“非礼也”，而为“货赂之物”（段玉裁《说文解字注》“赂”字注云：“货赂皆谓物”）。[③] 由此，我们就不难理解为什么《论语·阳货》有所谓“礼云，礼云，玉帛云乎哉”之语；我们就不难理解为什么礼是如此尊贵而不可让渡，孔子坚持“唯（礼）器与名，不可以假人”，而主张“不如多与之邑”（《左传·成公二年》）；我们也就不难理解为什么《周礼》虽主张“礼不下庶人”，但作为大梁守门人的一贫如洗的侯嬴，却可“意气兼将生命酬”，以自己的生命作为“礼物”回报信陵君对他的知遇之恩。“礼尚往来”是当时社会普世性的交往准则，但它并非可计算的有价的金钱，而是不可计算的无价的生命。礼虽是“象征”，看似为“如在”而非“实在”，却可以“执虚如执盈”，以生命为依凭，表现出真实、丰富的实存世界。

《周礼》之谜之二：礼的交往是什么性质的交往？也就是说，作为一种交

---

① ［法］让·鲍德里亚：《符号政治经济学批判》，夏莹译，南京大学出版，2009 年，第 45 页。

② 梅林（Merrin）这样描述鲍德里亚的象征：“节日与礼物的社会关联提升并参入了人性，但同时，更为关键的是，它也使人处于与他人的较量中。这种人际交流绝不是理想的：它包含了暴力、敌视、毁灭、抗衡、竞争、威胁、恐吓、狂乱、愤怒、情绪的紧张、（赌注的）增长、决斗、挑战、羞辱、屈尊、他人的黯然，或胜利、权力、荣誉与蜕变：这就是象征的场景。”（见“Television is Killing the Art of Symbolic Exchange”一文第 127 页。）

③ 关于这一点，可参看杨向奎：《宗周社会与礼本文明》，人民出版社，1997 年，第 257～258 页。

往方式的礼的交往，其实质上是“以物易物”的商业交往，还是人与人的生命交往？显然，答案同样也只能是后者而非前者。对于周人来说，“礼尚往来”决定了有来必往、有施必报，但是，“无言不雠，无德不报”（《诗经·大雅·抑》），真正的礼物交换与其说是物的交往、物的回报，不如说是在特定情境下的生命表达（言）、生命恩情（德）的交往和回报；与其说是商品的等价交换，不如说以身相许、以生相酬之道。古人之所以提出“敬之至也，大昏为大”（《大戴礼记·哀公问于孔子》），提出“大昏，万世之嗣也”（《大戴礼纪·哀公问于孔子》），提出“夫昏礼，万世之始也”（《礼记·郊特牲》），提出“昏礼者，礼之本也”（《礼记·昏义》），恰恰在于，婚礼作为一切礼的形式的“元型”，恰恰是礼的生命交往固有性质的至为集中的反映。婚姻关系中，我只能以自己的忠诚换取对方的忠诚，我只能以自己的信任换取对方的信任，这是夫妇间的“礼尚往来”，同理，“父慈”才能“子孝”，“兄友”才能“弟恭”，“君事臣以礼”才能“臣事君以忠”。夫妇婚礼承诺生命的对等交往，这是世间一切礼的真谛。或换言之，正如中国古代以“亲亲”为核心的《周礼》恰始于夫妇“成亲”那样，《周礼》“无言不雠，无德不报”的原则也恰发祥于夫妇的“匹俦”“配偶”。

《周礼》之谜之三：礼是否体现了一种“权力话语”？自现代以降，由于受“阶级分析”方法及的历史虚无主义的影响，礼被视为“以长责幼”“以尊责卑”“以上凌下”的统治者的工具，乃至有所谓“吃人的礼教”之恶谥，始终与“权力话语”联系在一起。穷原以竟委，这无疑是对礼的一种历史的误读，尤其对最原初的，尚未遭后儒所歪曲和篡改的礼来说更是如此。鲍德里亚依莫斯的礼物分析得出“馈赠是权力的源泉和精华本身”[①]的结论，也即权力源于馈赠，“权力属于那些能够给予却不可回赠的人”[②]。由是，鲍德里亚进而推出，礼物交换形成了礼物“馈赠一回赠”往复无穷的循环，它与其说使权力得以彰显，不如说使权力的“可逆性”得以实现，使至高无上、畅行无阻的权力得以颠覆、消解和中断。我们看到，这种礼物交换的“祛权力化”同样理所当然地出现在《周礼》里。《周礼》不仅使作为商品之物成为人生命象征之物，还使物的交往让位于人生命之间的交往，体现出的社会的平权。随着社会中权力的退隐，每一个个体在社会中恢复了他应有的生命尊严。这意味着，《周礼》中的理想社会乃是一个王国维所谓的“纳上下于道德”的

① ②Jean Baudrillard, *Symbolic Exchange and Death.*, trans, Iain Hamilton Grant. London: Sage, 1993, p. 49, p. 170.

道德共同体，在这个社会中，虽“普天之下，莫非王土”，但此处的“王”已并非法家“胜者成王败者寇”之“王”，而是“禹思天下有溺者，由己溺之也；稷思天下有饥者，由己饥之也”（《孟子·离娄下》）的儒家之“王”。这意味着，这种道德共同体既是一个人与人“对等交往”的社会，又是一个人与人“无限交往”的社会。在这个社会中，“礼尚往来”的持续不断，带给我们的不仅是和两姓之好的婚礼代表的生命在空间疆域上从家到国再到天下的无限扩展，还有以生者与死者对话的丧祭之礼为代表的生命在时间跨度上无限绵延。它以古人所谓的“事死如事生，事亡如事存”的方式，最终宣布了对被鲍德里亚视为绝对不可逾越的“终极性权力”的“死”的彻底逆转，宣布了“死”走在哪里，“爱”就在哪里出现——“爱”作为生命的回生术，作为生命的不死鸟，使我们每一个人转瞬即逝的生命如诗如歌般地长存于天地之间。

分析至此，笼罩于《周礼》上的重重迷障一扫而空，我们又一次看到了中国古代易、礼的相通：二者都把物视为有“生命象征”的涉身性之物，二者都以生动的“生命交往”为其交往内容，并且二者都通过无限交往最终宣告“权力话语”的寿终正寝。《周礼》《周易》的“周”字，与其说是特指“周人”，不如说是指无所不包的“周遍”“周到”；同理，《周易》《周礼》所属的“道”，与其说是特指“周人之道”，不如说是《诗经》中所谓“四牡騑騑，周道倭迟”的“周道”，即“大道”之“道”。既然同属于这一无所不包之大道，二者又何可须臾离乎，何可须臾间乎！

作者简介：

张再林，西安交通大学人文学院教授，博士生导师，文化哲学研究所执行所长。主要研究方向为身体哲学、中西哲学比较、中国哲学的现代阐释。

Author:

Zhang Zailin, professor of Xi'an Jiaotong University, executive director of Institute of Cultural Philosophy. His research interests mainly cover body philosophy, the comparative study of Eastern and Western philosophy, and modern interpretation of chinese philosophy.

E-mail: zzl@mail. xjtu. edu. cn

身体与符号*

张　兵

摘要：借助符号学的推动，“身体”以其社会建构的身体观与诸多领域相关涉而成为现代哲学研究的关键词，反之，“符号”也因其对身体的建构而后来居上，成为社会批判、权力诊断、文化分析的基本要素。然而，“身体”在借“符号”而“显”的同时又构成了“隐”的困境，即符号建构中的身体是一个沉默的、无声息的身体；在符号学的话语实践上，这一困境表现为话语决定论中的“能动性难题”。女性主义者巴特勒试图以其“操演”理论在话语符号系统内部解决福柯、拉康等社会建构论者理论中的能动性难题，但其最终所提供的策略——“作为被排除之物的身体的破坏性回归”，又构成了其身体建构论立场的反对项，这一悖谬或许促使我们超越西方的文化、哲学语境中重新思考身体的肉体性。

关键词：身体，符号，能动性问题

Bodies and Signs

Zhang Bing

Abstract: By virtue of the development of semiotics, "body" has been becoming a key term in contemporary philosophy's exploration of the notion of a socially constructed body. Conversely, "sign" has become the basic element of cultural analysis for its contribution to the construction of body. However, body is invested with a prominent image while

* 本文为教育部人文社会科学研究青年基金项目“中西哲学比较中的身体维度研究”（项目编号：13YJC720045），陕西师范大学中央高校基本科研业务费专项资金资助项目“‘性别操演’的‘身体’动因问题”（项目号编号：13SZYB19），陕西省教育厅人文社会科学研究基金项目“原罪的颠覆：身体美学的理论重构及其意义研究”（项目号：2013Jk0027）的阶段性成果。

simultaneously forming the problem of *hiddenness*, which can be stated as "the problem of agency". Butler has developed a theory of "performativity" to face the issues of discourse determinism, but she eventually falls into the conflict with the notion of flesh, which oversteps her constructed body premise. We are, therefore, compelled to rethink the flesh body in a new context, and even to explore the problem beyond the frame of Western cultural and philosophical thought.

Key words: bodies, signs, the problem of agency.

如果"转向"是基于过往运动历程的反动环节，则"身体转向""符号学转向"这些表述的流行不仅显示了"身体"与"符号"在当前理论运动中对哲学中央舞台的渴望，而且暗示了其声名鹊起的原因，即对自身被压制的隐秘历史的重述及重新肯定。在自我认定的努力中，"身体"与"符号"共同营造了当代哲学的某种氛围，并且在摆脱心理/身体、所指/能指的二元结构中相交织。然而，在身体与符号的汇流乃至重合之中，身体固有的疑难以一种新的形式呈现出来，并在这一新的形态中包含符号的"失败"，这一"失败"在肯定与否定意义上都与能动性问题有关，但能动性的内在要求又指向了符号化身体的反面，构成了身体运动的又一个反向环节。

一

在西方传统哲学中，人对自我身份的确认不是通过身体而是通过"祛身体"(decorporealize) 来实现的，在笛卡尔对"我思"的执着中，"我有一个身体"作为一个最明显的事实被搪塞过去。[①]"身体"是不在场的，对于身体

---

① "对身体的遗忘"浇铸了笛卡尔影响深远的二元结构丰碑，这一"密码"在胡塞尔自谓"20世纪的笛卡尔主义"中仍一脉相随，思维的"纯粹性"首先意味着纯粹于身体性（Leiblichkeit），对自我身份的肯定与对身体的剥离在同一行程。更大的问题在于，对身体的贬损不仅仅是在具有深度的高水平认知层面上，在不纯粹的感知层面上也有一个"忘身"的自然行为。我们暂且借用胡塞尔"原意识"(Urbewuβtsein) 和"后反思"(Reflexion) 一组概念，尝试分析布伦塔诺曾列举的一个与"内感知"——有时也被胡塞尔称作"原意识"——相矛盾的例子：当我想观察在我胸腔中熊熊燃烧的怒火时，那怒火必定已经冷却了。抛开胡塞尔及其他现象学家关于"后反思"定义的复杂争论，这里，在反思中，"怒火"已经失去了其强烈情绪的身体性特征，变成了意识的纯粹内容；在原意识中，在我不可遏止的暴怒中，虽然有剧烈的身体动作，我却意识不到我在发怒，怒火在我的注意力之外。这后一种情况通常被看作笛卡尔式二元结构的一个效应，但在 Drew Leder 看来，身体在身体活动中这种自然的"非对象化"恰恰"在鼓励和支持笛卡尔二元主义中扮演了一个决定性的角色"（具体论述可参见 Drew Leder, *The Absent Body*. Chicago: The University of Chicago Press, 1990)。

社会学的倡导者特纳来说，将“不在场”（absent）看作对身体的“忽视”“湮没”或许更恰当些，“因为社会学理论中的身体实有一段私下的、隐秘的历史而非全无历史”。[①] 特纳的“身体社会学”（sociology of the body，其《身体与社会》一书于 1984 年首次出版）常被看作身体诸问题的涌现节点，“自 20 世纪 80 年代起在人文社科领域关于身体的著作有一个大爆发”[②]，此爆发不仅指著作的数量，也包括讨论的领域，即身体不再局限于生物学之内，而是一个涉及面广泛的社会文化议题。

事实上，当代的身体研究之为人所瞩目应追溯到福柯，用特纳本人的话说，《身体与社会》“在某种程度上可看作是米歇尔·福柯哲学的一个运用”[③]。的确，福柯在《规训与惩罚》（该书于 1975 年首次出版）——这本福柯称之为“我的第一部著作”的开篇，描述了一个令人印象深刻的对身体施予惩罚的场面：

> 人们把挽马用的绳索系在犯人身上，再给马套上挽绳，把马分别安排在四肢的方向。……4 匹马分别由 4 名刑吏牵引着，向 4 个方向拖拽四肢。一刻钟后，又重新开始拖拽。最后，经过几次尝试，不得不对马拉的方向做些改变……接连试了两三次后，刽子手桑松和先前使用铁钳的刽子手各自从衣兜里掏出一把匕首，不是去切断大腿关节，而是直接在大腿根部切割身体。4 匹马一用劲，拖断了两条大腿，即先拖走了右腿，后拖走了左腿。然后对手臂、肩膀等如法炮制。刽子手切肉时几乎剔到骨头。马先拖断右臂，然后拖断左臂。[④]

这是福柯以谱系学方法从“羊皮纸文稿”中发掘出的历史事件。该引文不厌其烦地、细致地描绘了身体受刑的残酷场面，这种表达法与权力的控制意图和震慑效果相一致，而福柯丝毫不顾虑读者心中可能感到的种种不适，将达米安（Damiens）受刑的场面完整地摘录了下来。而这具象的身体，以一种触目惊心的方式呈现出来的身体，固然令人难忘，却绝不是福柯研究的主体，也不是特纳将其“身体现象学”归功于福柯启示的原因。不过，在这

---

① Bryan S. Turner, *The Body and Society*: *Explorations in Social Theory*, 2nd edn. London: Sage, 2004, p. 63.

② Mary Evans and Carolyn H. Williams, esd., *Gender*: *the Key Concepts*. London & New York: Routledge, 2013, p. 14.

③ Bryan S. Turner, *The Body and Society*: *Explorations in Social Theory*, 2nd edn. London: Sage, 2004, p. 63.

④ ［法］米歇尔·福柯：《规训与惩罚》，刘北成、杨远婴译，三联书店，2007 年，第 4～5 页。

个血腥的场景中也包含着福柯所要分析的内容：权力对人（身体）的作用。对达米安的惩罚是传统权力运作的典型方式，与现代的权力运作技术已大相径庭。现代权力运作的方式是温和的、道德的、科学的，而不是野蛮的。仍以惩罚来看，“人们不再（或基本上不再）直接触碰身体，而是触碰身体以外的东西”，身体的痛苦不是惩罚的目的，“人的身体只是一个工具或媒介”，从权力运作的有效性上看，“惩罚从一种制造无法忍受的感觉的技术转变为一种暂时剥夺权利的经济机制”。[①] 相应地，施罚者也不再是刽子手所代表的权力核心人物（比如君主），而是由看守、医生、牧师、精神病专家、心理、教育学家等组成，甚至还包括受罚者本人。因此，与传统政治权力的纯粹压制、强迫功能不同，现代权力的运作虽仍有控制性的一面，但其控制性恰恰要依赖于生产性——将权力的意图内化到其作用对象的灵魂之中使之成为权力的积极实践者。

在福柯所描述的权力运作方式的转换格局中，身体的形象也有一个相应的变化。身体不再是一个生物学的物理事实，有其自然的、固定的物质形态，而是一个总是由权力覆盖、赋予（invest）其意义的被驯化的温顺的身体。从这个方面来说，身体不仅仅是医学探究的纯粹生物学意义上的经验对象，“肉体也直接卷入某种政治领域”[②]，权力的运作给身体打上标记，使身体呈现为“政治的身体”[③]。由此，身体不是一个孤立、僵化、自然的存在，而是被权力、社会、文化不断塑造、建构的结果。从其现成性上看，被建构的身体是权力运作的结果，这为一种回溯性的研究提供了依据：身体以其被建构、以其所镌刻的社会密码而成为社会研究的棱镜，通过对“政治身体”的微观分析，可以探察其中所蕴含的权力运作“秘密”，将其解码并使之呈现出来。这可以看作“另类”的社会学研究，福柯自谓之“政治解剖学”（political anatomy），这一研究方式构成了当代“通过身体思考”（thinking through the body）的重要维度。

因此，也可以如特纳所说，“身体社会学”源自福柯的发明。自福柯开

---

① ［法］米歇尔·福柯：《规训与惩罚》，刘北成、杨远婴译，三联书店，2007 年，第 11 页。

② ［法］米歇尔·福柯：《规训与惩罚》，刘北成、杨远婴译，三联书店，2007 年，第 27 页。

③ ［法］米歇尔·福柯：《规训与惩罚》，刘北成、杨远婴译，三联书店，2007 年，第 30 页。考虑到福柯“政治”与“权力”相应的广义性，即政治无处不在，遍及社会的每一个角落，这里的“政治身体”也可以称为“社会身体”。此外，福柯所强调的“灵魂是肉体的监狱”（第 32 页），表明了现代权力对人的管控是不可见的、深入灵魂的，故可把灵魂“视之为与某种支配肉体的权力技术学相关的存在”（第 31 页），它不断在身体的周围、表面和内部产生出来，从而使身体成为一个文化的存在而非一个自然而然的事实。因此“政治身体”亦可被称为“文化身体”。

始，单谈论一个固定的、自然的身体已经不太可能，身体承载着丰富的社会文化信息，是被社会、文化建构的身体。以此之故，身体也成为文化研究的主要议题之一，身体就是一个“文-本”（cultural text），可以由文化在其身上书写。“身体是铭刻（inscribe）事件于其上的平面”，事件之迁流构成了历史，则“历史就是生成变化的具体的身体”。历史总是将其生成变化的谱系附着在身体上，则谱系学的方法，“作为谱系来源之分析，也就处在身体与历史的联结（articulation）之中。它的任务就是展露一个被历史标上印记的身体，展露一个历史对身体破坏的过程”。[①] 这一分析和研究，将不再是一个“‘观念史’，其中只根据身体被感知以及被给予意义和价值的方式来思考身体，而是一个‘身体史’，其中根据身体被赋予的最具实质性的和至关重要的东西的方式来思考身体”[②]。

福柯的“身体”是一个社会建构的身体，一个文化铭刻的身体，“如果我们想要理解它对人们意味着什么，我们需要去理解身体是如何通过象征、符码、符号、意指活动及话语实践来建构的”[③]。对于福柯来说，“身体”以及其晚期着重分析的“性”都是话语（discourse）实践的产物，权力的运作就是话语生产，话语承载着和生产着权力，则福柯的社会建构论也可谓是“话语建构论”。此处的“话语”，是一个符号学的概念或源于符号学，则“身体”概念的社会化，或许离不开符号的意指功能。

二

通常，索绪尔被看作现代符号学/语言学的开创者，他通过区分“语言”（langue）和“言语”（parole），确立了语言学研究的对象：不是异质的言语活动，而是其赖以存在的作为一个共时性结构的语言符号系统。作为符号系统的组织单元，“符号”的基本结构可表达为“所指/能指”，由于单个符号从属于整个符号系统，故符号的意义是从其与其他符号要素的区别中获得的，也是在这个意义上，符号结构中能指与所指的关系是任意的。

索绪尔关于符号的意义源于符号系统内部要素的“分节”（articulation）思想，对于强调符号的本源性地位有重要意义，即语言符号不再是传统表现

---

① Michel Foucault, *The Foucault Reader*, ed., Paul Rabinow. New York: Pantheon Books, 1984, p. 83.

② Michel Foucault, *The History of Sexuality* (*Volume Ⅰ: An Introduction*), trans. Robert Hurley. New York: Pantheon Books, 1978, p. 152.

③ Lisa Blackman, *The Body: the Key Concepts*. Oxford and New York: Berg, 2008, p. 22.

论意义上的思想传递媒介，而是思想所从出、所可能之地基。海伦·凯勒的故事仍然是一个极好的例子，下面是海伦的老师沙莉文小姐记述的海伦的“水之悟”：

> 今天早上，梳洗时她（海伦）想知道“水”的名称。当她想知道一件东西的名称时，她就会指着它并轻拍我的手。当时我拼了“w—a—t—e—r”，并没有想太多。直到早饭后我才意识到，借助这个新词，我可以成功地解决海伦混淆“杯子”“牛奶”这两个名词的困境。那时我们出去走到了水井房，我让海伦拿着杯子接在水管喷口下，而我来压水。当凉凉的水喷出来注满杯子时，我在海伦空着的那只手掌中拼写了“w—a—t—e—r”。这个词与凉水冲击到她手上的感觉联系得是如此紧密，以至于她看起来吃了一惊。她失手跌落了杯子，站在那里呆若木鸡。一道生气开始出现在她的脸上，她连着拼了好几次“water”，然后跌坐在地上问地面的名称，接着把手指向了水泵和水房棚，突然她又转过身问我的名字，我拼了“teacher”一词。……在回家的路上她一直处于高度兴奋中，学习她碰到的每样东西的名称，以至于在短短的几个小时内她的词汇量增加了三十个新词。①

这段文字亦曾被宣称“人是符号的动物”的卡西尔引用过，用来说明“符号的功能并不局限于特殊的状况，而是一个普遍适用的原理”② 这一原理。卡西尔的“原理”也许是对的，但海伦此处的“突破”还不是用来支撑这一原理的。海伦借“水之悟”所达到的由“指号”（信号）到“符号”的跃迁，不是因为她明晓了符号的普遍性，而在于她理解了符号所具有的意义之真正含义，正是符号之间的差异性赋予了符号意义，那“凉凉的水所提供的刺激”与那个已经强化过的拼写“w—a—t—e—r”为这一差异提供了生动的注解，借助这一差异，那个混沌、黑暗的世界才以明晰的面貌向海伦呈现出来。经历了这样一个曲折，最后，海伦才能领悟到“每一件东西都有一个名称”③ 的含义，否则，符号只是如亚里士多德对柏拉图“理念”批判，只是凭空增加了存在事物的数量，增加了点数的困难程度而已。

---

① Helen Keller, *The Story of My Life: With Her Letters and a Supplementary Account of Her Education*. Auckland: The Floating Press, 2009, p. 408—409.

② ［德］恩斯特·卡西尔：《人论》，甘阳译，上海译文出版社，2009，第 48 页。

③ Helen Keller, *The Story of My Life: With Her Letters and a Supplementary Account of Her Education*. Auckland: The Floating Press, 2009, p. 408.

如卡西尔所说，人不是生活在一个纯粹的物理宇宙之中，而是生活在一个符号宇宙之中，“在某种意义上说，人是在不断地与自身打交道而不是在应付事物本身”①。符号所意指的概念并不是事物本身，“是词语的世界创造出了事物的世界——事物起初是混杂在将要生成的此时此地的总体中——词语赋予它们的本质以具体的存在”②，上帝创世可以看作符号意义创造的隐喻，是语言符号使世界成为人们生活的世界与可被我们理解认识的世界，进一步而言，乃至人这一主体（subject）也是符号的创造物，用拉康式的表述来说就是，“人”是能指的效果，“人的本质变成由语言的结构显示其中的效果所编织的，其中他成了语言结构的素材”③。如果说在索绪尔那里语言符号还存在一个深度结构和表层现象的区分，拉康则完全颠覆了这一区分④，强调语言符号的创造性、建构性特征，不仅是人在说话，同时也是话在说人，人其实是“话语”的效果物。

借助符号学，拉康极大地改变了精神分析的气质，把弗洛伊德的生理主义发展为语言文化分析。在这一理论背景下，拉康理论极具哲学革命意义的内涵是对笛卡尔“我思”这一统一性主体的攻击，即作为主体的“我”是语言形构的效果。形构的关键源自一种“身体形态学”的展示，因此，作为功能的自我身份的建构也是身体的话语符号的建构，“身体”是符号意指功能的话语实践的效果。拉康对身体形态学的阐述有赖于其对弗洛伊德“身体自我”的镜像式说明，他将弗洛伊德的经由体验（例如痛苦）而知的身体分析为在语言中被意指的身体。在自我的形成上，弗洛伊德谈道：“自我首先是一个身

---

① ［德］恩斯特·卡西尔：《人论》，甘阳译，上海译文出版社，2009，第36页。

② Jacques Lacan, *Écrits: the First Complete Edition in English*, trans., Bruce Fink. New York & London: W. W. Norton & Company, Inc., 2006, p. 229.

③ Jacques Lacan, *Écrits: the First Complete Edition in English*, trans., Bruce Fink. New York & London: W. W. Norton & Company, Inc., 2006, p. 578.

④ 以符号的基本结构为例，索绪尔将其表述为$\frac{signified}{signifier}$，在拉康看来，如果两者以一种上项和下项平行结合而成的整体出现的话，这个算式就是一个谜一样的神秘符号，于是拉康将其改写成$\frac{S}{s}$，并将其视作现代语言学的一个基础算式。按拉康的解释，这个算式可读作如下：“能指在所指之上，‘之上’相当于分开这两个平面的横杠（bar）。”（Jacques Lacan, *Écrits: the First Complete Edition in English*. p. 415.）这个读法在两个方面与索绪尔截然不同：（1）能指以大写的S表示并被置于横杠之上，表明能指的优先性而非所指的优先性；（2）能指与所指中间的横杠不再表示二者的结合，而是意义对能指的抑制，能指总是抵达不了所指，只能靠引向另一个能指才能成立，因此，所指只是能指在能指链中不断滑动所产生的效果，即所指是语言符号的运动效果，是话语的产物。

体的自我；它不仅是一个表面的实体，而且它本身还是一种表面的投射。”[①] 在镜像形态学上，拉康同意这一观点，即自我是受身体在镜中形象的激发形成的，“这一点教导我们不要把自我看作居于感知－知觉体系的中心，也不看作是由‘现实原则’组织而成的”[②]，而是受惠于误认的功能。拉康用homelette[③] 一词指称六个月之前的婴儿，此时的“小人”是一个没有自我观念、未分化的存在，相应的，其身体的自我觉知是混沌的、杂乱的、碎片化的，借助于他偶然在镜子里瞥见的自我身体的形象（imago of one's own body），这个“小人”获得了对其身体统一性的把握，并在这种身体轮廓的统一性中获得了自我的确定性身份。相对于其实际的身体能力，这一完整的身体形象是超越其身体发展实际水平的，因而是早熟的，也是外在的，把镜中之像当作自我，其实是把“他人”误认为自我。这一误认亦发生在随后更具普遍性的以语言符号为镜的主体的确立中（想象域的故事情节可以看作符号域剧情的形象展示），借助符号之镜，想象域的“自我”（ego）在符号域中注册为“主体”（subject），相应的，在拉康所谓的符号域（symbolic order）中，可以说，身体是被话语建构的。

没有预先给定的身体，身体是符号建构的结果，前话语的身体也是不存在的。虽然晚期拉康谈到真实域的身体（body as real），但这并不构成对其符号建构的身体的挑战，“身体是真实的并不是因为它是前符号（pre-symbolic）的，而是由于它不能依赖于能指得到理解”[④]；同样，由内在感觉所确证的身体观也与拉康的符号建构论截然相反，如其所说，“他者的享

① 弗洛伊德：《自我与本我》，杨韶刚译，车文博主编，《弗洛伊德文集》，长春出版社，2006年，第127页。弗洛伊德在该书的英文版（1927）中给出了一个脚注：“意即，自我基本上是从身体的感觉中派生的，主要是从身体表面产生的那些感觉获得的。因此，可以把它看做是身体表面的一种心理投射，另外，如上所见，它代表心理结构的外观（superficies）。”巴特勒对此有一个评论，“尽管弗洛伊德在此试图解释自我的形成，并宣称自我源自被投射的身体表层，但他无意中建立了将身体切分（articulation）为形态的前提”，并将这一线索与拉康镜像阶段“重写形态学（morphological）的想象”联系起来。（参见：Judith Bulter, *Bodies That Matter*. London and New York: Routledge, 2011, p. 197, 41.）

② Jacques Lacan, *Écrits: the First Complete Edition in English*, trans., Bruce Fink. New York & London: W. W. Norton & Company, Inc., 2006, p. 80.

③ 这是拉康所造的合成词，由 homme（人）和 omelette 叠加而成，后者有“小”和“蛋”两义，故其既可指六个月大的“小人”——婴儿，也指“蛋形人”。该词借用了柏拉图《会饮》中阿里斯托芬所讲的神话中圆球人的形象，此“蛋形人”指尚无自我身份意识（例如没有性别身份意识）、尚未分化（分裂）的存在。

④ Sean Homer, *Jacques Lacan*. London and New York: Routledge, 2005, p. 121.

乐——为身体象征的他者——绝不是爱的记号"[①]，即，身体不是体验的、活生生的身体。

对于福柯来说，身体是被权力话语铭刻的，对于拉康来说，身体是被能指符码写就的。尽管表述上有着细微的差别，一个可谓社会建构论，一个可谓符号建构论，但二者在外在建构性方面是相通的，其中，身体因符号的意指而关涉于社会存在的各个部分，而符号也因其对身体的建构而后来居上，成为社会批判、权力诊断、文化分析的基本要素。

三

作为一种社会批判、权力诊断方式，身体建构论一度为当代女性主义的"翻身运动"诉求所看重，由此，女性主义的性别政治批评也体现了一个从生理的身体到话语的身体的位移。话语建构的身体观为女性摆脱"生理即命运"的生理本质主义枷锁提供了另一种可能，也成为后女性主义性别政治斗争策略的前提。从后女性主义的视角看，彻底摆脱两性之间的生理逻辑需要采取符号建构论的立场，即，甚至传统中有关两性生理身体的刻画也只是话语的建构，"本质的生理性别，真实的或固定不变的男性气质与女性气质这些概念本身也是作为策略的某一部分而被建构的"[②]，用福柯的话来分析，这些策略都是权力运作的一部分，它服务于男性。相应的，出于某种策略考虑，后女性主义采取了建构论的立场，并把它推到极致，其中朱迪斯·巴特勒的"性别操演"[③] 可谓其典型。

在巴特勒看来，身体是被建构的这一立场，其确立无疑与福柯有关。身体是一个话语和权力体制铭写自身于其上的场所，社会的变迁、权力的运作、文化的流行总是会在身体的表面上留下痕迹，如此，身体的表面就是一个写满了符号的文本，记载了社会、权力、文化运作的轨迹。这些轨迹就是身体

① Jacques Lacan, *On Feminine Sexuality: The Limits of Love and Knowledge*, trans., Bruce Fink. New York and London: W. W. Norton &Company, 1999, p. 39.

② Judith Butler, *Gender Trouble: Feminism and the Subversion of Identity*. New York & London: Routledge, 1999, p. 180.

③ "操演"的原文为 performativity，有人将其译为"表演"（将其与剧院的 performance 相联系）或"施为""述行"（这种译法考虑到该词的 performative 这一语言学渊源以及巴氏对奥斯汀"以言行事"理论的借重），本文采用《性别麻烦》一书中译者宋素凤的译法，原因在于，巴氏本人已澄清用 performativity 一词首先在于将其与 performance 区别开来；其次，该语虽有奥斯汀的语用学线索，但还包含福柯、拉康、德里达等的话语思想，已经成为巴氏本人的概念，似不应专属奥氏；此外，中文"操演"一词既可表达建构的外在管控性，又含有个体的强迫重复乃至生产的积极性，可承载 performativity 的丰富含义。

的“身世”，如巴特勒所引福柯《谱系学》中的文字，“身体是铭刻事件于其上的平面”，相应地，谱系学的任务就是“展露整个被历史标记的身体”，借助于身体这一具体事物的微观分析就构成了社会文化分析。“在许多文本中，福柯明确质疑存在一个物质性的身体，这一身体断然有别于在专门的社会领域内建构身体的那些观念的和文化的意涵”①，比如在《性史》中，福柯明确宣称不存在一个先于律法的“身体”，也不存在一个与权力关系绝缘的“性”，但福柯有关铭刻的身体的分析模式，却潜在地包含着一个可以推论出的矛盾，即“权力必定要外在于身体本身”，“福柯描绘这一建构机制——身体经由文化建构形成——的努力，引出了这样一个问题，即在事实上是否存在一个外在于其建构的身体，一个其建构中不变的身体，以及，事实上代表了一个对于文化本身给予抵制的动态位置”②。从字面意思上看，“铭刻”即书写于其上，在书写之前应有一个承载体、一个空白的场所，类似于洛克的白板（tabula rasa）——一个便于刻写的空白平面，则“铭刻于身体之上”是否预设了一个等待被书写的身体，一个尚无任何意义、等待文化形式赋义的质料？如果把建构理解成福柯所说的铭刻，则此处理应存在一个先于铭刻的身体，作为一个预先给予的稳定的存在物成为建构的地基，成为接受诸建构的受体。

再回想一下我们文章开头所援引的福柯关于惩罚场景的生动描述。传统的“体罚”是将酷刑加诸身体，近代以来的惩罚则转变为将体面的、温和的、道德的管控技术加诸身体，同理，后者仍需要一个痛苦或意义的承当者，在这个意义上，“身体被理解为一个工具或媒介”③，福柯仍然会陷入“生理的身体/社会的身体”二分的僵局之中。对于巴特勒来说，身体的物质现实性总是早已在一个社会情境中被定位并被规定的，以性别身份为例，并没有一个不被性别化了的身体，即，没有一个前话语的、作为一个自然事实的先定的身体，由此，巴特勒区分了表演（performance）与操演（performativity）。以表演来说，在一个异性扮装舞会上，人们清楚地明白一个人所扮演的性别（gender）角色与他本人真实的生理性别（sex）并不相匹配，人们知道在他（她）的如此妆容、如此举止之后有另一个行为主体，舞台情景支持了这一区

---

① Judith Butler, "Foucault and the Paradox of Bodily Inscriptions", *The Journal of Philosophy*, 1989, 86 (11): 603.

② Judith Butler, "Foucault and the Paradox of Bodily Inscriptions", *The Journal of Philosophy*, 1989, 89 (11): 602.

③ Judith Butler, Foucault and the Paradox of Bodily Inscriptions. *The Journal of Philosophy*, 1989, 89 (11): 604；米歇尔·福柯：《规训与惩罚》，刘北成、杨远婴译，三联书店，2007年，第11页。

分意识；但如果是公交车上一个坐在我们座位旁边的易装癖者，则很难被视作在表演，他的如此妆容往往构成了对我们严重的挑战。[①] 因为生活中我们是从他们的体容、体貌、体态读出他们的性别身份的，这些诸行为、品性本身就是主体，主体是由这些属性构成的而非先在的，也不是支配这些行为的意志体，如其所引用的尼采的话，"在所作所为、施行、生成的背后并没有'存在者'；'行为者'仅仅是附加到行为之上的一个虚构——行为就是一切"[②]。故对于操演来说，并没有那样一个生理的身体，并没有那样一个行为主体，主体（包括生理性别和社会性别）是机构、话语和实践的效果而非原因，身体亦如是。借助一种彻底的话语建构论，巴特勒可以对异性恋的男权统治霸权展开攻击。异性恋身份只是话语建构的诸形态之一，此外还有跨性别主义者、变性性欲者，男同性恋、女同性恋，话语建构为我们展现了多种可能，女性可以有一个更广阔、自由的表现空间。

排除了福柯在身体问题上可能的形而上学残留，我们看到，巴特勒又将陷入新的困境之中，即摒弃了作为行动者的身体和作为选择筹划的主体，性别操演所具有的积极意义又如何可能？既然一切都是话语的建构，我们又如何选择建构的方向和样式？这个问题对关注"自我呵护"的晚期福柯同样有效。在福柯那里，身体是被动的，被动承受权力运作的烙印；它是灵魂围剿的目标，灵魂以其无上智慧把身体作为碑石刻写自己的丰功伟绩，身体在文化的覆盖中沉默失声。因此，虽然"身体"因福柯而声名鹊起，但在福柯的建构论中却是一个缺席的在场（absent presence），福柯的微观分析只是一种呈现，一个沿着谱系的回溯，无法为自我的未来提供有益的线索。如克莱茵评论的，"我从后女性主义者的作品中读到的身体没有呼吸，不会欢笑，也没有心跳"[③]，身体只是话语的效果物，我们很难指望通过身体影响或者回击那作为规训权力的话语。

这个"能动性问题"（problem of agency）[④] 与作为另一种决定论的话语

---

① James Loxley, *Performativity*. London and New York: Routledge, 2007, p. 142.

② Judith Butler, *Gender Trouble: Feminism and the Subversion of Identity*. New Yok & London: Routledge, 1999, p. 33.

③ Jane Pilcher, Imelda Whelehan, *50 Key Concepts in Gender Studies*. London, Thousand Oaks & New Delhi: Sage Publications, 2004, p. 8.

④ "能动性"的英文词为 agency，有时它也被译为"代理"，此处所讨论的问题也与这个方面的含义有关。在话语建构论者看来，没有一个先在的、统一的、实体的主体，主体也是被建构的，因此，相比于传统的主体观，此处的主体只是一个空洞的主体，如拉康所引用的诗词，"我们内中空空/我们塞得满满/彼此靠在一起/头盔里填的全是稻草。唉！"（参见：Jacques Lacan, *Écrits: the First Complete edition in English*. p. 234.）我们只是空心人、稻草人，只是一个转换词（shifter），主体这个词只是一个代理，没有自主权，其被动性就构成了个体自主选择的难题。

建构论有关，对于许多学者来说，“将社会建构的身体视作对于自然主义的身体的替代方案，这一趋向只是从一种形式的决定论——本质主义，变为另一种形式的决定论——话语或社会决定论”[①]，如此，后者只是前者更复杂的形式而已。话语建构论的这一两难典型地体现在拉康作为女性主义者“不可思议的盟友”（strange bedfellows）这一角色中；当代女性主义者借用了很多拉康的思想，但在根本性上又将拉康定位为男性中心论者、菲勒斯中心主义者，因其理论仍使女性陷入男性话语体系的决定，符号建构论变成了先验建构论。

能动性这个概念主要关涉的是个体抵抗、协商或者拒绝规训权力起作用的能力，对于女性主义者来说，能动性是其性别政治的核心问题。福柯的话语谱系可以揭示女性在权力运作中的不利地位，但女性主义更关心的是如何改变话语实践中已建构的女性形象，那么，能动性问题在女性主义这里又可表述为：如果性别是经由建构变成的而不是一个先天如此的存在状态，那么，是什么决定了这个变成？更进一步，对于巴特勒的“操演”理论来说，操演所具有的自由存在来自话语的重新意指（re-signification），那么改变已有话语的意涵的动力何在？简言之，“能动性问题被重新表述为意指和重新意指如何运作的问题”[②]。

四

一种对“操演”错误理解的观点是，“操演是个人意志运用语言的有效表达”[③]，例如，性别身份的获得，就像某人早晨醒来，打开摆满各种样式、各种花色服装的衣橱——隐喻各种性别身份的集合（由话语建构的诸效果物的陈列室），随当天的心情与愿望选择其中心仪的一种“穿上”或“脱下”。将与这种流行性见解相关联的“能动性悖谬”向前推进一步，则其理论前提为：“（a）只有诉诸一个前话语的“我”，能动性才得以建立，即使那个“我”存在于一个诸话语的交集中；（b）被话语建构就是被话语决定，此决定排除了能动性的可能性。”[④] 在巴特勒看来，回答能动性的问题，不必回归一个先于意指过程存在的“我”，因为那个“我”是建构的结果而非原因。与清晨的妆

① Lisa Blackman, *The Body: the Key Concepts*. Oxford and New York: Berg, 2008, p. 28.

② Judith Butler, *Gender Trouble: Feminism and the Subversion of Identity*. New York & London: Routledge, 1999, p. 184.

③ Judith Butler, *Bodies that Matter: On the Discursive Limits of "Sex"*. London & New York: Routledge, 2011, p. 139.

④ Judith Butler, *Gender Trouble: Feminism and the Subversion of Identity*. New York & London: Routledge, 1999, p. 182.

扮相比，操演否定了那样一个类似表演结构中服饰之下的自主身体的承当者，“表演预置了一个前存在的主体，而操演则对这一主体观提出质疑”①，甚至，操演所关涉的政治伦理道德诉求首要在于对此主体观的破除，“服务于某种形式的权力的统一主体观必须遭到质疑并得到消解，因其意指某种类型的男权主义，这一主义抹杀了性别差异并确立了对生活领域的统治权”②。

不存在一个自我决定、自我选择、自我谋划主体，与这种主体能动性相应的具有强烈情感与坚强意志的物质性的身体也被抹除了。“能动性”在主体性上的悖谬在于，主体只是一个代理（agency），其形成依赖于我们永远无从选择的话语，同时，这些话语也产生并供养我们的能动性（agency）。坚持话语建构论的立场，则不能从身体方面而应当从符号角度去寻找话语建构论中的能动性。从其最初意义上，社会建构论的建构即是一种能动性的表现，这一建构作为符号之建构是符号之能动性的表现，其根源，在索绪尔那里是使个体言语活动成为可能的作为深层结构的整个符号差异系统，在拉康那里是作为大他者的无意识的话语，具体言之是能指在能指链上的回溯性意指。总之，把建构中的能动性归结为符号，在于符号的意指行为是由于符号系统自身产生的而不是依赖于所指，强调符号的意指实践能力及建构能力，则使符号成为与权力运作一体两面的生产性的“话语”。对于巴特勒的“操演”理论来说，符号能动性的另一个来源是奥斯汀的言语行为理论（speech-act theory），即奥斯汀区分出的不同于陈述性言语的另外一种言语，如婚礼上面对牧师“你愿意这个女人成为你的妻子吗？”的征询，新郎坚定而喜悦的“我愿意！”一语，不是在描述一个事实，而是本身即构成了一个行为：“很明显，在这些例子中说出一句话（当然，要在合适的情境下）不是描述我所做的事情或陈述我正在做的事情：说这些话就是在做事。”③ 奥斯汀将这一类型的话语称为“施行话语”（performative utterance），因其表明“言语的发出就是在实施一个行为”。奥斯汀的以言行事场景与阿尔都塞著名的警察询唤场景很相似：警察过“嗨！叫你呢！”这一言语询唤（intepellation），大街上被询唤

---

① Judith Butler, “Gender as Performance: An Interview with Judith Butler”, *Radical Philosophy: A Journal of Socialist and Feminist Philosophy*, 67 (Summer): 32.

② Judith Butler and Athena Athanasiou, *Dispossession: The Performative in the Political*. Cambridge&Malden: Polity Press, 2013, p. ix.

③ John Langshaw Austin, *How to Do Things with Words*. Oxford: Oxford University Press, 1962, p. 6.

的那个人“仅仅做了一个一百八十度的转身，他就变成了一个主体”①。这里，符号的能动性变成了话语的决定性，是话语产生了那个主体，就像拉康的律法以其强制性使那个“它”在符号域中注册从而成为主体（“他”或“她”）。

话语的建构成为一种排除了能动性的决定论。在巴特勒看来，问题在于“阿尔都塞把这种‘招呼’或‘询唤’设想为一种单边行为”，“没有考虑到这一询唤律法所可能引出的一系列违反。律法不但有可能被拒绝，而且有可能被破裂，被迫进行重新表述（rearticulation），使其自身单边运转方式的一神论式的强制性受到质疑”②。这一施行的构成性失败又与德里达所说的符号的失败有关。德里达的符号思考起因于对胡塞尔的“意谓”（*Bedeutung*）概念的思考。为了保证意向性行为构成的含义的纯粹同一性，胡塞尔坚持与意谓同一性相应的符号表达的无限可重复性。“一个只此‘一次’发生的符号将不是一个符号”③，意向性的、观念的纯粹性要求符号能够无限地自我重复，即在符号的意指中“能指总能绝对地达到所指”，从而维护“在场”的优先特权。在德里达看来，符号的重复性不能保证意指的统一性，而恰恰是意义分裂乃至增衍的根源，原因在于，如前所引的奥斯汀关于施行话语的论断：一个施行话语或询唤必须在合适的情境下才有效，而符号的可重复性又要求符号“必须能够将其从其生产的当下在场与单一意向中剥离出来”④，从而有一个符号的失败。这一超出了其原初语境的再次使用固然是历史意指的失败，但也可以看作新的意指及与其相应的情境生成的无限可能性。因此，符号的重复不是保持其意义自我统一性、保证话语建构同样有效性的构成机制，而是意义延异、撒播的路径，因为，符号的任意性所代表的差异性一开始就植根于符号的内在结构中，符号与其被看作一个忠实于能指的所指，不如看作一个意谓不断位移的踪迹（trace）。“踪迹”是对在场形而上学和本体论神学中那个起核心作用的超验所指的解构，同时“它的功能也动摇了符号的形而上学的决定性”⑤。

---

① ［法］阿尔都塞：《哲学与政治——阿尔都塞读本》，陈越译，吉林人民出版社，2011年，第306页。

② Judith Butler, *Bodies that Matter: On the Discursive Limits of "Sex"*. London & New York: Routledge, 2011, p. 82.

③ Jacques Derrida, *Voice and Phenomenon: Introduction to the Problem of the Sign in Husserl's Phenomenology*, trans. Leonard Lawlor. Evanston: Northwestern University Press, 2011, p. 42.

④ Jacques Derrida, "Signature Event Context", *A Derrida Reader: Between the Blinds*, ed., Peggy Kamuf. New York: Columbia University Press, 1991, p. 107.

⑤ Niall Lucy, *A Derrida Dictionary*. Malden, Oxford & Carlton: Blackwell Publishing, 2004, p. 144.

德里达关于符号重复性的解释，有助于我们理解巴特勒赋予“操演”的特别的能动性含义，“如果借助德里达的征引概念重新思考，操演将对诸政治能指的操演性特征给予说明，其中一个根本的民主理论将被发现有其价值”[①]。但是德里达有关重复性征引及其中可能的失败等的说明，只是对霸权话语形态的解构，其能动性所蕴含的解放的民主含义只停留在“去中心化”的意义上，其所提供的只是解构之后的诸多可能性，缺乏能动性所特有的在积极方向上的要求。由此，在由符号的重复性所导致的话语的重新意指方面，巴特勒要彻底解决的能动性难题是如何使这一重复性朝向某一个所需要的方向运动，或者说，如何使那些曾被规范话语所压制的存在从话语中建构出来。在这里，巴特勒又借助了精神分析对“重复性”的解释。弗洛伊德关于忧郁症机制的解释将“压抑”视作生产性力量的可能，在忧郁症中，那对欲望的压抑既是对欲望的拒绝也是对欲望的保留，欲望总是以各种不同的形式在现实中表现出来，这也是福柯曾经分析过的抑制与生产合为一体的律法（话语）的本性。在精神分析的维度中巴特勒又需要重新思考身体的物质性问题：身体的物质性如何体现？肉体生命真的可以在理论上化约为一个符号的存在吗？巴特勒虽然坚持身体的物质性，但她并没有把身体看作与其周遭具体情境一齐活灵活现的身体，而是看作——如其 *Bodies that Matter*（可以译成《麻烦的是身体》）一书的副标题所显示的——话语的界限，是话语实践和符号意指所遭到的抵制。在这一抵制中，话语建构身体的物质性喻示的是某种超出话语体系的外在，“但它并非一种绝对意义上的‘外在’，即超出或反击话语边界的存在论意义上的‘在那儿’（thereness）”[②]，而是一种构成性外在，它指示的是话语边界的脆弱性以及运动性。以女同性恋者为例，异性恋的菲勒斯话语将身体作为令人嫌恶的对象排除为“外在”，这一“外在”作为“压抑”下的“无意识”[③] 总是试图回归话语形态，从而使那些曾被贬黜的、嫌恶的存在在话语中建构出来。因此，事关一种能动性的抵制，巴氏又不能仅仅将身体当作一种话语的边界，而需要对欲望的身体、身体的欲望的额外援引。

---

① Judith Butler, *Bodies that Matter*: *On the Discursive Limits of* “*Sex*”. London & New York: Routledge, 2011, p. 143.

② Judith Butler, *Bodies that Matter*: *On the Discursive Limits of* “*Sex*”. London & New York: Routledge, 2011, p. xvii.

③ 在这里，巴特勒显然是整合了福柯的权力-话语理论与精神分析的话语理论，权力对身体的规训一方面将主体按照话语的结构建构出来，同时将那种与规范性（normativity）相冲突的身体要素排除在外。这些被排除在外的“剩余物”（remainder）构成了压抑机制中的无意识冲动，这些无意识冲动因子总会以种种变形重复出现在意识中，构成对意识话语的和已建构主体的某种威胁。

这里不再是符号自身的分裂逻辑，而是欲望的生产逻辑。被压抑的欲望的重复性，实质是渴求在话语秩序中的回返，曾经被符号秩序拒绝的东西试图重返回来。重复不仅是某种主体化未能出现的标记，同时也是主体化失败的标记，“在主体中所重复的是彻底排除于主体的形构之外的东西，是威胁到主体自身的边界和一致性的东西”[①]。这些曾被排除之物的回归不仅是对不可抗律法的破坏，也是“一个有效的分裂，一个对符号域进行彻底的再表述的时刻，其中身体变得至为关键了”[②]。

让我们在此处把巴特勒有关能动性的复杂解释简化一下。(1) 性别身份与主体性都是由话语建构的，并不存在话语之外的身体，谈论话语之外的物质性是没有意义的；(2) 建构论中主体的能动性被让渡给话语的能动性，在某种程度上递变为话语决定论而排除了能动性；(3) 话语决定论中的规范话语的霸权统治依赖于对“他者”的排除，这一排除对“他者”来说构成了精神分析意义上的压抑；(4) 被压抑的欲望作为一种原初性创伤构成了对话语秩序的抵制，它总是要不断地表现自己；(5) 曾被排除之物（痛苦的身体）在话语秩序中的破坏性回归构成了对现有话语形态的挑战，从而使话语的重新意指成为可能，这也是话语自身所包含的能动性之所在。在这些解释中，话语所包含的两面性充分体现出来：一方面，话语建构了主体，建构了身体；另一方面，话语又包含了主体活动的广阔空间，为主体提供某种能动性。但是需要注意的是，对此能动性的说明并没有忠实地存在于话语符号之内。在能动性证成的关键——符号的重复性上，我们不得不引入一个异质性的外援，即与感知和物质性紧密联系的身体的欲望，这身体并非如福柯、拉康、巴特勒等社会建构论者所坚持的那样，完全是由符号建构的——这构成了身体建构论的一个内在矛盾；再者，身体的物质性也并不如巴特勒所宣称的那样只是一个话语意指的界限。以符号吞噬身体也许与自索绪尔以来的能指/所指的二元区分有关，只不过符号建构论者采取了将所指消融到能指中的策略，这一“文化”覆盖“自然”的策略在解决身心二分、以心控身的传统模式中恰恰是沿着笛卡尔的道路行进并将其推到极致的。综合来看，这一立场的极端性，也许预示了另一个议题——梅洛-庞蒂的身体观，即作为活现（embodiment）的身体的重要性，其要走出同样可能极端的肉身性立场，跳出西方文化的框

---

① Judith Butler, *Bodies that Matter: On the Discursive Limits of "Sex"*. London & New York: Routledge, 2011, p. 190.

② Judith Butler, *Bodies that Matter: On the Discursive Limits of "Sex"*. London & New York: Routledge, 2011, p. 27.

架去思考也许是一个有益的尝试。

作者简介：

张兵，哲学博士，陕西师范大学政治经济学院讲师，主要从事中西哲学比较研究。

Author:

Zhang Bing, Ph. D. in Philosophy of Xi'an Jiaotong University. Currently he teaches philosophy at Shaanxi Normal University in Xi'an. His research centers on comparative study of Eastern and Western philosophy.

E-mail: zb18zb18@163. com

消费社会和符码统治：鲍德里亚消费社会理论批判性研究*

李军学

摘要：随着生产力的飞速发展和科学技术的突飞猛进，晚期资本主义从早期物质匮乏的生产主义时代走向了物质丰裕的消费主义时代，如何刺激消费以缓解频发的经济危机，成为晚期资本主义社会的重大问题。借助符号学思想和媒介力量，鲍德里亚建构了一套刺激消费欲望，缓解社会危机的符号政治经济学理论，从而将社会的阶级矛盾转向了对商品的符号价值追求。这种转变不仅无助于从根本上解决资本主义社会日益严重的社会问题，反而使人们陷入了不幸的异化境地和生态危机之中。毫无疑问，理解鲍德里亚的这些思想对于我们当代经济社会的发展具有重大的建设价值和理论启示意义。

关键词：消费社会，符号价值，异化，符码统治

Consumer Society and Code Control：Critique of Baudrillard's Theories on Consumer Society

Li Junxue

Abstract：With the rapid development of science and technology, post-capitalism, which developed from productivity to consumerism, faces the important problem of how to address material deprivation by stimulating people towards consumption. In response to this question,

* 本文是教育部人文社会科学研究专项基金（项目编号：13JD710032），陕西省社科联科研项目（项目编号：109-211208）。陕西省教育厅人文社会科学研究基金项目（项目编号：2013JK0027），校博士基金项目（项目编号：109-211201）的阶段性研究成果之一。

Baudrillard constructed a semiotic political economics. However, his theories haven't solved our capitalist society's increasingly serious crisis, as our society continues to fall into greater alienation and ecological danger. This critique will explore Baudrillard's theories in details, and outlining their significance as well as their falterings.

Key words：consumer society, signal value, alienation, code control

在鲍德里亚看来，晚期资本主义社会的一个明显事实是，人们已经摆脱了早期资本主义社会的物质匮乏状态，实现了物质财富的极大繁荣，摆在人们面前的重大问题已经不是如何生产更多物质产品，而是如何把更多商品销售出去。如何销售这些产品？鲍德里亚在借鉴巴塔耶“普遍经济学”和索绪尔、巴尔特等符号学思想基础上，提出了有别于马克思政治经济学的符号政治经济学，且将其视为消费社会的重要理论指南。那么，鲍德里亚符号政治经济学是如何成为消费社会理论指南的？这一理论对于晚期资本主义社会产生了怎样影响？这些是我们值得探讨和思考的重要问题。

一、消费社会中符号价值的理论缘起

由于晚期资本主义社会一方面进行经济制度的自我更新，吸收了计划经济的有益成分，使得资本主义频发的经济危机有所缓解；另一方面，随着科技的发展和经济的增长，人们的物质生活水平得到了大幅提升，从中受益的被统治阶级于是接受和认同了现行社会体制，革命热情逐渐丧失，因而晚期资本主义社会反而使力图取代资本主义的社会主义革命一再受挫，法国“五月革命”的失败就是一个极为典型例子。那么，导致这一现象的深层原因何在？在我们看来，除了晚期资本主义经济政策自我调整外，造成这一深层变化的根由无疑是晚期资本主义社会思想文化的重大转变，这一重大转变就体现在从早期市场资本主义为了完成资本积累所主张的禁欲主义思想，向晚期垄断资本主义为促进商品消费而倡导的纵欲主义观念的转变。① 这一转变把人们从关注资本主义早期阶级斗争的革命热情引向了晚期对商品符号价值的

① 在关于资本主义的起源问题上，从文化根源上，有两种截然不同的说法，一种是马克斯·韦伯的《新教伦理与资本主义精神》，韦伯认为正是新教伦理的禁欲主义思想为早期的资本积累乃至资本主义的发展奠定了基础；与之相反，桑巴特在《奢侈与资本主义》一书中，却认为早期资本主义的发展与封建贵族阶级及新兴资产阶级的奢侈型消费有关，正是他们奢侈型消费才促进了资本主义的发展。

追求。一如瑞泽尔所言："想象一场由那些整天成为'宝马'轿车而不是'现代'轿车的消费者所需的金钱而忙忙碌碌的人们来承担社会革命是极其困难的。"[①] 而对符号价值的追求是从刺激人们的消费欲望开始的。

对于社会发展而言，人的欲望具有举足轻重的作用，正如马克思所言，自古以来人的贪欲和权势欲是推动社会发展的有力杠杆，但在生产力落后和物质财富极为有限的时代，"人们对欲望的追求还处在仅仅满足于生理需要和使用价值为目的，人在这种状态下生产的东西不多于他直接的需要，他需要的界限就是他生产的界限"[②]。欲望被视为"被诅咒的部分"，因而禁欲主义思想历来是古代统治者所倡导的一种价值观念。统治阶级总是通过宗教、道德、法律、禁忌等种种手段来抑制普通大众的物质欲望，这一方面是为了促进扩大再生产，另一方面是为了满足自身穷奢极欲的物质享受。所以在早期专制社会和资本主义发展初期，"无论在物质上和精神上，臣民几乎处于禁欲状态，而君主的欲望却得到了充分的满足，臣民的欲望转化成君主之欲望的欲望……于是，前者无个体的欲望可言，后者的个体欲望却无限膨胀，专制体制使君主变成了社会体"[③]。但是，到了资本主义社会发展晚期，随着科学技术的发展，人们的物质财富实现了极大繁荣，"存在着一种由不断增长的物、服务和物质财富所构成的惊人的消费和丰盛现象。……富裕的人们不再像过去那样受到人的包围，而是受到物的包围"[④]，加之封建社会的社会地位及等级界限被打破，摆在人们面前的不再是基本生存和生产问题，而是如何消费以及使人们自觉地实现对商品的购买问题。如果仅仅局限于人们实际生活需要而满足于购买商品的使用价值，显然不能解决生产过剩问题，更不能实现商品的最终目的和促进经济发展的，因此，在人们的基本需求得到满足之后，不断制造和刺激人们的消费欲望，以便让人们心甘情愿地购买在实际生活中并不具有多大价值，但却能满足他们某种欲望的商品，才是晚期资本主义社会面临的首要课题。因而在晚期资本主义社会，消费比生产更重要。正如鲍德里亚所说："关于消费的一切意识形态都想让我们相信我们已经进入了一个新纪元，一场决定性的人文'革命'把痛苦而英雄的生产年代与舒适的消费年代划分开来了，这个年代终于能够正视人的欲望。"[⑤] 但是，人的欲

① ［美］乔治·瑞泽尔：《后现代社会理论》，谢立中译，华夏出版社，2003 年，第 113 页。
② 《马克思恩格斯全集》第 42 卷，人民出版社，第 33 页。
③ 韩桂玲：《吉尔·德勒兹身体创造学研究》，南京师范大学出版社，2011 年，第 124 页。
④ ［法］鲍德里亚：《消费社会》，刘成富、全志钢译，南京大学出版社，2008 年，第 1 页。
⑤ ［法］鲍德里亚：《消费社会》，刘成富、全志钢译，南京大学出版社，2008 年，第 64 页。

望却是一个无法定性和定量的变数，之所以人的欲望难以确定，就是因为在人的心理世界中，人的欲望始终处在一种欲壑难填的“匮乏感”之中，而这种“匮乏感”也正是在我们与周围世界“他者”的比较中产生的。而在消费社会中，刺激消费者进行消费就是要不断地制造消费者不断寻求承认的欲望，让消费者永远活在“他者”眼中的“匮乏感”之中，使其永无休止地走在试图消弭自我“匮乏感”的路上。这是借助“能指符号”来完成的。因为“倘若不借助于能指符号，我们将不能再遭遇真正的欲望对象……能指成了欲望机器的真正内驱力”①。在这种符号价值的引导下，消费者从未面对过自己的真正需要，它内在于那些符号的召唤。那么，鲍德里亚是怎样发现物的符号价值的呢？我们有必要追溯鲍德里亚物的符号价值形成的来龙去脉，以便于更为清楚地把握其消费社会的符号价值逻辑。

鲍德里亚符号政治经济学思想的形成在很大程度上受巴塔耶普遍经济学思想的影响。正是借助巴塔耶的普遍经济学思想，鲍德里亚提出了物的功利性价值之外的物之非功能性的符号价值。相对于巴塔耶普遍经济学思想而言，古典经济学是从狭隘功利主义思想出发来看待经济发展的，认为生产发展的目的就是经济的增长和财富的积聚。巴塔耶则认为正像生命有机体成长过程中能量生产总要多于能量消耗，而多余能量必须被“排泄”出去一样，资本主义社会也必须想办法把自己生产的剩余价值“消耗”出去，否则便会导致晚期资本主义经济危机频发，从而使经济发展处于停滞和恶化状态，因此晚期资本主义社会中的消费比生产更重要。要实现消费，也就是说要刺激人们去购买除了满足自己生活资料所需之外的其他商品，就必须借助超出商品自身的符号价值，因为“无论在符号逻辑还是象征逻辑里，物品都彻底地与某种明确的需求或功能失去了联系”②。而这一点也像费瑟斯通所指出的那样，“在鲍德里亚看来，面向大众的商品生产运动的重要特征，是在资本主义交换价值的支配下，原有的‘自然’使用价值消失了，从而使商品变成了索绪尔意义上的记号，其意义可以任意地由它在能指的自我参考系统中的位置来确定，因此，消费就绝不能理解为对使用价值、实物用途的消费，而应主要看作是对记号的消费”③。另一方面，促使鲍德里亚从马克思的政治经济学走向符号政治经济学的还有莫斯、列斐伏尔等的影响。在莫斯《礼物》一书中，作为

① 张一兵：《不可能的存在之真——拉康主体理论研究》，人民出版社，2005年，第7页。

② ［法］鲍德里亚：《消费社会》，刘成富、全志钢译，南京大学出版社，2008年，第1页。

③ ［英］迈克·费瑟斯通：《消费文化与后现代主义》，刘精明译，译林出版社，2000年，第124页。

商品的礼物已经丧失了其自身所具有的实用价值，而成了商品拥有者自身地位和身份权力的象征。而受列斐伏尔“消费受控官僚制社会”观点的影响，鲍德里亚借助索绪尔、巴尔特等符号学理论完成了消费社会的符号价值的创制。

众所周知，索绪尔对于符号学思想的重大贡献在于建立了符号学独立自足的体系[①]，也就是说，符号学中的符号并不是对现实事物的指涉，而是由能指（signifer）和所指（signified）构成的。前者指语音信息的接受者所听到的口语词汇的听觉形象（sound），后者指能指的刺激在接受者心中所唤起的意象（mental image），能指和所指之间并无内在的联系，而是具有任意性，它们的结合是特定社团的契约使然。“符号的任意性并不是意味着符号本身的选择完全交由言说者来决定，而是意味着符号本身与它所表达的对象内容之间不存在自然的联系，事实上，在社会当中使用的每一个表达中介都必须以约定俗成的集体行为为基础。”[②] 如果说索绪尔的符号学还仅限于符号学自身的理论建构的话，那么，巴尔特在继承索绪尔符号学理论的基础上，进一步修正和改变了符号学的发展方向，打破了符号学自我封闭的狭小天地，进入对各种社会生活现象的分析，从而使符号学由普通符号学发展至社会符号学，从而极大地拓展了符号学的表现范围。

相较而言，如果说索绪尔的语言符号只注重语言符号的形式而不注重语言符号实质的话，那么，巴尔特的符号学则依据具体的非语言的实物，是这些实物的“实用”关系和意义；此外，如果说索绪尔的语言符号的理据性来自社会的约定俗成，来自社会的契约关系，那么，巴尔特则认为符号的这一理据性是由少数的技术专家、决策集团来制定，并通过杂志书写、媒体展示等形式传达出来，而被大多数群众所接受的。[③]

鲍德里亚正是立足于马克思的政治经济学思想，并在继承以上符号学思想的基础上，建构了消费社会的符号学理论。受索绪尔语言符号学思想的启发，索绪尔发现，符号学中能指和所指二者之间的关系类似于马克思政治经济学中商品的交换价值和使用价值之间的关系。正如符号学的能指凌驾于所指之上一样，商品关系中的交换价值也最终凌驾于使用价值之上。但在马克

① 关于符号是否指涉外在事物的问题，是符号学中的一个关键，本维尼斯特曾就此批评过索绪尔的符号学思想，认为符号学的符号就是对外在事物的指涉，而这一点又遭到了巴尔特的反批评，认为本维尼斯特根本不是符号学家，符号学只有在不再指涉外在事物时才是真正的符号学研究。

② 林信华：《社会符号学》，东方出版社，2011 年，第 114 页。

③ 项晓敏：《零度写作与人的自由——罗兰·巴特的美学思想研究》，复旦大学出版社，2003 年，第 116~117 页。

思那里，商品的交换价值的价值量还取决于商品生产过程中社会必要劳动时间的多少，而在鲍德里亚这里，商品的符号价值则完全超越了社会必要劳动时间，而完全由马克思政治经学之外人们所赋予的商品的意义来决定。一如凯尔纳所言："商品之于鲍德里亚如同语言之于索绪尔，二者都具有能指和所指结构，具有抽象、等价和可互换性这些索绪尔所赋予语言符号的特点，也就是说，对于符号学家来说，语词是抽象的概念，这些概念根据等价、交换、可替代性等具体的规则在语言结构中可以被整合在一起，同样，商品也构造了一个系统，在这个系统里，交换价值——商品的价格、市场价值等——和商品符号构造了价值的形式系统，其中个人或物品可以被相互替代。因此，鲍德里亚证明，商品被结构化为一个符号价值系统，受到规则、符码和社会逻辑的制约。"① 如果说马克思曾把交换价值对使用价值的超越看作人类社会的"惊人一跳"，在我们看来，鲍德里亚符号价值超越于商品的使用价值和交换价值的思想，便是更为惊人的一跳。那么，符号价值又由什么决定呢？鲍德里亚认为，符号价值并非由符号自身的价值来决定，而是由其社会的差异逻辑来决定，是以它们带来的社会声誉以及所展现的社会地位和权力来衡量的。实际上，鲍德里亚在他著作的《物体系》和《符号政治经学批判》中，分别为我们阐述了"古物""收藏品"和"艺术品"等游离于物品使用价值之外的物品的符号价值。② 这其中，人们之所以对"古物"情有独钟或对"艺术品拍卖"趋之若鹜，就在于人们看重的并非物品本身的使用价值，而是物品的符号价值。而这一符号价值的建构不是来自商品自身的使用价值或这一商品本身所付出的社会必要劳动时间的多少，而是来自人们对于符号的"赋义"行为。正是基于此，人们认为鲍德里亚的符号政治经学已经完全脱离了马克思主义政治经学的历史唯物主义基础，消费不再是一个经济学的问题，而是一个人们如何赋予符号意义的文化问题，而这一符号价值的"赋义"行为，恰如巴尔特所言，在现代社会越来越由社会的媒介组织建构和完成。

二、消费社会中符号价值的建构之途

如前所述，消费社会中商品的符号价值并不完全由生产商品所耗费的社

① Douglas Kellner, *Jean Baudrillard: From Marxism to Postermodernism and Beyond*. Cambridge: Polity Press, 1989, p. 21.

② 鲍德里亚在《物体系》和《符号政治经学批判》中分别阐述了"古物"和"艺术品拍卖"中物品非功能性的价值和意义，这些物品超越了物的使用价值而体现了其符号价值。可分别参阅鲍德里亚：《物体系》，林志明译，上海人民出版社，2001年，第85～95页；《符号政治经学批判》，夏莹译，南京大学出版社，2009年，第101～114页。

会必要劳动时间来决定，也不完全由商品的使用价值来决定，而是由商品的符号价值来建构。体现商品外观的符号价值比商品的内在本质更重要。一方面，在消费社会中，当人们生活的基本需要得到满足之后，符号价值就在刺激人们购买更多的商品中发挥着非常重要的作用。在此，鲍德里亚曾给我们描述了这样一种购物实验：让消费者进入超市，让他们免费在有限的时间内尽可能多地拿走他们所需的东西，结果发现消费者在琳琅满目、美轮美奂的商品世界里，拿到的也不过是一些价格低廉、微不足道的东西。由此可见，在充斥着令人目不暇接、眼花缭乱的商品世界里，如何引导人们购买商品，符号价值的引导作用就显得异常重要。另一方面，在商品的功能和使用价值基本趋同的情况下，如何提高商品自身的价格或吸引人们来购买该种商品，商品的差异化的符号价值就发挥着至关重要的作用。因此，在消费社会中，符号价值显得越来越重要，它带你进商场，教你买东西，帮你花钞票。

这一符号价值的建构在某种意义上已经超越了当初符号的契约关系，在很大程度上由某一特定的社会团体或利益集团通过广告媒介等方式来完成。那么，媒介又是如何完成符号价值的建构作用的呢？媒介建构符号价值主要还是利用消费社会中符号的差异逻辑。

媒介完成符号价值的建构任务必然要基于符号。一如我们在前面所论述的，符号是由能指和所指构成，而在符号的发展过程中，符号的能指凌驾于符号的所指之上，造成了对所指的任意“赋义”。但是符号的这一任意“赋义”行为必然受符号差异逻辑所主宰，而使符号所指涉的物品因此而“增殖”。因此，在符号价值建构活动中，符号的能指就可能脱离符号的所指而完成对商品的价值重构。正如鲍德里亚所说：在消费社会中“财富和产品的生理功能和生理经济系统（这是需求和生存的生理层次）被符号的社会学系统（消费的本来层次）取代”[①]。因此，在消费社会符号建构过程中，符号的能指一撇符号自身的指涉对象，而径直进入符号价值的社会建构系统，由符号的指涉功能走向了符号的意义建构功能。[②] 而在符号价值的社会建构过程中，作为替商品生产者宣传的媒介本来应就产品的产地、性能、生产过程以及使用价值向消费者如实地介绍以促使消费者购买，但实际上，媒介与广告商却

① ［法］鲍德里亚：《消费社会》，刘成富、全志钢译，南京大学出版社，2008 年，第 50 页。

② 在这里，有必要提及的是，针对经济学中的功利主义思想，美国经济学家萨林斯提出了“文化理性”的概念，提出了文化理性制约经济发展的思想，这一点对我们理解鲍德里亚的符号价值的意义理论具有重要的启示。相关论点可参阅马歇尔·萨林斯：《文化与实践理性》，赵丙祥译，上海人民出版社，2002 年。

做着“挂羊头卖狗肉”的工作，总是“将所提供的使用价值全面最小化，并且同时通过对商品进行包装和展开广告，将表象的魅力最大化，最终使商品尽可能地对人们的愿望和渴望产生咄咄逼人的效果”①。独具匠心的广告，能够把罗曼蒂克、欲望、美、成功、舒适、进步等意象附着于肥皂、洗衣机、摩托车及酒精饮品等平庸的商品上，其结果是我们并非是在购买我们所需要的东西，而是在购买符码告诉我们应该购买的那些附着在商品上的“意义”。而这种符号的“能指游戏”使得商品的真实成分越来越稀薄，它所反映的不是对实物的迷恋，而是对符码的迷恋。正是商品的符号价值建构，极大地培育和提升了消费者的消费欲望。② 而媒体的符号价值建构往往采取以下的方式来进行。

首先，这种符号的价值建构往往同人们的社会身份认同联系在一起。在建构符号价值的过程中，如果说在封建社会人们的身份认同更多地取决于世袭的地位，那么，到了资本主义工业社会，随着人们政治分层的逐渐弱化和经济分层的不断强化，人们的社会身份认同就更多地取决于一个人在社会上占有财富的多少和相对购买力。人们不是通过自己的力量来实现自我，而是通过消费实现自己的身份认同。人们购买“宝马”轿车的热情胜过购买“现代”轿车的热情不是因为“宝马”比“现代”更有用处，而是因为在轿车的物体系中，“宝马”比“现代”居于更高的地位，更能体现消费者的成功人生和其不同凡俗的身份地位，这样，炫耀性消费作为提高声望和社会地位的手段越来越重要。特别是在后工业社会，“交通的发达与人口的流动，使个人的接触面有了扩大，这时他所接触到的广大群众要推断他的声望和地位，除了以在他们直接观察之下所能夸示的财物（还有仪态和礼貌）为依据外，已别无其他方法”③。因此，在商品符号的价值建构过程中，广告商正是在这一点上大做文章。一方面，广告商和生产商总是要寻找社会名流或影视明星为产品代言，似乎人们购买了名流和明星们代言的商品，自己会和他们一样身世

---

① ［德］沃尔夫冈·豪格：《商品美学批判》，董璐译，北京大学出版社，2013 年，第 54 页。需进一步说明的是，实际上，许多商品的广告都采取了这种“避实就虚”的伎俩，包括一些“套牌”的商品和商品生产黑作坊，一旦其不为人知的实际状况被曝光之后，其商品连同符号价值也随之一跌千丈。国内外许多一味注重产品包装而忽视产品质量让百姓深受其害的商品，就是在媒体的曝光下而声誉扫地，从而退出消费市场的。

② 在 1970 年的美国，大概有 2%的人想要一部以上的电话，3%的人想要第二台电视，20%的人想要第二辆汽车，而到了 21 世纪，经过大众传媒不断地制造欲望，相应的比例变为 78%、45%和 59。参阅阿兰·德波顿：《身份的焦虑》，陈广兴、南治国译，上海译文出版社，2009 年，第 193 页。

③ ［美］凡勃伦：《有闲阶级论——关于制度的经济研究》，蔡百受译，商务印书馆，1964 年，第 65 页。

不凡、富贵荣华；另一方面，广告商也处心积虑地竭力开发同一产品的不同型号，即使这些型号在性能和用途上大同小异，他们也要煞费苦心地赋予各种不同型号不同的意义和价值，以此作为将产品兜售给消费者的“卖点”。也正是符号建构过程的认同机制决定着我们消费什么和不消费什么，进而决定我们在社会上的地位——我买故我在。也正如此，在消费社会里，“人们从来不消费物的本身（使用价值）——人们总是把物（从广义的角度）用来当作能够突出你的符号，或让你加入视为理想的团体，或参考一个地位更高的团体来摆脱本团体”①。

其次，这种符号价值身份区隔也竭力和社会时尚联系在一起。在符号价值建构过程中，符号价值在引领时尚方面发挥着两种重要的功能。一方面，符号价值起着维护购买者某种社会地位的同化功能，费瑟斯通称之为“地位性商品的获得”；另一方面，符号价值也承载着社会地位的分化功能。“时尚变化的两种推动机制——同化和分化——都为了阶级区分。同化是为了寻找阶级集团内部的相似性，分化是为了寻找阶级、集团的差异性。尽管同化和分化是一个不断变化运动、变化的过程，但同化和分化的结果，最后都将形成一个阶级分明的社会结构”②。也就是说，一旦代表较高阶层的社会时尚潮流的某种符号价值的商品为大多数较低阶层消费者所拥有时，生产商就会制造出某种新的能代表社会新潮的商品并赋予该商品更为前卫的符号价值，以满足那些追求时尚的较高阶层消费者的需求。这样，“为获得‘地位性商品’，为获得表明步入了上流社会的商品而展开的斗争，使得新商品的生产率不断提高。而这使人们通过标志性商品获得上层社会地位的意义，反而变得只具有相对价值了。经常供应新的、时髦得令人垂涎的商品，或者下层群体僭用标志上层社会的商品，便产生了一种‘犬兔’越野追逐式游戏。为了建立起原来的社会距离，较上层的特殊群体不得不投资于新的（信息化的）商品”③。这样，我们在商品社会中，常常看到同类商品新品迭现、各领风骚，不断推陈出新、升级换代的现象，而广告就这样在不断引领变动不居的“时尚”风潮的同时，蛊惑人们陷入不断追逐时尚和流行品牌的符号游戏之中。

这样，在消费社会里，广告并不指涉商品的自身性能和使用价值，而只彰显商品拥有者社会地位或身份认同的符号价值，成为引领人们消费的行为指南。但是，这样的一种严重背离商品自身的实际价值而任意夸饰的符号操

---

① ［法］鲍德里亚：《消费社会》，刘成富、全志钢译，南京大学出版社，2006 年，第 34 页。
② 姚建平：《消费认同》，社会科学文献出版社，2006 年，第 70 页。
③ ［英］迈克·费瑟斯通：《消费文化与后现代主义》，刘精明译，译林出版社，2000 年，第 27 页。

控活动，会给我们带来什么样的后果呢?

三、消费社会中符号政治经济学批判

如果说在初期资本主义的生产主义时代，在生产力尚不发达的情况下，资本家通过对工人阶级赤裸裸的剥削和压榨来实现资本的原始积累，资本符号以其显性的力量体现了其对人的异化统治，那么，到了晚期资本主义的消费主义时代，这种统治则借助传媒的力量，以不张声势的更加隐秘的形式来实现对人的变本加厉的统治。如果说早期的统治体现了两种阶级之间的对立和抗争，那么，晚期的统治则表现为消费者对资本家的自动缴械和自觉归顺。鲍德里亚曾写过一本题为《忘记福柯》的著作，在该书中，他认为后现代的权力已经发生了很大的变化，已经从诸如学校、监狱、医院等实体性的权力结构的统治转向了由电子媒介、符号价值等更为微观的符号权力的统治。如果说前者还使我们能隐约感受到一种"意识形态国家机器"等外在力量对我们的钳制与灌输，那么，后者则是使我们身陷其害却莫知其名的符号暴力对我们的渗透和濡化。这种符码统治给晚期资本主义社会带来了意想不到的后果。

首先，这种符码统治进一步加深了对人的异化。我们知道，在资本主义社会早期，在商品的生产过程中，凌驾于使用价值之上的商品的交换价值成为抹平一切差异的货币符号。为了追求更多的剩余价值来扩大自己的商品生产规模和提高资本有机构成，资本家以延长工人的劳动时间和劳动强度来加强对工人的剥削和统治，使生产者处于动物般凄惨的异化境地：生产者在劳动中不是肯定自己，而是否定自己；生产者在其中不是感到幸福，而是感到不幸；生产者肉体受摧残，精神受奴役；生产者为别人建筑了宫殿，却为自己生产了贫民窟。而到了后工业社会的消费主义时代，虽然工人阶级生活的整体状况有所改善，但其被异化的处境并未改变，不过是更加令人浑然不觉，消费主义时代符码统治的背后依然是不变的资本逻辑的统辖和宰制。正如有学者所言："在资本主义里，符号化的过程是受到经济力量支配的，说得具体一点，也就是被生产者企图攫取更多剩余价值的私心所支配着。"[①] 也就说，19 世纪资产阶级主要关心对工人的控制，而到了 20 世纪，资本主义则要确保人们积极地和以各种特殊的方式投入消费社会。前者将消费者的控制留给了消费者自己，后者则将对消费者的控制留给了媒介与广告商。这样，到了

---

① ［美］苏特·杰哈利：《广告符码——消费社会中的政治经济学和拜物现象》，马姗姗译，中国人民大学出版社，2004 年，第 229 页。

晚期资本主义社会，从劳动者所创造的剩余价值中，不但生产商攫取了一部分财富，而且媒介和广告的经营商也分得了一杯羹。[①] 这无形之中加重了对劳动者的剥削和奴役，而这种剥削和奴役似乎并不是外在强力作用的结果，而是在电视、报纸、网络等广告媒体影响下人们自愿的臣服和归化。人们越来越沉溺于自己所创造的一种外在的、万花筒般的、难以企及的符号召唤之中，不断追逐身份而实际上又丧失身份，周而复始。这不但进一步加剧了使我们自身的不幸感，而且我们失去了生存的内在根基。

其次，这种符号统治更加激起了人们的"流行性物欲症"，导致了人们的价值迷失和身份焦虑。"物欲症"（affluenza）在《牛津英文字典》中指一种传染性极强的社会病，人们不断渴望占有更多的财富，从而导致心理负担过大，个人债务沉重，并引发强烈的焦虑感，它还会对社会资源造成极大的浪费。[②] 也就是说，在消费社会里，由于符号价值凌驾于使用价值和商品价值之上，成为体现社会地位和彰显身份认同的重要途径，而体现符号价值的商品则成了竞相追逐的对象，所以人们把对物欲的满足当作了人生价值追求和个人生活的全部。这样，人们即使实际上并不需要某种商品，也会在符号价值的诱惑下疯狂购买，以彰显自己不同凡俗的社会身份。正如马尔库塞所言："人们似乎为商品而活，小轿车、高清晰的传真装置、错层式家庭住宅以及厨房设备成为人们生活的灵魂，把个人束缚于社会的机制已经形成，而社会控制就是在它所产生的新的需要中得以稳定的。"[③] 所以，随着网络技术的发展，现实生活中，一些被时尚操控而精神空虚和价值迷失的财富拥有者不就是通过在网络平台炫富来证明自己的身份和地位吗？这种注重物欲追求而躲避崇高的现象不仅让个人退化到动物的原形进而迷失了自我，而且在侵蚀着这个社会机体。"现代文明以金钱为最通用的价值符号，以不同等级不同档次的商品符号来标识人生意义。它要人们相信，你的人生有没有意义，成不成功，你的个人价值是否得到实现，就看你能赚多少钱，你的消费档次、消费品位是怎样。现代社会就是以这样一种方式来引导人们的价值需求。"[④] 当今拜金主义、虚无主义等价值观念充斥社会，与这种物化的符码统治有着不容回避的关系。

---

① 关于这一点读者可进一步参阅苏特·杰哈利在《广告符码——消费社会中的政治经济学和拜物现象》一书第三章的精彩分析。

② ［美］约翰·格拉夫等：《流行性物欲症》，闫佳译，中国人民大学出版社，2006年，第3页。

③ ［德］马尔库塞：《单向度的人》，刘继译，上海译文出版社，2006年，第10页。

④ 杜维明，卢风：《现代性和物欲的释放——杜维明先生访谈录》，中国人民大学出版社，2009年，第7页。

最后，这种符号统治是导致生态危机的重要原因。如前所述，消费社会中的符号价值既不反映物的实用价值，也不反映物的交换价值，而是反映人的心理需求。正如鲍德里亚所言："物品在其客观功能领域以及其外延领域之中是占有不可取代地位的，然而在内涵领域里，它便只有符号的价值，就变成了多多少少被随心所欲替换的了……无论是在符号逻辑还是象征逻辑里，物品都彻底地与某种明确的需求或功能失去了联系。"① 这样，人们消费的目的就不是实际需要的满足，而是体现身份地位和权力的符号意义。这一符号意义是以欲望的满足来体现的，而当消费以符号的差异逻辑来显示的时候，它永远不会有满足的时刻，因为，在日益差异化的社会里，在符号引导下人们不断攀升的虚假欲求就会以拥有商品的方式来体现，在这样一种心竞身逐、对符号盲目而贪婪的追求游戏中，整个自然界都成为满足人类欲望的原料库，从而失去了它作为人类家园的诗性光辉，异化为个人的利己对象和满足其自身经济利益最大化的手段，进而转换为赢获个人身份地位的社会符码，从而对我们的生态环境造成了巨大的压力。

公允而言，鲍德里亚对晚期资本主义消费社会的分析和批判，在某种程度上，确实反映了消费社会的镜像，是对马克思早期政治经济学思想的进一步发展和完善。但是由于他过分夸大了物的符号价值维度而忽视了物的使用价值的维度，故其思想不免带有某种程度的片面性。甚至可以说，鲍德里亚的符号政治经济学思想也没有走出马克思的理论视野，他的符号价值仍然是资本逻辑在媒介力量作用下导演的结果。但无论如何，鲍德里亚的对晚期资本主义消费社会的分析和批判对于我们当下社会经济的发展都具有重大的建设价值和理论启示意义。

作者简介：

李军学，哲学博士，西安理工大学人文与外国语学院副教授，四川大学符号学－传媒学研究特约研究员，研究方向为西方马克思主义。

Author:

Li Junxue, Ph. D. and associate professor of philosophy at Xi'an University of Technology. He has also been appointed as the researcher of Institute of Semiotics and Media in Sichuan University. His research mainly foucuses on Western maxism.

E-mail: 13186118976@163. com

① ［法］鲍德里亚：《消费社会》，刘成富、全志刚译，南京大学出版社，2006 年，第 47～48 页。

书 评

声音与叙述：评大卫·利特菲尔德与萨斯基亚·路易斯《建筑的声音：聆听老建筑》

胡一伟

作　者：［英］大卫·利特菲尔德，［英］萨斯基亚·路易斯
译　者：王东辉，康浩
书　名：《建筑的声音：聆听老建筑》
出版社：电子工业出版社
出版时间：2011 年
ISBN：978－7－121－14151－5

建筑是否会发出声音？《建筑的声音：聆听老建筑》一书给了我们一个肯定的答案：建筑是有声音的，并且值得聆听——无论是一座废弃的大教堂、一家以前的妓院、一幢雄伟的房子，还是一家皇家邮局分拣处，透过作者的耳朵，都重新呈现出了它们各自的声音。该书作者是从建筑学角度来阐述声音的：他们通过对老建筑的修葺与重塑，仔细调查了建筑物是如何引导建筑师和艺术家的，即让我们知道建筑也是会说话的，而“各种各样的建筑会向我们诉说民主与专制、坦率与傲慢、热情与威胁，甚至可以憧憬未来或回到过去”①。这本由知名建筑作家大卫·利特菲尔德和科班建筑师萨斯基亚·路易斯所著的书融会了他们各自的专业优势。如，大卫专攻建筑空间设计领域并有丰富的写作经验——他曾获室内及空间设计硕士学位，目前在伦敦艺术大学（切尔西）和巴斯大学教授设计课程，同时也为一系列建筑杂志撰稿，

---

① ［英］大卫·利特菲尔德，［英］萨斯基亚·路易斯：《建筑的声音》，王东辉、席浩译，电子工业出版社，2011 年，第 9 页。后文引用此书仅随文标注页码。

其中包括《建筑设计》这类刊物。而萨斯基亚·路易斯在建筑领域则有着丰富的实践经验——她目前在英国建筑联盟学院和伦敦大学巴特雷建筑学院教课，同时也做伦敦艺术大学、威斯特敏斯特大学和伦敦都市大学的项目。她曾就职于伦敦、巴黎和纽约的多家事务所，也曾举办过个人作品展（作品涉及记忆、腐朽和时间流逝等概念）。而这两位作家不同的从业经验以及相契合的设计理念，使该书别具一格，正如阿兰·德波顿所说，“这本书的好处就在于把争论的焦点从苛刻的视觉和技术角度转向建筑自身所提升的价值，从而使我们能够把握我们所谈的的确是关于建筑的，而不是关于人、思想或者政治议程等其他的东西”（9）。

概言之，该书独特的风格主要体现在以下三个方面：

第一，作者对建筑的考察跨越了时空的局限，也打破了技术对建筑品质的禁锢。即作者从对建筑技术层面的分析转向了人们对建筑的感受（涉及对建筑空间的记忆、情感与想象等），人性化的建筑便成了该书的研究对象。譬如，在《痕迹的代表》一章中，建筑设计师默里提到：如果他找到的建筑只是没有了人性的一堆物质，那是“非常无聊”的。对于找寻声音和生命在建筑的什么地方这一问题，默里更注重人对建筑的感觉，他认为声音不只存在于建筑自身当中，而是存在于一个地方的符号、湿度、味道、杂物中。如果声音有任何物质性的话，那么它的厚度可能也是原子级的，只要轻轻地就能清理掉它。而有的时候声音却非常难以清除，他在维米岭坑道的感觉就是典型的例子——那里的空间太紧凑、太幽闭，并且会让你孤独地忘却了那里的气味。虽然默里承认人们对一个地方的感觉和回应可能大相径庭，但他确信在维米岭坑道里的声音并不是由那里以前发生过的事所发出的，因为声音早已融入坑道的结构。默里说：“直到一些人提出了科学证据来反驳前，我还是相信我自己的感觉。”（59）又如《消失的力量》一章中，艺术家杰力·犹大认为，真正的建筑的声音并不是建筑所告诉你的东西，而是你能从中辨别出来的东西。要把自己的感情投射到建筑上，你必须为这一点留出空间。对这位善于表现消失之物的艺术家来说，参观者对于建筑永远都不仅仅是一个旁观者，而是要屈从于建筑所发出的信号和暗示，融入建筑的生命当中。若真的“听到”什么的话就必须真的做些什么。像布莱希特一样，犹大希望我们有一种积极的聆听方式，这种聆听是用个人记忆去进行的。（101）而在《乳白色的空隙——对一个采矿建筑的重新解读》一章中，怀尔德（在切尔西有一个室内和空间设计的硕士培养项目）则从人们对建筑的感觉与想象中，进一步阐释了建筑与人的“互动”关系。如他深信建筑会通过人们对待它们的方式积累下一种心理状态——“这些建筑残破的状态、失调的比例和设计形式集中到一个建筑身上就会使它们很容易让人们产生遐想”（141）。因此，对某一空间声音的想象，取决于一个人的内部反应（感觉）与空间外部（现实）之间的相互作用。怀尔德进一步说：“我们可以把内心的世界搬到现实。我感觉任何共鸣是我们按照内心世界设计一个建筑的结果……但是建筑的一些东西却向我们述说着失落，要阻止这种失落，我却无能为力。”（141）

第二，该书提供线索多过于直接给答案。书中提出的问题多于给出的答案，但我们往往能从诸多的问题中寻找到一丝线索。譬如，在《马舍姆街2号的音景》一章中，设计师马修·埃米特的一系列疑问可以给我们很多启发：“一座消失了的建筑的声音真的能够保留在原有建筑所在的空间里吗？一个超音速的录音带能够揭示过去和现在空间的声音吗？如果能，我们如何才能听到这个声音呢？这将是一个什么样的声音呢？一个人能够感觉到这个‘声音’吗？……在建筑和它的声音被移除后这里发生了什么：一个空间被创造出来了，或者周围的声音渗入到了人们未曾居住过的位置，只留下嘈杂和渐渐消逝的回声吗？当旧的建筑形式被新的所取代，残余声音会不会继续环绕着它呢？还是转变形式后聚集于新建筑当中呢？……”（206）这些问题，将引导着我们不断地思考、探索。另外，书中不论是提出的问题还是给出的答案，多半都建立在不稳固的和松散的记忆、联想和比喻之上。这又从另一个侧面印证了作者对建筑的研究注重体验与直接感受，并通过与建筑有关的人（和他们交流）与建筑周围的环境找寻线索。

第三，该书作者在凸显建筑与人们的日常生活、与人的感觉密切相关之时，并非就建筑论建筑，还融会了其他文化艺术门类（小说、电影、绘画、音乐等）的例子。如《圆形铸造厂》中，作者以爱伦·坡的《厄舍里屋的倒塌》为例，说明被破坏或者抛弃的建筑常常被一些东西打上烙印，而通过触摸一座建筑会与曾经居住在里面的人有更直接的交流。在《记忆、意识和痕迹》一章中，作者以电影《石头记》（导演彼得·萨斯迪，主演珍·亚瑟，该影片描述一群科学家发现一种新的记录介质——房子里的石头，从这以后他们开始琢磨为什么墙上的石头可以像记录设备一样“记录”和“播放”）为例，说明建筑空间里的确有一些真实存在的东西和以前发生过的事情有关，这些东西或者一些情感因素会被吸收到建筑的空间里，直至今天也仍然回荡在这个空间里。而当人们居住于建筑中时，这些东西一被触发就可以还原。

可以说，约翰·罗斯金的观点始终贯穿于该书——“建筑能够和我们说话，说所有我们认为重要的东西和需要经常提醒我们、能够唤起记忆的东西”，该观点甚至对体现此书的创意和价值起到了很大的作用。由此，我们也会发现该书论及的建筑的声音，并非都是建筑发出的实实在在的物理声音。书中“发声”“诉说”等词汇的运用体现出了一种修辞的方式——听觉譬喻，以此比拟出建筑似乎在向我们说话、与我们交流的情景。如负责修葺、重建的工作人员会将干衬和墙面之间的缝隙称之为“声音的力量”，他们认为建筑和人一样会有口音和语调，会表现出可爱、忐忑；又或者把圣巴尔纳巴斯大教堂形容成一个“放大器”，一个“播放我们自己经历的大音箱”，它随时提醒我们，唤起我们的记忆。诸如此类的譬喻一方面再一次印证了建筑是活生生的，是人性化的；另一方面也触发了我们对视听叙述的思考。尤其是《马舍姆街 2 号的音景》《关于背景噪音的遐想》等章节，为我们指出了一个全新的研究领域——建筑的听觉空间。在这个空间里，我们可以“化无形为有形，化无声为有声”。这也从某种程度上触动了我们对听觉叙述的思考。

(1) 声音可以标示空间，黏合故事情节。

故事的发生需要一定的空间场所，而不同的空间场所具有的声音不同。譬如该书中提到的马舍姆街 2 号，就与其他街道的音景不同。那里充斥着各种声音，包括大本钟、泰晤士河、风、雨、川流不息的车、人以及城市的白噪音，甚至还有地下的噪音。这样的音景也只有在威斯敏斯特声音环境最丰富的地区才会形成，所以在那样的音景下所发生的事件与乡村或北京胡同里发生的事件必然有区别。然而，声音的此类效应还能通过其他艺术门类体现出来，此处不妨以电影《声梦奇缘》为例。这部电影讲述了一个来自爱尔兰的年轻但天资非凡的酒吧歌手与一名年轻的女大提琴家在纽约华盛顿广场相遇，迅速坠入爱河，但却立即被迫分开后的故事。两人的一夜情的结晶——奥古斯特·拉什也因此成了孤儿。10 年后，长大了的奥古斯特只能在纽约街头卖艺为生，后来由于得到许多人的帮助，奥古斯特开始利用其非凡的音乐天赋来寻找在自己出生之日便被迫分离的父母。可以说，整部影片均体现出了声音是如何推动故事发生发展的。电影开场奥古斯特感受麦田与其第一次来到城市中心区这两个场景都是通过声音来标示空间的不同的。不仅如此，整个故事也体现出了声音与空间的关系：美妙的乐音使得他的父母在屋顶偶遇，尔后有了他，又使得分离多年的一家三口最终在音乐广场团聚，声音总是引导着他们从不同空间来到同一个地点。此外，当特定空间下的声音具有“核心”事件的功能，或者声音成为一种“迹象”时，它就不仅能暗示出被叙述空间之特别，还能预示故事的发展趋势。这点在侦探悬疑小说或影片中可以得到鲜明的体现。

（2）声音可以改变空间，影响叙述效果。

在该书中，声音改变（扩展）空间的方式有两种，以《关于背景噪音的遐想》一章为例。其一，化无形为有形。作者以城市景观中的阴影、奥登《美术馆》一诗中表现出来的背景噪音的活跃性以及皮耶罗·弗朗西斯卡的《理想城市》对艺术与声音的理解，来说明声音可以使空间扩展到看不到的领域（提供第四维的空间——透视空间），“而看不见的物体和丰富的细节的影子就是这个隐形领域的表现”（198）。这是从视觉角度论声音的扩展。另一种则是从听觉角度来论，即化无声为有声。作者以先锋派作曲家约翰·凯奇的作品《4分33秒的寂静》为例，来说明我们的身体（身体作为发声体，如呼吸声、血液流动的声音）与我们所在空间的即时互动，也即在寂静的大厅中，我们能听到这个空间里的声音。类似情况还见于其他门类的艺术中，譬如在近期上演的3D版电影《了不起的盖茨比》（莱昂纳多主演）中，声音起到扩展建筑空间的效果。如，黛茜第一次出场时的音效（电影配乐、黛茜的笑声、风声）不仅使那被风吹动的窗纱显得更加飘逸、浪漫、虚幻，还在无形中使人感觉声音在扩大建筑的空间。又如，汤姆带尼克来到他情妇住处嬉闹时，对面那栋楼上黑人乐手吹响的爵士乐音，将窗里房间内的场景与窗外的场景连接了起来，使得楼与楼相互连通。可以说，通过窗口传出或传入的声音，将不同的场合、场景联系了起来，这也于无形中让人感觉到空间仿佛在扩展。而从电影的主题上看，此类诉诸听觉感受的音效，往往会影响电影所要达到的叙述效果。若忽略声音所能达到的效果，将其变成无声电影，或者改换其他音效，不仅达不到其叙述效果，恐怕电影里表现别墅之华丽、生活之奢华的视觉画面都会受其影响。

（3）声音可以穿越时空，甚至跨越叙述层。

在《关于背景噪音的遐想》一章中，作者还以银行总部、高级诊所、丹尼斯·莱斯登的国家大剧院为例，进一步揭示出声音具有带我们穿越建筑空间的作用。之后，作者从舞台本《哈姆雷特》末尾，舞台导演要求结束后要有嘹亮的号角声展开，说明声音不仅能穿越时间，还能穿透第四维空间。此类穿越甚至穿透的效果，也见诸其他文化艺术，例如，在小说或电影中，人物往往随着钢琴声的响起，或者脚步声的响起穿越到其他场景中（梦境、回忆等）。当然，这是在被叙述的空间内谈声音的穿越作用，而当我们考察叙述者所处的空间时，会发现叙述者的声音（言语）也可以带我们穿越时空，甚至跨越叙述层，如小说作品中的批注与评点、电影中的画外音等。甚至，这种声音还会扩展到荧幕外、舞台下。譬如戏剧中，台下观众对台上演员的干预（喝彩、互动、搭话等），跨越了台上与台下、戏里与戏外的区隔。有时，观众也可以像皮兰德娄的《六个寻找作者的剧中人》这一剧本中的情形一样，从台下转到台上，扮演起故事中的人物。

总之，声音与建筑空间有着密不可分的关系：其一，声音能占据空间，比方说在建于1083年至1097年间的法国勃艮第圣埃蒂安教堂里，格里高里的素歌会像黑色葡萄酒倒进一只沉重的大杯子里一样充满整个教堂。[①] 在这里，勃艮第圣埃蒂安教堂变成了一个声音大教堂——音乐承载起了整个教堂。其二，声音能标示空间，比如像巴黎圣母院这样的哥特式大教堂，由于里面有凹室、走廊、塑像、楼梯、壁盒、结构复杂的石头赋格，格里高里的素歌会变得支离破碎、残缺不全，而在圣埃蒂安教堂或西斯廷教堂中，可以同时响起多个声部，它们相互交融，变成辉煌的歌声，回荡在整个复杂的空间。[②] 同一种歌声在不同的空间中有不同效果，恰恰说明了声音能标示出不同的空间。其三，声音能穿透空间，正如19世纪法国乡村的钟声一样，声音可以散播到广场、十字路口以及所有宣告布公告和民众聚集的场所，甚至这片地区以外的人也能听到这里钟声。而声音与空间的关系经常通过其他艺术门类呈现出来，起到上述黏合故事情节、影响叙述效果，甚至跨越叙述层的作用。

当然，该书也为建筑的图像叙述研究提供了众多线索，同时还涉及味觉、触觉等方面的研究，这在某种程度上与作者独特的设计理念相呼应。在此，该书作者用建筑的声音来引发我们对听觉感受的关注，触发我们认识声音与空间的关系，意在说明声音会影响我们对空间的认知，而对听觉空间的选择又会影响到故事的讲述。

作者简介：

胡一伟，四川大学文学与新闻学院博士研究生，四川大学符号学—传媒学研究所成员，从事符号学与叙述学研究。

Author:

Hu Yiwei, Ph.D. candidate in college of Literature and Journalism, Sichuan University, and member of the ISMS Research Team. Her academic interests cover semiotics and narratology.

E-mail: huyiwei321@163.com

---

① ［美］戴安娜·阿克曼：《感觉的自然史》，路旦俊译，花城出版社，2007年，第241页。

② ［美］戴安娜·阿克曼：《感觉的自然史》，路旦俊译，花城出版社，2007年，第241页。

城市文本的媒介解读：评王安中、夏一波《C时代：城市传播方略》

吴迎君

作　者：王安中，夏一波
书　名：《C时代：城市传播方略》
出版社：新华出版社
出版时间：2008年
ISBN：978-7-5011-8504-7

现代城市是现象、历史过程与社会变迁的动力和表征，正如传播学者埃利胡·卡茨（Elihu Katz）所言，"大众传播研究的重心之一即是城市社会的符码系统研究"[①]，换言之，城市研究亦须进行传播学向度的解读与阐释。由此，由城市传播的一系列问题所形成的问题域（problem domain），亟待建构一个现代城市传播研究的新学科。基于"现代性"知识立场，则可发现城市并非本质上的自然范畴，而是处于关联性空间生产关系中的节丛，始终进行着一系列的符号运作和意义生产。而迄今为止，现代城市学（Urbanology）理论由于缺少传播范式的介入，基本把城市视作纯粹物质性载体加以解读，不可避免地陷入某些研究误区，从而遮蔽了对于一系列城市发展关键性问题的有效剖析。另一方面，传播学创立于现代性的城市空间，研究焦点亦主要集中于城市场域中，传播学对于城市问题研究的学理性进路，必然推进总体性把握城市传播学的系统研究范式建构和实践。对此，西方传播学界有所意识，蒂莫西·吉布森（Timothy A. Gibson）等主编的论文集《城市传播：生产，文本，语境》（*Urban Communication: Production, Text, Context*）于2006年底出版，编者意图勾勒出"聚焦于多个理论和现实问题的城市和传播

① Elihu Katz, "Communication Research and the Image of Society Convergence of Two Traditions", *The American Journal of Sociology*, vol. 65, no. 5 (Mar., 1960).

研究之间的总体性地图”[①]，但是，此论文集并未完成城市传播学作为一门新学科的建构，相反更加突出显示城市传播学系统性建构的高难度和紧迫性。正是对于上述一系列问题的有效回应，中国学者王安中、夏一波“构思五载，数易其稿”的城市传播学学科的拓荒之作——《C时代：城市传播方略》（*C-times：Urban Communication Strategy*）于2008年问世，初步“厘清城市传播的域值轮廓”[②] 关涉的问题域，并系统界说、阐释、实践例证了“城市传播学的研究路径与方法”（11）。作为中国学者“第一部系统阐述城市传播理论和实践的著作”，该书既在学理层面完成了作为全新学科之城市传播学的系统性建构，某种程度上在世界范围切实推进了传播理论的发展；又始终以紧密联系中国现实问题的实践应用为导向，从而达到了重构性运用“传播学的研究范式和出场路径为我们思考并试图解决我国当前的很多城市问题提供了另一种研究视角和现实途径”（307）。由此，则可通过对《C时代：城市传播方略》的有效阐释，从学理性和应用性两个层面，发掘城市传播诸多问题的症结所在，有效启发和推进中国传播学研究的发展。

城市传播学系城市研究和传播研究的跨学科研究，其贯通之基点何在？吉布森和马克·洛斯（Mark Lowes）初步设想，把城市视作“生产－文本－语境”（production-text-context）[③] 的循环而加以解读，即城市作为文本，处于此文本的生产关系和具体语境中。而王安中和夏一波则明确指出“城市文本”的符号学学理基础，称“城市文本不仅仅是一个物质性的课题，又是一系列意义的集合体。……城市特别是现代大都市或区域中心化城市……已经是‘文本化城市’”（51）。城市传播学将城市视作文本，重新照亮了城市本身作为符号意义生产传播者的重要价值，而此重要价值却长期遭到遮蔽。如彼得·纳斯（Peter J. M. Nas）所指出的，长期以来“城市（文本）的符号象征主义是一个极具吸引力而同时常常被忽略”[④] 的场域。而只有在文化研究进行空间问题转向，传播理论将城市视作一个“永远处于现在时”的符号生产体系进行文本解读，社会学、经济学、建筑学偏重于城市物质载体分析的片面性才能得到充分揭示。对城市文本进一步追问，则可察知与其内在关联

---

① Timothy A. Gibson, Mark Lowes, Mark Douglas Lowes, eds., *Urban Communication: Production, Text, Context*. Lanham: Rowman & Littlefield, 2006, p. 5.

② 王安中、夏一波：《C时代：城市传播方略》，新华出版社，2008年，第10页。后文引用此书仅随文标出页码。

③ Timothy A. Gibson, Mark Lowes, Mark Douglas Lowes, eds., *Urban Communication: Production, Text, Context*. Lanham: Rowman & Littefield, 2006,. p. 12.

④ Peter J. M. Nas, ed., *Urban Symbolism*. Leiden: Brill Academic Publishers. 1993. p. 2.

的消费社会语境，即“文本消费性日益突出”的现实景观，包括“有形”消费和“无形”消费。城市文本始终进行着各种意义的符号生产和传播，由此“城市文本的符号消费策略”（85）解读则成为城市传播学的重要维度。沿此脉络，《C时代：城市传播方略》提出“C时代”的原创性命题，指出“人类在21世纪将整体性地迈进‘C时代’，即迈进了城市（City）的世纪、创意（Creativity）的世纪、消费（Consumption）的世纪和传播（Communication）的世纪”（内容提要）。在此基础上进而指出，空间文本化延展消费的重要问题，即城市“无形”空间的符号在场和指涉，启示城市文本媒介接触策略的方法论。而城市媒介文本的路径传播，同时也是城市文本符号意识形态消费性的提纯，《C时代：城市传播方略》由此创造性地提出“传播即消费”（87）的重要命题：城市文本之消费语境即传播媒介，亦即符号能指。由此可见，城市传播学即城市文本消费/传播的研究，一方面，它不同于古典城邦的城市学研究，因其始终将城市符号系统置于消费社会的语境中进行解读，具有现代性；另一方面，传播学研究肇始于消费社会之文化工业语境中，始终具有现代性学科意识和观照意识，是城市传播学的学理支撑，城市传播学的学理和现实基点始终建构于对“现代性”的解码意识上。《C时代：城市传播方略》虽然没有明确予以阐述，但其行文始终渗透此意识。需要强调的是，如其所指，城市传播学是“一门交叉性、横断性的学科，它既不属于自然科学，也不属于社会科学，而是一门学科横跨性较强的应用性学科”（10）。作为一门前沿性学科，城市传播学既具有与时俱进的实践意识（中国已将“城市化战略”确定为现代化进程第三步走的重要方针），又具有逻辑理据反思下的前瞻性指示，集前沿性、前瞻性于一身。

城市传播学的新意既在于前瞻性的预见展望，亦在于对于城市问题全新视域的解读。以中国城市发展中的“旧城改造”个案分析为例，一旦进行城市传播学的学术追问，则可廓清同时具有“完成时”和“现在时”的“旧城”本质，揭示社会学、经济学、城市学、建筑学所存在的认识盲区，彰显“旧城”所不可替代的符号价值和代际传播功能。城市传播学循此对“旧城改造”进行了富于创见的学术阐释，指出“从城市传播的角度来看，旧城是‘城市记忆’的空间载体，承载着城市代际传播的功能，沟通城市的历史、现在与未来、彰显者城市‘地脉’与‘文脉’特征并将之传承与延续。……旧城是城市历史的一种‘言说’”（199～200），既是久远历史的遗存，又始终活在现实当下，具有当下的“生产性”。换言之，旧城一方面是过去历史创造出的具有完成时态的“旧媒介”，另一方面则是现代城市文化生产不可或缺的“新媒介”，具备现有媒介所匮缺的符号意义。由此可见，“旧城”和“新城”的性质界定和价值确定具有双重层次。在第一个层次，古代建筑文物等是历史的“旧物”，似乎欠缺“现代性”，而新兴现代建筑之“新城”则是当下的和现代化的。而在第二个层次，大量现代建筑往往是机械复制式的，有着同质性，单调、雷同；而古代建筑相对于现代建筑异质性和独有的差异化特征正是被有被后现代奉为圭臬的“小叙述”。在此意义上，古代建筑是对现代建筑的一种“间离”性媒介，是具有现代建筑匮缺之特殊所指的“新”能指，始终在进行现代性的符号意义生产和再生产。由此可见，“旧城”作为传播媒介既在进行代际传播，亦在进行现代性关系传播。《C时代：城市传播方略》虽未进行上述两个层次的界说，但对“旧城”兼具的“完成时”“现在时”两种时态详加阐述，由此逻辑可有效推进至关于两个层次的省思。

与之相对，其他研究范式由于缺乏对城市传播学维度的体察而产生集体性“失语”，进而导致“旧城改造”的盲目化。由此，中国城市发展陷入诸多误区：苏州在世界文化遗产评选中因历史街区毁坏严重而落选，历史文化名城襄樊市的千年古城墙在“新建设”中被摧毁殆尽，城市符号系统遭到破坏并形成断裂，城市传播也因而患上某种“失忆症”，城市形象的传播效果大打折扣。《C时代：城市传播方略》追问招致“旧城改造”盲区的思维盲点：无知于历史文化名城的文化符号价值及其媒介，无知于“旧城”有效保护的资本效益，更无知于“旧城”中所蕴含的“最先进最科学的因素”，即如北京四合院周围住房、中间庭院植育花草的结构可以保持水土、防止噪音、减少灰尘，自成绿色小气候而远胜现代郊野别墅的建筑理念。基于上述认识，城市传播学提出“赓续与复兴：旧城现代性利用与开发策略”（215）的启发性思路，指出“旧城”现代性保护与开发的基本原则：真实性原则——以保持“旧城”不可复制的历史媒介价值；整体性原则——基于城市文本符号系统的和谐统一，总体上把握“旧城”；可持续原则——使“旧城”的现代性符号意义得以不断生产和在生产。在上述原则指示下，针对“旧城”的不同生存样态进行多元化应对，则有封闭独立的博物馆式或纪念馆式开放利用、半开放性的历史街区规划、“旧城”空间纳入现代式生存的“意义转场”等具体方法论。由此可见，城市传播学对于“旧城改造”和其他现代城市发展问题，可进行有效的城市文本“症候阅读”，厘清其盲区背后的症结，从而“对症下药”，给出一系列行之有效的具体策略，实践其以现实应用为导向的理论品质。

“旧城改造”的城市传播学症候阅读，即对于城市空间多重性之符码解读的典型案例，背后蕴含着对于消费社会空间观的省思。亨利·列斐伏尔

（Henri Lefebvre）提出“感知/构想/生活”的空间三元论，而爱德华·索亚（Edward W. Soja）则基于对消费社会中现代城市的研究提出“第三空间”（thirdspace）的重要命题，有效启迪了对城市传播问题的剖析。索亚指出，物质化城市是第一空间，想象构想性空间是第二空间，在此之外，存在着“可被视作关注‘真实性’物质世界的第一空间和通过‘想象性’构想的第二空间两者的有机结合和延展的‘第三空间’”①，呈现出极大开放性。现代城市的“第三空间”中，主体性与客体性、抽象与具象、真实与想象、重复与差异、精神与肉体、意识与无意识汇聚一体，融化于无间。《C时代：城市传播方略》循“第三空间”的开放性思路，富于启迪地提出“流城市”（Stream City）的未来城市形态说，即在当前“实体城市”和“虚拟城市”的基础上形成的“实体城市内部要素、虚拟城市内部要素以及由实体与虚拟城市相互影响所生成的复合要素之间将呈现出高度流动且复合同构的特征，促使形成实体城市与虚拟城市之间的万象流动与深度融合，两者边界日益消弭，从而建构而成的一种新的城市”（259），进而详细阐释流城市所具有的去地方性、弱结构化、万象流动性、超变异性四个基本特征，由此提供一种现代城市发展的未来指向，对现实实践予以启示。由此，城市传播学的“城市文本”解读转化至“城市超文本”解读。城市的诸多要素皆具有超文本特性，其传播方式随之发生跨越性变化，体现出城市传播学研究的持续必要性。从某种意义上说，“流城市”理论阐述和“旧城”传播读解一脉相承，同样是对于现有思维框架的超越，它开放、流动而且始终保持着学术的敏感性。正是由于独具如此之学术敏感性，城市传播学完成了其学理性推进亟待、实践性应用必需的学科拓荒；同样由于如此之学术敏感性，城市传播学总体勾勒出并进而深入论述城市文本的各个问题域，而中国传播学研究的切实推进亦可由以得以深入。

作者简介：

吴迎君，复旦大学中文系博士后，广西大学文学院副教授。

Author:

Wu Yingjun, postdoctoral researcher of pepartment of Chinese Language and Literature, Fudan University; associate professor at the College of Literature, Guangxi University.

E-mail：townlet@qq. com

---

① Edward W. Soja, *Thirdspace*. New Jersey: Blackwell Publishing, 1996, p. 6.

“其出弥远，其知弥夥”：评张汉良《文学的边界——语言符号的考察》[①]

彭 佳

作 者：张汉良
书 名：《文学的边界——语言符号的考察》
出版社：复旦大学出版社
出版时间：2012 年
ISBN：978-7-309-09229-5

翻开张汉良的文集《文学的边界——语言符号的考察》，开篇序言便是一位求知者踟蹰于家园与异乡之“十字路口”的告解：“长久以来，比较文学者喜用‘十字路口’的异乡，描述他的专业面临十字路口……在‘边界’之内，生活是安逸的，生命似乎是牢靠的；然而，一旦‘出其东郭外’，‘道路’岂仅‘阻且长’？除丘坟点缀，四顾野茫茫。虽然如此，学术的探索与诠释学惯用的古典隐喻颇有启示：吾人由安身立命的、熟悉的环境：‘家园’，德语所谓的‘家园的’（hemlich）局限，往外探险，面临的是陌生的（unheimlich [非家园的]），甚至危险的世界，犹更有不幸者，则如但丁笔下再度离家出走的尤里西斯（奥德赛斯），终至舟覆人亡。但这则传奇岂非道尽了知识探索的真相?”[②] 诚哉斯言，边界的泯灭的确可以赋予人的认知以更大的弹性与自由，但另一方面，一旦我们走向未知的疆野，与陌生相伴的恐惧亦会不期而至。在不同的学科、地域、语言之间，似乎耸然矗立着分明的壁垒；要跨越林立的界限，不仅需要在各个语言和知识体系之间游刃有余地进行符码转换的能力，还需要宽广的视野，需要勇者的开拓精神。张汉良《文学的边界》一书，让我们得以窥见一位智者与勇者所开辟的广阔疆域；作者学术积淀的

---

① 本文受西南民族大学中央高校基本科研业务费专项资金资助（项目编号：13SZYQN01）。

② 张汉良：《文学的边界——语言符号的考察》，复旦大学出版社，2012 年，第 1 页。后文引用此书仅随文标注页码。

幽深丰饶，以及对知识永不疲倦的探索与叩问，都让人击节赞叹。

一、对比较文学疆界的拓展

尽管比较文学研究已经出现了一个多世纪，但从它的诞生之日起，比较文学论者便为了它的范畴界定争论不休：如果我们大致阅读过早期比较文学研究的代表，法国学派的著作，就会发现，不论是梵·第根（Paul van Tieghem）对“国别文学”“比较文学”“一般文学”三个领域的主张，还是巴尔登斯伯格（Fernand Baldensperger）在创办《比较文学评论》时明确提出的对文学作品类似点进行随意拉扯和拼凑的反对，都没有超越影响研究的范畴。而美国学者关注的，则是比较文学的另一个面向，即文学的平行研究。这两大分支如今被公认为这门学科的两个主要部分，但是却鲜有人思考：文学何以在这两种维度上形成比较？比较文学这两种关系的成立，和我们基本的思维模式之间，是否有着某种深层的联系？在《文学的边界》一书的前两篇论文中，张汉良即为“文学何以比较，如何比较”的问题提供了一个清晰的答案。

在《符号学与诠释学——比较文学研究的基础》一文的第一段，作者便旗帜鲜明地亮出了自己的观点：“构成关系的要件有二：第一是两个个体，可称为 releta；第二是使这两个个体相互连接的逻辑……它们属于建构关系的第三元（tertium relationis）。”（3）因着国别、语言的划分而看似泾渭分明的文学史，其下埋藏着相互牵动的种种暗流；然而，倘若我们暂时按下文学作品在不同语言间的历史流变不提，在世界文学的共时截面上，亦可以寻见种种意象、主题、文体的彼此映射，即比较文学研究者常常提到的“类比”（analogy），也就是韦勒克（Rene Wellek）所说的内涵研究。借用雅柯布森（Roman Jakobson）的符号学传播模式，作者首先是改写了梵·第根的文学跨国传递模式，一改渊源学（crenologie）和舆誉学（doxologie）单方面注重发送者（emitteur）或接收者（receoteur）的样态，将文本（text）放置在传播的中心环节，而构成文本的信息（message）或者说符码（code），在整个传播过程中起到了关键作用。如果我们以语言为边界，而文本中不同语言符码的转换包含了表意（signification）和传播（communication）这两个符号过程（semiosis）中的主要阶段，那么文本的编码（coding）和解码（decoding）之对称/不对称，就成了比较文学研究的焦点所在。作者进而引入雅柯布森对人类思考的基本模式，即转喻（metonymy）和隐喻（metaphor）的区分，对比较文学的两种基本面向进行了讨论。雅柯布森的转喻/隐喻二分法，实则是建立在索绪尔的组合轴（syntagmatic）和聚合轴（paradigmatic）的二分关系之上的，只不过他运用了相似性关系的概念，“把符号文本的双轴，都拉到显现的运作平面上”①，这一学术概念上的发展过程，与本文无关，暂且不提。张汉良在此处对雅柯布森的借用可谓妙极：“影响关系是连续、换喻式的；类比或平行关系是非连续性、空间置换的。”（7）比较文学的两种基本模式在思维范式上的科学性由此得以确定。

在确证了比较文学研究的两种基本模式之后，作者进一步探问：比较文学从“眼前”到“陌生”的航程，经历过、或者说面临着什么样的危机？在《再论比较文学的“恒常危机”》一文中，作者回顾了韦勒克和姚斯在文学研究范式上的不同，指出韦勒克及其追随者孙竺瑾所信奉的“透视主义”（perspectivism）即“视野”理论实则是站不住脚的。作者认为，所谓客观的视角不过是一种幻觉，“文学作为对象语言已然被研究者所选择的‘后设’语言（也就是他的视野）所建构”（25）。这种反本质主义的立场解释了具体的比较文学关系得以建立的缘由，即后设的语言可以使看似无关的作品产生相关性，从而得以比较。作者进而指出，“被观察者没有透明的存在，他的意义要靠观察者的输入”（25）。

在这里，颇为有趣的是，张汉良作为华语界生物符号学研究的先行者，其思考方法与生物符号学的基础概念——乌克斯库尔（Jacob von Uexkull）的环境界（umwelt）理论在哲学范式上是不谋而合的。简言之，环境界是由生命体对环境的感知而形成的世界，它的意义是与生命体的感知同时形成的，也就是说，对生命体而言，世界的意义并非透明的、先验的、可发生在自身感知覆盖范围之外的。从文学的角度而言，完全超越的视角是不存在的，意义必须依靠文本接收者的解释才能建立。如果我们采用这样的思维方式去看待文学作品，种种本质主义的神话与寓言便可以随之瓦解。

生物符号学对于比较文学的启发在此处已经有所显现，然而，作者并未驻足于此，他进一步将生态论述分为两类：（1）生态政治学的、伦理性的文学文化研究，（2）具有科学实证性、系统性的文学研究。后者正是他的主要研究方向。在这方面，作者发表于《符号系统研究》（*Sign Systems Studies*）上的论文《寄生符号学刍议》（“Notes towards s Semiotics of Paratism”）堪称典范。该文从文学寄生的比喻出发，援引生物符号学家乌克斯库尔和梅图拉纳（Humberto Maturana）的理论，对社会结构中的寄生现象进行了详尽

① 赵毅衡：《符号学：原理与推演》，南京大学出版社，2011 年，第 165 页。

的论述。[①] 令人遗憾的是，该文并未收入本文集，但它在华语学界所开创的对生物科学进行文学研究的范式，意味着比较文学在第三元关系，即后设语言上的创新，具有重要的学术意义。在此之后，张汉良的学生、现任长庚大学教授的叶玉慧完成了她的博士论文《国家文学的生物学架构：新加坡作品举隅》（*Towards a Biosemiotic Model of National Literature*：*Samples from Singaporean Writers*），可视为对这一研究课题的承接和发展。可以说，作者为比较文学的关系建立设定了全然不同的后设语言，从而开拓了新的领域。

二、对世界符号学的重写

身为比较文学研究者，在进入符号学研究领域时，张汉良的视野也是放诸世界的：这或许是他积极参与符号学史的重建工作，努力在中西文化的古典文献中为符号学探源的原因所在。从 20 世纪 90 年代后半期开始，张汉良就从皮尔斯的符号学三分体系出发，对中世纪符号学与教育之间的关系进行了深入探讨，并在国际知名期刊上发表了系列文章。在本文集收入的《符号学的兴起与人文教育——重读拉丁文学〈神凡配〉》中，作者将自己对西方上古至中古时代的人文教育课程进行了精要的总结，验证了三门、四科及七艺与符号学的种种渊源，尤其是以皮尔斯的三分体系对中世纪的教育课程进行了重新审视。尤为精彩的是，作者引证罗兰·巴尔特对音乐的符号学批评，介入对卡佩拉的文本《神凡配》的讨论，从而以语言符号系统与其他符号系统的转换关系为基点，指出了卡佩拉的逻辑讨论之皮尔斯和格雷马斯思想的启发可能。这无疑是构建符号学“史前史”的一个重大突破，但作者对这一事业的贡献还不止于此。在《互文性与系统转换—试论古代文论的起源》一文中，他对《易经》和《文心雕龙》的互文指涉进行了详尽的辨析，并引入一度符号系统和二度符号系统的概念，对“辞”与“象”这一后设语言与对象语言的交互关系进行了讨论。如果我们将该文与作者稍早时期发表的关于西塞罗等人和中国先秦典籍的论文进行对照阅读，就会发现，作者对逻辑学与修辞学的兴趣是一以贯之、有迹可循的，而他通过对古代哲学与文学典籍的追索与考察，为世界符号学史前史的构筑作出了重要贡献。

除了在历时方向上将符号学推向纵深之外，在当今符号学的共时版图中，

---

① Han-liang Chang，“Notes towards s Semiotics of Paratism”，*Sign Systems Studies*，2003（31，2）：421－439.

作者也进行了相当程度的开拓。首先，作者是第一位提出“灾难符号学”（disaster semiotics）这一术语的学者。在《从“全球符号学”到“灾难符号学”》一文中，作者从西比奥克“全球符号学”（global semiotics）理论无所不包的视野出发，就人与自然灾难的关系提出了一个问题：何以包含一切的灾难现象不被“全球符号学”关注？紧接着，作者艾柯、皮尔斯和瑞德（Thomas Reid）的符号理论，尤其是克拉克（D. S. Clark）的“表意爆发”（significate occurrence）概念，勾画出自然灾难作为符号文本，在人类的经验领域内被传播和解释的过程，以此来说明灾难符号学的任务在于阐明“自然与社会符号系统之间的关系如何被建码即解码”（129）。作为全球符号学的重要分支，灾难符号学研究势必在将来引发更多的学术思考。

除了在符号学新领域的开辟上有所建树之外，作者的城市符号学研究也显露出其学术思维的敏锐与开阔。收入本书的两篇城市符号学论文，其一是借由格雷马斯的符号分离律（the rule of disjunction）对彼处的遥想，辨析德昆西作为观看者和被观看者的身份激荡与其文本表现之间的关系，从而推演出一个虚构的符号帝国；其二涉及电脑科技与文学之间的关系，以林耀德等人的作品为研究对象，描述电脑科技在台湾文学媒体行为、在文化阶层中的作用，以皮尔斯的符号过程（semiosis）三元式来解释泛科技符号世界空泛的循环指涉。应当说，即使是在世界符号学的范畴内，作者的研究也是具有前沿性和创新性的，这种学术上的创新能力，既来自作者多年的学术积累，也来自作者为了追求真知，随时愿意重新学习的谦逊精神。据作者自述，为了厘清生物符号学的发展脉络，他曾经和台湾大学的学生一起听了半年生物学课程。这种对新的知识领域永远保持开放的心态，的确值得当今的符号学人学习和传承。

三、对电影语意世界的探索

在本书的第三部分，作者对诗学问题进行了系统批评，该部分与作者今年出版的英文论文集《符号与言谈：比较诗学的实践》（*Sign and Discourse: Dimensions of Comparative Poetics*）有颇多相互印证和激发之处，将另文探讨，此处暂且存而不论。对于我这样一个既钟爱电影，又喜欢叙事学研究的读者而言，本文集最有趣味的章节，在于它的第四部分，“戏论影片的语意世界”。作者将自己对电影的散论自谦地称为“戏论”，其实当中不乏令人称妙的见解。

在该部分的第一篇短论《小说与电影之间的“墙”——兼论文学的“改

编”》中，作者就以呈现式（presentational）和断言式（assertive）两种叙述模式的差异对电影和小说叙述的方式进行了区分，点明电影叙述具有视觉细节饱和的特点，这种媒介转变带来的叙述方式变化值得人们深思。在接下来的几篇短文中，作者对《绘图师合约》《向玛丽致敬》《凝视水晶球》等几部影片的文本互涉、意义诠释和电影文本内部的双轴关系转换等都进行了简短而精要的分析，令人读来趣兴味盎然。例如，在《“性趣”的空虚与幻灭——奥布洛维奇影片分析》一文中，作者从影片叙述视角的自限谈起，论及影片中不同动作的意符指涉，从而引发我们对影片的性意符之空洞、音画断层现象的思考。在这里特别要指出的是，这些影评写成的时间多是20世纪80年代，彼时的电影叙述学研究正处于从“第二电影符号学”阶段到“第三符号学阶段”，即结构过程研究向精神分析过渡的阶段。[①] 和主流的电影研究类似的是，这些影评也注重电影文本结构与意义的产生：作者对意义的开放保持了相当的自觉。在《〈向玛丽致敬〉的诠释问题》一文末尾，作者的谈论收束于影片中人物的离合关系，并写道：“其实所有的影片难道不是由剪（cutting）和辑（editing）构成的吗？密耶维尔和戈达尔的影片与福音书的关系，难道不也正是离合的辩证吗？让我在陷入浪漫的呓语无限衍生之前，就此打住，让这篇正文开放，它的罅隙为后来的诠释者填补。”（280）在意义的传达阶段，将无限衍义的权利让渡给随后的接收者，不得不说，这正是一个符号学者的智慧。

四、结语

多年漂泊在家园之外的诗人保尔·策兰曾为自己的漂泊写下这样的句子：“你改变钥匙，改变词语，和雪花一起自由漂流。”诗人的钥匙在于语言本身，而学者的钥匙，在于他的理论视域：视域的改变，可以为文本注入不同的意义。在张汉良的研究中，我们可以看到，这种视域上的“远游”可以为文学研究、为知识建构打开相当宽广的天空，是达到“自由漂流”之境界的必需。“其出弥远，其知弥少”的箴言无助于学术素养的养成，而对未知领域的渴求与探问，才是推动我们靠近真知的永远的驱动力。

① 马睿：《电影符号学：西方与中国》，唐小林、祝东主编，《符号学诸领域》，四川大学出版社，2012年，第327～334页。

作者简介：

彭佳，西南民族大学外国语学院副教授，四川大学符号学－传媒学研究所驻所研究员。研究方向为理论符号学、生态符号学以及民族文学。

Author：

Peng Jia，associate professor of Southwest University for Nationalities，member of ISMS Research Team. Her research fields include theoretical semiotics，eco semiotics，and minority literature.

E-mail：pj8024@163. com

实现自然、社会和文化的衔接：评保罗·科布利《劳特利奇符号学指南》

蒋诗萍

编　者：保罗·科布利（Paul Cobley）
译　者：周劲松，赵毅衡
书　名：《劳特利奇符号学指南》
出版社：南京大学出版社
出版时间：2013 年
ISBN：978-7-305-11363-5

就学界的长期使用习惯而言，“符号学”有两个可以与之对应的英文单词词：semiotics 和 semiology。学界对于这两个名称是否有区别，存在争议。特伦斯·霍克斯（Terence Hawkes）在《结构主义和符号学》一书中指出，semiology 和 semiotics 两个词的唯一区别就在于：前者来源于索绪尔，欧洲人出于对他的尊敬，喜欢使用这个名词；后者来源于皮尔斯，说英语的人出于对他的尊敬，喜欢使用这个名词。

西比奥克（T. A. Sebeok）并不认为二者的区别仅体现为一种单纯的地域性，更强调划清这两个词的界限，他认为这是了解符号学、进行符号学研究的首要问题，这直接关系到符号学的适用范围与符号学的疆域问题。他很早就用“以偏概全的谬误”的提法来说明 semiotics 与 semiology 之别，意思是“把仅限于人类语言和文化的符号作用错误地等同于全部符号作用”[①]。semiology 的适用范围只限于语言与文化，因为索绪尔所建议的符号学“关注的仍然是一切以任意性为基础的系统的整体”[②]。他倾向于由洛克（John Locke）最早提出的 semiotics 传统——洛克提议符号的一般研究将是一门自

---

① ［美］约翰·迪利：《符号学基础》（第六版），张祖建译，中国人民大学出版社，2012 年，第 3 页。

② ［瑞士］索绪尔：《普通语言学教程》，刘丽译，中国社会科学出版社，2009 年，第 103 页。

主的独立科学，它将一方面与自然科学相互协调，一方面与关于文化的科学相互协调，探索利用什么样的手段获得、发展和交流任何领域的知识。据此，西比奥克告诉我们“指号过程应当被视为一种兼属自然和文化的普遍属性”①。

约翰·迪利（John Deely）继承了西比奥克的符号学研究思想，他的《符号学基础》一书从欧洲和北美两种符号学传统的区别出发，论证了皮尔斯符号观的合理性，并通过意指作用把自然界、社会和文化各个层面衔接起来，形成了一种大的综合性的符号学理论。近日由南京大学出版社出版，伦敦城市大学交流学高级讲师保罗·科布利编著，周劲松、赵毅衡翻译的《劳特利奇符号学指南》（以下简称《指南》）是又一次对西比奥克观点的继承，也是对洛克关于符号学在自然科学和人文科学当中的地位的佐证，更为重要的是向读者展示了当前符号学研究所取得的新成果和开拓的新领域。

《指南》由“理解符号学”和“符号学中的核心主题和重要人物”两个部分组成。“理解符号学”这一部分是关于符号学的前沿思考，文章均出自国际符号学领域的领军人物之手，其中不乏获得“西比奥克奖”的大师，如约翰·迪利、卡列维·库尔（Kalevi Kull）、苏珊·佩特丽莉（Susan Petrilli）、叶斯柏·霍夫梅尔（Jesper Hoffmeyer）。该部分由11篇文章组成，《绪论》《古代符号学》《自然符号学》《环境界与模塑》《逻辑与认知》《唯实论与认识论》《皮尔斯、现象学和符号学》《索绪尔的遗产》《社会符号学》《关于媒介与文化的符号学》《符号伦理学》。

这些课题汇集在一起，形成了当前符号学研究的重要论题和方向，它表明符号学已经超出文学和语言学，扩大到生物形式乃至一般意义上的进化过程，这无疑为符号学研究描绘了一个更大和更新的研究框架，与此同时还表明了符号学最为本质的特点，即跨学科性。正如该书的编者保罗·科布利在绪论中写的：“知道诸种动物行为学和生物学等学科以及其他科学的诸多方面对于理解交流的启迪，意义十分重大，这不仅是因为它鼓励了跨学科性，而且因为它促进了更具综合性的知识”。②

不仅如此，该书中译本的出版，对于想要在符号学研究上有一番作为的中国读者来说意义重大。符号学的理论渊源极其深厚，中国读者对西方现代

---

① Thomas. A. Sebeok. ed.，“Ecumenicalism in Semiotics”，in Sebeok，ed.，*A Perfusion of Signs*. Bloomington：Indiana University Press，pp. 182－183.

② ［英］保罗·科布利编：《劳特利奇符号学指南》，周劲松、赵毅衡译，南京大学出版社，2013年，第3页。

理论往往不甚了了，这让中国学者的符号学研究难上加难。而一些学者外语水平有限、获取先进理论的途径有限，直接导致其难以摆脱自话自说或者被牵着鼻子走的研究困境。该书的中译本无疑为中国读者了解西方关于符号学的最新理论成果提供了捷径。该书对符号学理论进行了溯源：符号学的发展由古希腊的占卜、医学始，之后历经中世纪唯识论与认识论的斗争与交错发展，继而在索绪尔与皮尔斯两位巨人手中完备成形，最后经过西比奥克对两种研究传统的梳理和区分，得以完整，并因其所从事的“动物符号学”开辟了非人类符号活动研究新领域，打破了传统的以语言学为核心的符号学（semiology）疆域。

那这一疆域将扩展至何处，也就是符号学研究的边界到底在哪里？该书主题便是对符号学研究领域的开拓。尽管“理解符号学”部分只有 11 篇文章，但涵盖的主题甚广，包括符号学的历史、发展和应用，索绪尔、皮尔斯、西比奥克等人的核心理论，生物符号学、社会符号学和符号伦理学等当代重要的符号学论题，媒介符号学、文化符号学、自然符号学和认知符号学。这使得符号学的研究领域大大打开，实现了社会、自然和文化等各个领域的衔接；这自然得益于西比奥克充分理解了由皮尔斯提出的“解释项”的价值，他认为在意指过程中该项不可或缺。

该书向大家所展示的符号学领域，从社会、自然到文化，涵盖了今天被称为人文与社会科学的全部领域，让我们看到了符号学的活力，看到了符号学的普适性。这对于符号学学者来说，自然是一件激动人心的事。但另一方面，这却可能遭到来自其他学界的质疑，认为这是一种“泛符号学论”（pan-semiotics）。这种质疑是不对的，因为尽管该书所展示的研究范围如此之大，但还没能完全涵盖符号学可以触及的领域。赵毅衡先生认为，“说普天下学问都是符号学的范围，不是没有道理，因为都卷入意义”①，在阐释这一观点时，他引用了王夫子的界定：“乃盈天下而皆象矣。诗之比兴，书之政事，春秋之名分，礼之仪，乐之律，莫非象也，而《易》统会其理”。② 中国古人已经看到《易经》符号学“统会天下之理”③。

说到此，我们不无遗憾地发现这样一个事实：中国的符号学思想积淀已久，早在数千年前，《易经》就建立了一个完整的符号系统，到春秋战国时

① 赵毅衡：《符号学》，南京大学出版社，2012 年，第 19 页。

② 王夫之：《船山全书》第一册，《周易外传》卷六，岳麓书社，1996 年，1039 页。转引自赵毅衡：《符号学》，南京大学出版社，2012 年，第 19 页。

③ 赵毅衡：《符号学》，南京大学出版社，2012 年，第 19 页。

期，各学派开始关于“名实”的论争，这种论争延续了两千年之久。但是，这些思想却没能发展成为一个独立的“符号学”学科。而《指南》一书对东方的这些符号学思想只字未提，说明中国的符号学传统至今也未能充分融入现代符号学。这跟众多西方学者认为中西方文化不具有可通约性有关。

确实，由于所根植的文化土壤具有极大的不同，许多貌似具有类同性的文学和文化文本有着深层本质的差异，但这也恰好说明了将符号学与中国传统思想结合进行研究的迫切性。运用符号学的阐释方式，对中国文化传统进行新的解读，将有利于促进中西方的跨文化交流。更为重要的一点是，“符号学研究中明显的缺项，就是未能充分吸收中国的先秦名学、禅宗美学、唯识宗和因明学的成果。东方资源的启示，将把符号学理论推进到一个全新的境地”①。

这一方面为中国符号学学者创造了弥补符号学缺陷的学术机遇，另一方面也对国内研究者提出了更高的学术要求，首要的一步就是掌握现代符号学知识与理论。这本《指南》不仅是一部理论著作，更是一部符号研究的工具书。这样的一本书，似乎充满魔力：给我们一个偷懒的机会，一夜之间获得了符号学的所有知识。不管是否真有这个魔力，但书如其名，它绝对没有指北。

作者简介：

蒋诗萍，四川大学文学与新闻学院博士研究生，四川大学符号学—传媒学研究所驻所研究员，从事品牌符号学研究。

Author:

Jiang Shiping, Ph. D. candidate of College of Literature and Journalism, Sichuan University, and member of the ISMS Research Team. Her research field is semiotics of branding.

E-mail:jshiping@gmail. com

① 赵毅衡：《符号学》，南京大学出版社，2012 年，第 18 页。

本书在编辑过程中，得到了四川大学人文社科期刊资助项目、四川大学文学与新闻学院985工程文化遗产与文化互动创新基地，以及211工程子项目“中外文学与俗文化”的支持，特此感谢。